I0797312

BERGHAIN NIGHTS

BERGHAIN NIGHTS

A JOURNEY THROUGH TECHNO AND BERLIN CLUB CULTURE

LIAM CAGNEY

REAKTION BOOKS

For Indrani

Published by
REAKTION BOOKS LTD
2–4 Sebastian Street
London EC1V 0HE, UK
www.reaktionbooks.co.uk

First published 2025

EU GPSR Authorised Representative
Logos Europe, 9 rue Nicolas Poussin, 17000, La Rochelle, France
email: contact@logoseurope.eu

Printed and bound in Great Britain by Bell & Bain, Glasgow

A catalogue record for this book is available from the British Library

ISBN 978 1 83639 083 1

CONTENTS

The music comes from the void, the nothing, in response to the burning need for something else.

SUN RA

There was much of the beautiful, much of the wanton, much of the bizarre, something of the terrible, and not a little of that which might have excited disgust.

EDGAR ALLAN POE,
'The Masque of the Red Death'

TechNoWhere

Techno is the art of nowhere.

Techno is a musical art for those who feel like they're nowhere all the time. When they're on the top deck of a bus, or shopping in the aisles of a supermarket, or laying their head down on the pillow and staring up at the ceiling: nowhere at all these times, yet somehow inexplicably *there* all the same.

Techno affirms the reality of nowhere.

Within the club's darkness – through immersion in out-there sounds and rhythms like insect heartbeats – techno envelops you in silence. Then, techno whispers that, yes, what you feel despite it all *is* real, that history is madness and selfhood a fantasy.

The dance floor becomes a liberating zone, what remains when everything is wiped away, past personhood and place.

It's no coincidence that techno clubs were founded in no-man's-lands: history's borders, a place for the alien, the other.

Techno always came to us from aliens.

From Detroit to Düsseldorf, from Tokyo to Sheffield, techno was born of marginal types, born of the community of those who don't fit in – of the community of those without a community –

the community of the reviled –

the community of the loners –

the community of those, like you, in thrall to the nothing.

These were my thoughts that muggy summer morning at the Berlin techno club Berghain – thoughts raging like a hillside of ferns and grass in a hurricane – as my body sat cowering in a dank toilet cubicle, taking refuge from the abject madness into which my morning had devolved, trying in vain, as so often, to think myself out of trouble.

I had come to Berghain that morning excitedly but without expectations, accompanied, improbably, by the tall, polo shirt-clad Jürgen, a Dutch neoliberal economist I barely knew. Jürgen had spent the preceding Saturday night, as we toured Kreuzberg's dive bars, praising the free market and iPhones and dating apps. He was full of himself. I was hanging out with my friend David, a bohemian economist of whom Jürgen was an old acquaintance. When I mentioned that I had two Berghain guest-list spots for that night, Jürgen's ears pricked up. And when David, my expected plus-one, fell ill and went home, our unwelcome club date was sealed.

To make things more complicated, it wasn't actually me who was on the guest list: it was my Scottish friend John, a former football hooligan turned ingenious music producer (he was dating Berghain's accountant). But since I knew John wasn't going, I had prudently decided to assume John's identity at the door.

All of which should have been fine. Except that, at 5 a.m., as, under a radiant dawn firmament of summer blue, Jürgen, in his Louis Vuitton jacket and preppy chinos, and I, in my unkempt red T-shirt, stood on the gravel before Berghain's hulking mountain, eyed by the moustachioed muscular bouncer with his clipboard, my vision began to shimmer: the mushrooms I had been idly microdosing earlier that night had gone *macro*. A lysergic tint washed over me; my tongue thickened; and I fumbled. When asked my name, I mistakenly gave not the guest-list name but my own.

I'd been mooching around Berlin a month or so by this point, a recent musicology graduate, an overqualified dropout. I was well enough acquainted with Berghain not to have bothered going for years. I'd first partied there as a student in 2006, and in 2010 had kissed an eyelinered blonde woman there, Emma, who for a few years after was my life partner in crime. I already knew the gothic concrete interior, the brute gay energy firing the former East German power station's industrial corridors and stairwells, already knew the excess, the genderfuck, the drug lunacy, the endless opening hours. For years, Berghain had held little interest – I assumed that clubbing had been a fixture of my early twenties, whereas now, a hard-won PhD under my belt, I'd moved on to more mature things. I was paid to review operas and write classical music programme notes.

But it turned out my clubbing past until then had been merely a prologue.

Jürgen sighed dramatically. 'That was worse than the border crossing into Israel,' he muttered as we passed the security check and paid the cashier. After the bouncer had asked me my name and I replied 'Liam – I mean John!', and following a stern stare and Jürgen shifting his feet, and an excruciating moment of deliberation, we were waved in, skipping with relief past a queue of black-clad hopefuls that stretched off for miles.

A Bavarian musicologist friend, Karin, had given me the shrooms as part payment for some copy-editing (yes, how very Berlin), suggesting that gentle microdosing might help my depression and dissociation. The shrooms were an ungodly synthetic cross-breed of Mexican psilocybin and some unnamed species, and, as I discovered, this singular hybrid granted you all the awesomely intense visuals with none of the comforting giggles.

By the time Jürgen and I left our things in the cloakroom and, passing under the colossal Dionysus statue, began ascending the vast iron staircase to the club proper on the first floor – from which darkness the brutal pounding techno kindled our excitement – it had become abundantly clear that, through my drunken hands, I had fucked up the whole microdosing thing: I had tasted and tested too much. My dread rose with each wobbly step up that stairwell. I gazed in dilated-eye wonder at the pillars of purple light stretching upwards, and trembled at the sound system's oceanic roar, knowing full well that I was hurtling headlong into a full-on psychedelic trip in the most trip-uncongenial setting.

We quickly decamped to the mellower upstairs Panorama Bar. But the red halogen strip lights ululated; the music's jazzy piano morphed into android laughter; my left hand's fingers stretched away like fleshy measuring tapes; not to mention the overwhelming purpleness of the gender-fluid Prince lookalike before the DJ box, nor the deafening cigarette smoke swirling round the two bald red-kimono lesbians dancing together in silky synch, and my heart pounded, and it was all too much. Berghain was sensory overload – reality turned up to eleven.

I began panicking. I desperately needed some respite, desperately needed quiet, desperately needed grounding contact with comforting normality. But when I turned to tell Jürgen, he was gone: now that we were inside, this smarmy neolib had ditched me. I was alone with my terror.

That's how I ended up cowering in a metallic toilet cubicle. There was nowhere else in Berghain where you could escape the sensory onslaught. I was trapped in a madness machine with my mind amplifying everything a hundredfold.

My encounters with techno up until this point had been few and casual. In the 1990s, in our rural Donegal bedroom, our nearest neighbour a kilometre away, my beanie-hatted older brother Éamonn had exposed me to rave and ambient music. As a musician in my early adulthood, I'd ended up playing in noise bands and eventually did a PhD on post-war French electroacoustic music. In my spare time during my London grad student years, as my long-term relationship with Emma painfully disintegrated, I often whiled away evenings dreaming on the sounds of Drexciya and Plastikman and Underground Resistance.

I knew about techno's history. I knew that when club techno arose in 1980s Detroit – America's first de-industrialized city – Black producers were reimagining their urban environment as a site of futurist fantasies. Cybotron's dystopian 1984 track

'Techno City', one of the first to foreground that term, was inspired by Fritz Lang's *Metropolis* (1927) and the Tokyo of Yellow Magic Orchestra's earlier track 'Technopolis' (1979). 'I extrapolated the necessity of interfacing the spirituality of human beings into the cybernetic matrix,' said Cybotron's Rik Davis, 'between the brain, the soul and the mechanisms of cyberspace.' As well as the music, techno meant a whole conceptual vision – a post-human vision not unlike that of Donna Haraway's contemporary 'Cyborg Manifesto'. 'The cyborg would not recognize the Garden of Eden,' Haraway wrote in a feminist context. 'It is not made of mud and cannot dream of returning to dust.'

Jeff Mills, the second-wave Detroit artist who pretty much invented modern club techno's style, similarly spoke of shedding his human form through music. 'I'm becoming the third person,' he told *The Wire* in 2009, comparing his productions to robot probes of alien territories. Along with Mike Banks, Mills was co-founder of the Detroit techno collective Underground Resistance (UR). UR sought to harness techno's power of anonymity to de-programme people from the 'dominant mindbeam': the false reality by which, through mass media, we're conditioned to accept an untrue sense of who we are. Everything around us may not be real, UR sang on their 1998 album *Interstellar Fugitives*: it might be a mirage.

In my tripping state I leaned my elbows on the bar's glass counter; the contact made liquid ripples. Around me the walls were charnel-house black. The sensory barrage remained relentless, overwhelming. I hoped a shot of Jäger would take the edge off the psychedelics.

Berghain's gay clones and butch queens seemed like emissaries from the future. Beside me was a characteristically bizarre trio. One of them was a haggard white SO36 punk with a red mohawk; dressed in red tartan, he swayed woozily in his Doc Martens. The second, steadying him, was a topless Black woman; I admired her spangly gold hoop earrings, though her teeming snake-like green hair extensions gave her the unsettling aspect of a gorgon. The third was a toking man of East Asian origin, with a bare chest, baggy white cargo pants and a ludicrous Dalí moustache.

Did I look that weird, too? Or, on the contrary, did I look *sufficiently* weird?

It was as if, in this club, pushed to the limit – humans at the limit of being human, music at the limit of being music – everything was finally revealed as it truly was; I was being granted a vision of life in its monstrous nudity. *That was what this club was*, I thought, as a sweet smell filled my nose, *a vast black box where –*

'Toke?' the East Asian man asked kindly: he was brandishing his magic wand towards me with Salvador Dalí realness.

I shook my head. 'I don't take drugs, thanks.'

Under the glass counter, what had at first glance appeared to be a row of glowing rotisserie chickens on closer inspection proved to be a debauched amber sculpture: running the length of the seedy bar, it showed a series of recumbent bald male clones, naked, making love. The dance floor was full of those hypermasculine types – brawny, poppers-sniffing, near molten.

Berghain, with its fathomless corridors and experiential intensity, was like an immersive artwork. Berghain's founders, Michael Teufele and Norbert Thormann, had reportedly said something to that effect to the DJ and writer Daniel Wang back in 2004, when they showed off their new club to friends. The owners 'stated that they wanted to create a club as a work of art', Wang said, as I'd read in an article he'd written.

I connected this, given the Soviet design of Berghain's power station building, to what the Russian Formalists of the 1920s had written about art. The artwork exists to explode our world's narcotic everyday fug, said Viktor Shklovsky. It does this through the act of defamiliarization:

> Art exists that one may recover the sensation of life; it exists to make one feel things, to make the stone stony. The purpose of art is to impart the sensation of things as they are perceived and not as they are known. The technique of art is to make objects 'unfamiliar'.

In our everyday life, habit is the engine of normality. Habit is a great deadener. You learn to put on one shoe and then another; you learn to take the train to work, to have the same conversations as others at the water cooler, to wear a smile, to go on the same holidays as everyone else, to consume the same goods. 'Habitualization', wrote Shklovsky, 'devours work, clothes, furniture, one's wife, and the fear of war.'

Berghain, by contrast, served up life defamiliarized, life rendered in its true strangeness. Perhaps this techno club, this colossal black box, signalled a new mode of art, with nameless electronic sounds at its core.

Back on the dance floor my state of panic peaked. Far away through the night-time forest of bodies, I knew the DJ currently playing was called Function, an underground techno luminary. Yet he appeared to me in the DJ box like an imperious stag with yellow fur and glowing green antlers.

The techno he played was way too big, the lights way too streaming, my fingers way too long. All of it was beyond me. It was a profoundly disturbing yet elating experience that, in the end, I only got through when I realized that, rather than try to escape it, I had to embrace it. I internally repeated to myself Nietzsche's stoic mantra *amor fati*: love of one's fate. Love all of this. Submit to this terrifying experience unreservedly and in every fibre.

Do with me what you will.

With this, the peaking state magically evened out. I merged with my dance floor surroundings; I found composure, relief – even joy. Delirious but lucid, I was swept along in the undulating techno to which the thousandfold revellers around me, naked or in fetish gear, were swinging their tattooed limbs.

I was finally at ease enough to listen to the music properly. Function's bare pounding kick drum pulse sounded steady and alone, drawing in your ear to its periodicity. Gradually over this, an explosive, harmonically rich bass note was resounding, once every two bars. The huge bass note's resonant decay flowed slowly out, expansive and tidal, to submerge the hall, fusing your body to the expanse of teeming nothingness.

As in much modernist music, everything recognizably musical was stripped away: no melody, no harmony, no verse or chorus, no formal structure, nothing that could contain or pin down the electricity of the sound itself, which poured all over us like a roaring river of intoxicating wine. The music's goal, achieved through extreme repetition, seemed to be to strip away everything historically determined – in other words, sullied by having been assigned the vulgarity of an identity – and to let sound resound in its true voracious anonymity, its core nothingness, unconstrained by musical forms.

After a while, I leaned back against the latticework barrier spanning the back of Berghain's dance floor. Behind me was a fall of 20 metres, down to the concrete ground level and the Dionysian guardian statue of the threshold. I arched my head up.

Red laser lights were making slow sweeps as on a painted canvas, flickering and configuring into polygons. Then, at once, the laser lights turned blue. And the room, too, full of dry ice, turned blue. And staring at the boundless static blue, I had the sense of my individuality evaporating. I was united with the blue and with the droning bass, pouring out of myself through my eyes, pouring out of myself through my ears, pouring out of myself through myself, becoming the faint scintillations, becoming the space between things.

It was annihilation, if you like – merging with the nothing, here in this staged nowhere. But it wasn't pessimistic. It felt like the experience I had had at Tate Modern before a Rothko canvas when, having stared at it for half an hour, I abruptly found myself *become* the canvas; since for your vision and your hearing, there is no inertial frame of reference, no changeless object. It briefly shows you that a universe subsists outside your body with which, through the artwork, moving beyond the tyranny of personhood, you can be united.

All of which is very high-flown indeed. And all of which disappeared, like a dream upon waking, the moment I shakily stepped back outside that grand GDR building. There I stood, dazed in the squint-eyed afternoon light. I shuffled past the hundreds of bodies queuing outside the club (so many, so many). I unlocked from the wire fence the rickety second-hand bike Jürgen had gifted me in exchange for the guest-list entry. I briefly thought of Jürgen, who before leaving I had spotted near the toilets but decided to ignore, sat as he was with protruding jaw between two men whom he was telling about his experience of love on a recent corporate Ayahuasca retreat.

Then, I cycled all the way back to my home in a Weißensee squat, out on the city's northern edge. The tree-fringed streets and redbrick buildings rose to meet me, glowingly unconcealed as if they were in on the whole thing.

Few things are more tedious than a drug memoir – someone droning on about how wasted he got in Berlin. For this brand of storytelling, I love the catty phrase with which Carl Solomon, dedicatee of Allen Ginsberg's poem 'Howl', dismissed Ginsberg's Beat epic: 'crypto-bohemian boasting à la Rimbaud'.

I open with a tripping anecdote not to boast or vice signal. The drugs were only a catalyst for taking off my blinkers and seeing a wide vista of life I'd up until then ignored. That summer weekend, techno entered my life more or less unannounced, a doppelgänger that, from then on, began following me around and mimicking my movements. Eventually I took notice and wisely resolved to follow it. Because maybe *it* was the original and I was the copy.

It was a time in my life when I was looking for something. I had arrived in Berlin that July for a long summer break. Ireland had exhausted me and I'd exhausted Ireland. I was disillusioned, depressed and lost. I had no stable job and few remaining prospects. I was no longer young, my academic career had been stillborn, and I ended up in Berlin simply because I'd lived there a few years earlier and knew the lay of the land.

I rented a room in a remarkably bizarre place even by Berlin standards – a huge former Stasi base called the ECC. Looming up high from grey industrial storage yards, the ECC had a house-of-Usher vibe, an uncanny artefact of a dead past, telling something no one cared to hear. Inside, it comprised hundreds of rooms, most of them empty, linked by echoing stairwells and extensive corridors. It housed artists and students, anarchists and Syrian refugees, assorted lost souls and me. One day in the basement one of my fellow tenants, a ponytailed Spanish guitarist, found filing cabinets full of old Stasi files on GDR citizens. Something like that happened every day.

My studio you might call ruin chic: whitewashed walls, a threadbare carpet, no curtains, exposed piping, sparse furniture. A decades-lingering smell of industrial cleaning products filled my nose each morning. At night I lay awake staring at the pipes, wondering what I was doing there. To buoy myself, I listened to Natalie Dessay singing Mozart arias. Every now and then, bursts of laughter resounded down the corridor from the Syrian men playing video games. I felt disoriented. How had I come to be nowhere?

When I invited my musician friend Barry von Liz over for dinner one evening, he casually remarked that the building had 'a stench of death' about it. Barry wasn't wrong. In a storage space beside my room lay the unclaimed possessions of a young woman who had died at the ECC, whose body supposedly hadn't been discovered for weeks. Among her leftover belongings were disturbing pen drawings, a Sinéad O'Connor biography and a black-and-white photograph of her smiling with a boyfriend. In an empty studio one evening a few of us gave her a makeshift posthumous art exhibition.

David, my economist friend, also lived at the ECC. And it was David who urged me to take another look at Berghain. He insisted the club owners wanted someone like me to write about clubbing – to take it seriously. 'The thing about Berghain', he said, 'is that it's all about the music. It's not the hedonism but the music that comes first.' Alongside that, he said, the club showed you to yourself. 'The club experience reflects the person who's having it. Because inside you're free to do anything and everything, you're forced to ask yourself: what is it that I really desire? And that can really mess some people up.'

I brooded on this. My vague idea on leaving Ireland had been to return there in September and reluctantly sign up to join the civil service. The bureaucratic life beckoned like a prison sentence. But I was beginning to reconsider. Maybe I could contribute to saying what these clubs meant. After all, I had not only the requisite academic training but the requisite caution-to-the-wind underground spirit. Not to mention a dash of Irish madness.

David seemed to think so anyway, and he encouraged me. But I knew that whatever I wrote couldn't be musicology; it wouldn't be a pseudo-objective report typed up to fence off a tranche of academic dominion. I was done with that game. No, this would be more like gonzo music writing, oozing out my being on the page. I would be my own large lab rat, my own case study.

A techno artist I spoke to about the Berlin scene was Ellen Allien. Having started off DJing in the 1990s in clubs like Tresor and

E-Werk, Allien was these days one of Berlin techno's biggest international stars, equally at home behind the decks in an industrial warehouse or chatting over dinner on an episode of Anthony Bourdain's series *Parts Unknown*. She was to Berlin what the Ramones were to New York City.

'Techno is based on community vibes,' Allien told me. 'You meet so many nice people in the club, open-minded and modern. You can talk easily with them, have conversations, hear their life stories very quickly, if you are not on the dance floor. And if you're on the dance floor, you can close your eyes and nobody disturbs you much.'

Berlin's clubs, Allien said, drew together people who, for different reasons, were searching for an alternative lifestyle. The atmosphere of openness in clubs meant learning to have impromptu conversations, moving beyond the usual formalities and social barriers. 'Before I became a DJ, I was a very shy person,' she said. 'Nightlife changed my attitude completely. I lost the shyness I still had from the school system.'

More than just an electronic musical genre, then, techno was a catalyst for community-building. 'The club is full of people searching for little spots or islands where they can express themselves,' she said. 'Tripping with the music and with the people and with the lights and even with the bar people. Everything has a rhythm from the DJ who is playing, so the whole club is literally on the beat. Even when you are in some areas where you can sit, you can still hear the music quietly. So, everything is about the beat, the tribe.'

In her career, Allen had spent a lot of time socializing in clubs, simply being present in the scene. 'Being a part of the community means you create islands, working spaces, creative zones, which somebody can't give you. You have to create them by yourself. This has something to do with courage, and something to do with strength and love.'

If techno was the art of nowhere, as I'd been inspired to think – a musical art for those who feel like they're nowhere all of the time – how could such an art have any form at all? Wouldn't the art of nowhere be destined to be inchoate and formless?

Another artist I chatted to about this was Ireland's pre-eminent techno DJ Sunil Sharpe. Having come up as a DJ in early 2000s Dublin, Sharpe was an internationally renowned techno artist, playing regularly at Berlin clubs like Tresor and Berghain, and he was the focus of a striking episode in *Resident Advisor*'s 'The Art of DJing' series. As a DJ, Sharpe had a virtuosic ability to mix with up to four turntables at once. He was also an activist for changing Ireland's night-time licensing laws.

'I think it's just basic expression most of the time,' Sharpe said when I asked him what techno was as an art form. 'First and foremost, it's escapism: it's moving yourself out of the mundane and the day-to-day repetition of life, which is quite boring for a lot of people. That's what techno did for me – gave me new options, expanded my mind.'

I asked Sharpe how he would account for the range of techno. 'Techno can be whatever you want it to be,' he answered. 'It can be simple, it can be complicated, it can involve all types of instruments, found sounds or electronic instruments. I think techno still now is only scratching the surface of what it can be. The problem with techno is its having been defined. You could argue that there are a lot of forms of music out there that are not called "techno" that *are* techno.'

This last point resonated with my recent listening habits. Since that weekend at Berghain, I had been listening a lot to Jeff Mills and to Drexciya, two pivotal techno axes, each from Detroit but each having a different style. Sharpe helped me bring that diversity into focus.

Mills's DJ sets, through their frenetic mixing and relentless intensity, generate a sort of organized delirium. On his classic mix album *Live at the Liquid Room*, recorded in 1995 at a dingy Tokyo club, Mills weaves a continuous texture through micro-modifications to perceptual units, layering successive vinyl records and loops within each record. (Mills mixes mostly his own productions on *Live at the Liquid Room*'s first segment.) Accelerated over a steady beat, recognizable sound elements are transmitted so as to become an unfamiliar delirious stream.

As in the contemporaneous films of Martin Arnold such as *Pièce Touchée*, where fierce repetition of micro-second segments subverts the dreary dominion of domesticated time, Mills's deranged repetitions open a different temporal sense. Mills's work sounds gritty, and occasionally it reminds me of looking at a person in a photograph and seeing not only their face but the image's cracks and flaws, part of the image's vitality. In Mills's music, it's the perceptual unit that's being composed, corroded and radiant. Mills's febrile sound is built on scrambled everyday elements, witnessed from some nowhere that his music accesses.

Drexciya's techno, by contrast, was more introverted. Each record by James Stinson and Gerald Donald in their Drexciya guise – or by their many alter egos (Der Zyklus, Abstract Thought, Japanese Telecom, and so on) – is like a musical signal sent from an imaginary universe. Where Mills's DJing is expansive and quickening, Drexciya's music, particularly the late period music, is contemplative. Albums like *The Opening of the Cerebral Gate* and *Grava 4* at base explore the fundamental disjunction of subjectivity, between outer identity (the everyday world) and inner universe (the anonymous, the nowhere).

In his final interview before his premature death, James Stinson, who invented the Drexciya concept, described the duo's music as 'an infinite journey to inner space within'. The music's aim was 'to find the beauty that's inside and bring it out'. Drexciya's narrative concept on *Grava 4*, of a return by Afro-diasporic mutants to their true home not on the Earth but in the stars, resonated with earlier music of the Black Atlantic, such as Bob Marley and the Wailers' *Exodus*. But it also had a wider application, a dualism whose tension is felt by the socially marginalized of all types. On this earth, you are always at once both here and nowhere.

I had gone through life feeling like someone pretending to be a person. Where some faked their own death, I faked my own life. Adulthood had presented a catalogue of my shortcomings: not academic enough to be academic, not Irish enough to be Irish, not straight enough to be straight, not queer enough to be queer, not working class enough to be working class, not middle class enough to be middle class. I realized that that was part of what a techno club touched on. This darkness, this sensory deprivation, this cut with the everyday world: they allowed you to meditate on your non-self – that is, on your true being.

When I began clubbing regularly in the weeks and months and years afterwards, I did so to get a dose of reality. The everyday world is strange already; being a person with a name is alienating already. Berghain's club environment exaggerates that strangeness to the furthest degree, such that the everyday starts to stretch and tear apart and show what's underneath: to let you feel at one with the strangeness, at home in the nowhere.

September arrived. David moved back to Ireland to take up a fixed-term academic position, and other ECC heads I knew also left. The ECC's bleach-haired owner, Herr Potso, a Klaus Kinski lookalike prone to cocaine psychosis, lost his mind and walled up our common living room area, siloing us ECC tenants further – unironically dividing a group of Berliners by a wall. I reflected that if my setting was surreal, my marginality could perhaps be an advantage, inhabiting as I did a view from nowhere. Scraping by through freelance editing and copywriting gigs, I resolved to hang on into the winter. I wouldn't be going back to Ireland.

My first task was to learn more about the history of techno. How did the concept of techno emerge? In answering this, I learned that before there was club techno, there was techno pop.

Your Roots Are Fabulous

The name 'techno' goes back to the 1970s. That was the era of the oil crisis, of Detroit's auto-industry entering freefall, of flared denim jeans and ambitious writing on pop music (remember that?). It was the era of *Futurist* magazine on newsagent shelves and *Tomorrow's World* on BBC television. And it was in 1977 that the music weekly *Sounds* ran a short piece on Kraftwerk, penned by Ingeborg Schober, using the term 'Techno Boogie' ('Kraftwerk: Techno-Boogie aus der Neonröhre').

By 'techno boogie', *Sounds* meant a synthetic electronic, European sub-branch of the disco music that was shaking up the charts and which would peak the following year with the film *Saturday Night Fever*. Techno boogie followed from similar descriptions of Pink Floyd and the MC5 as techno rock (*Creem* had called the Detroit band 'techno rock' in 1971). Literally, 'techno boogie' meant electronic dance music, music fusing *kosmiche* synthesizer lines with disco rhythms, and it took in the music not only of Kraftwerk but of Giorgio Moroder and Cerrone. As a descriptor for looping electronic grooves, it's not far off the later Detroit branding of techno.

A year after that *Sounds* piece, Kraftwerk released its signature concept album, *The Man-Machine*. That 1978 album was where the Düsseldorf four-piece first adopted their red-shirt robotic personas; where they first used a sequencer to layer continuous electronic loops. It is the album of the machine-funk of 'The Robots', of the glistening 'Neon Lights', of the catchy 'The Model'. And it was in the press release for *The Man-Machine*, inspired by *Sounds*, that Kraftwerk casually, fruitfully referred to their distinctive music using the word 'techno': 'Long in the vanguard of techno-pop music, Kraftwerk's music is irresistible to even the most electronic-resistant ear,' remarked the press release.

Here things start to get confusing. Because as I learned, the prefix *techno-*, once emitted, soon went solo and began flashing around like an unruly electrical signal on a global network grid.

Reviewing *The Man-Machine* in 1978 in Japan's *Rock Magazine*, Tokyo-based critic and record label founder Yuzuru Agi expounded upon the term 'techno pop'. Agi's review of Kraftwerk's album (which seemingly neglected to mention that he'd taken the term from the band's press release) was read by the members of the soon-to-be-launched Japanese three-piece electronic group Yellow Magic Orchestra (YMO). YMO liked the term 'techno pop' and adopted it for their music, and on the back of their surprise hit single 'Firecracker', YMO toured the West, influencing New York City's B-Boys and appearing on the television show *Soul Train*. 'The Japanese technopop of Yellow Magic Orchestra is poised to invade America,' ran a 1980 *Rolling Stone* headline. By that stage, it was forgotten that the term 'techno pop' had been used for Kraftwerk, with YMO releasing the single 'Technopolis' and later an EP called *The Spirit of Techno*.

Name aside, the futuristic image was also influential. Kraftwerk's androgynous robot chic inspired acolytes not only in Japan but in England and West Germany, as if the group, having performed a conjuring act, had called forth an army of cyborg clones, each model slightly modified. In England, the band Buggles released a 1980 B-side called 'Techno Pop'

('I loved *The Man-Machine* by Kraftwerk,' said Trevor Horn, 'this idea of a band that were totally techno'). In West Germany, the androgynous Wolfgang Riechmann on his 1978 album *Wunderbar* reprised Kraftwerk's epicene froideur and streamlined electronic pulses, and at the outset of the 1980s, Liaisons Dangereuses and Deutsch-Amerikanische Freundschaft (DAF) infused that template with underground queerness and punk edge – local traits that would subsist in Berlin's 2000s techno aesthetic.

As the 1980s began, the new generation of Kraftwerk-influenced acts looked to the future as a liberating escape from a decaying industrial present. In the UK, Cabaret Voltaire spoke of harnessing in their music Sheffield's dark Satanic mills; the Human League started life as a band called the Future, with a manifesto saying they would only use electronic instruments; while John Foxx, erstwhile singer with the Conny Plank-produced Ultravox, sang of wanting to be a machine ('The ideal is to be invisible,' he told Nick Kent in 1980. 'I've always wanted that kind of anonymity, because it's quite romantic not to have a specific identity.'). The cover of Foxx's album *Metamatic* (1980), too, spills into that of Cybotron's subsequent *Enter* (1983). Futurism infused new music, in part because of how the release of affordable mass-market synthesizers like the Sequential Prophet-5 and Korg MS20 democratized electronic sounds.

Common among English and American techno pop acts was their growing up in discomfiting urban sprawls amid the decline of manufacturing-based economies. Paul Morley in the *NME* noted in a piece on YMO in November 1980 that motivating such instrumental electronic dance music was a futurist urban poetics:

> This is city-music. In Japan the happy alternative madmen call it 'Techno-pops'. The city: complex, concentrated, a symbol of achievement and self destructiveness. YMO instrumentals reflect the multi-facets and pressures of complex city existence: speed, repetition, noise, stimulation, flashing lights, non-stop, sensurround, roundandround, closeness, out of control. YMO songs capture the cities, the twentieth century's centres of civilization, on the edge of breakdown.

The themes of earlier artistic modernism were reprised in early techno. 'The city is a motor. Its core is *dynamo-electric*,' Hirato Renkichi had similarly written in 1921 in his 'Manifesto of the Japanese Futurist Movement'.

The Detroit act Cybotron was founded in 1979 by community college classmates Rik Davis and Juan Atkins. In their early material, like 'Alleys of Your Mind' (an imitation of Ultravox's 'Herr X'), Cybotron responded to the English bands with their own cold North American paeans to the city, cars, underpasses, cybernetics. By the 1980s, Detroit was on the way to becoming America's first de-industrialized city. Atkins later said: 'When the new technology came in, Detroit collapsed as an industrial city, but Detroit is Techno City. We're at the forefront here.' Cybotron's NYC electro-inspired 'Clear' – which pointed the way for Atkins's subsequent groove-based techno – encouraged *techno-fying your mind*.

For theorist Kodwo Eshun, Cybotron and other Detroit-based electronic musicians affected European elements in their music to scramble their expected identity, the essentialized Blackness culturally foisted upon them. Just as 1960s British rockers had mimicked Robert Johnson, 1980s Detroit producers mimicked Ultravox:

> the guys listening to this stuff coming out of Europe, coming out of England, listening to the whiteness of the synthesizer and using it because that sound would make them alien within America. That's the secret behind all of the early Detroit records. All those guys – Model 500, Cybertron [*sic*] – they've all got these affected Flock of Seagulls type accents. Why do they have this? Because they want to be alien in America. How do they do this? By singing like white New Romantic English kids. So it's the idea of white music being exotic to black American ears. So it's more or less like trying to turn the exotic eye back onto the English . . . in this case, it was America bastardising, taking English music and doing strange things with it . . . In techno, Kraftwerk is the delta blues, Kraftwerk is where it all starts. In techno, Depeche Mode are like Leadbelly.

Like Funkadelic before them, Cybotron scrambled codes through hybridizing elements of white and Black music. They were musical hackers. Eshun comments: 'Black Americans are synthetic; the key in techno is literally to synthesize yourself into a new American alien.' Rik Davis called himself 3070, a digital identifier nodding to the transhumanist author FM-2030 and not unlike the designations of characters in George Lucas's film *THX 1138* (1971).

This conceptual level is what I'd call techno's prehistory. Techno's origin is as a networked transmission on a global grid spanning Düsseldorf, Tokyo, London, Detroit, Sheffield, Berlin, Brussels. And by 1982, the name 'techno' really was everywhere. English duo Vicious Pink called their music techno; Madonna, too, in a 1984 *MTV* interview, spoke of her love of techno. Frankfurt record store City-Music, at the initiative of staff member and DJ Andreas Tomalla, had a 'techno' section. Ava Cherry released 'Techno Lover'; Testpattern released 'Techno Age'; Patrick Cowley produced 'Tech-No-Logical World' (for singer Paul Parker); YMO released the album *Technodelic*; Kraftwerk advertised a forthcoming 1983 album (never released) called *Techno Pop*; Cybotron released the 1984 single 'Techno City'. Techno at this time meant sleek pop music with predominantly electronic elements extolling, through new technology, the liberating romance of a high-tech future.

The name 'techno' zipped off in yet another direction in Los Angeles's early hip-hop scene. Techno Hop was an LA-based hip-hop scene using predominantly electronic sounds and Techno Hop Records was its node. The 1982 single 'Techno Trax' by Man Parrish probably inspired the name, although he was originally from NYC. LA's Knights of the Turntable released tracks like 1983's 'Techno Scratch', full of scratching synth lines and Roland TR-808 drum machine workouts. And here, Juan Atkins comes back in. Having by the mid-1980s broken from Cybotron, who had released music independently through LA's Fantasy Records, and given the success of 'Clear' in California, Atkins relocated to LA, where he produced music under the new moniker Model 500.

Looking for a market for his music, Atkins released more LA-techno-friendly material, like the tracks 'Technicolour' and

'Time Space Transmat', West Coast developments of NYC's Kraftwerk-inspired electro template. When in 1988, through the auspices of Atkins's younger friend Derrick May, a compilation album of new Detroit electronic music was being put together, Atkins submitted the track 'Techno Music', a fabulous slab of electronic funk recalling percussively a mash-up of New Order's 'True Faith' and Alexander Robotnick's 'Problèmes d'amour' with his new LA aesthetic. For the album's title, given house music's recent commercial success in the UK, Virgin Records and May had mooted *The New House Sound of Detroit*. This branding was eventually vetoed in favour of *Techno! The New Dance Sound of Detroit*, which Atkins, proud of his Cybotron work, wanted. Thus was born Detroit techno.

All of which meant that, by 1988, Kraftwerk were yesterday's men – or rather, yesterday's robots, rendered obsoletely fabulous by their younger clones. In an interview that year for the Japanese magazine *Silverstar Club*, Kraftwerk's Florian Schneider was asked how he felt about the development of techno pop. Given the thrilling cutting-edge music of the Art of Noise, asked Sachiko Shikata, did Kraftwerk consider digital sampling 'the future of techno music'? Schneider (robotically warping his voice on the recorded answer) replied: 'the whole evolution of techno pop music is very gradual.' Addressing the origin of the name techno, Florian Schneider commented that 'one day, maybe a journalist found this word from technology and from pop music and combined it and said "techno pop". I think that's how it happened. And now it's a label for a lot of different musics.' Schneider's comment, I realized, heralded a general future amnesia about the pre-Detroit sense of the term 'techno'. History is based less on remembering than on forgetting.

Did you get all that? I don't blame you. Techno's prehistory isn't simple. Picture your narrator in his squat, deep in the Berlin winter, scouring scans of old newspapers online and reading library books, trying to get a grasp on it all. The techno concept, I concluded, was always about liberation, through technology, from outmoded pre-industrial narratives. There's a dollop of media theorist Marshall McLuhan there ('Art as a radar environment takes on the function of indispensable perceptual training rather than the role of a privileged diet for the elite,' as he writes in *Understanding Media*), filtered through futurist Alvin Toffler and the visionary Sun Ra. It's about loners inventing themselves anew: as a cyborg, as a cloud of particles, as a synthesis resulting from anonymous fields of forces interacting. Techno encourages hybridity: techno becomes itself precisely through differing from itself. It's a play of masks, with each mask having under it another mask.

Sun Ra and Kraftwerk had kinship in this regard. In the film *Space Is the Place* (1974), directed by John Coney, asked by the incredulous Black kids if he's for real, Sun Ra replies that he is not – and neither are they. 'You're not real. If you were, you'd have some status among the nations of the world. I come to you as a myth. Because that's what Black people are: myths.' Fabulations such as Ra's mean artfully skewing your inherited narrative to arrive at a deeper truth.

Techno history, reflecting this play of masks, is built on anonymous networks. Interconnected by technology, the world becomes a feedback system evading terrestrial borders. In considering techno's development, I realized that rather than imagining a family tree with one sturdy line, it was better to imagine a frenetic multidimensional rhizome: a system of spontaneous bifurcations, lacking any one centre, befitting our world's digital networked era. Nonetheless, within this dynamic system, Detroit in the 1980s was the principal nodal point – at once generator and amplifier, carrier signal and distorter signal.

In light drizzle on a noirish winter afternoon, Stefan Schwanke and I were walking down Bergmannstraße in west Kreuzberg. I was looking for a vegan restaurant in which to chat to Schwanke, a youthful middle-aged man with dark hair and two black circle earrings, dressed in a black BOY jacket and black glasses, and an authority on Berlin's techno scene. By the time we slid into a bamboo-panelled room and ordered our meals, I was somehow spilling out my life story (rave childhood, wandering adulthood). Holding in his hand a leftist book on social media, he nodded as I told him about how I'd ended up in Berlin and wanted to make sense of my experiences.

I asked Schwanke about a remark of his I'd read in the book *Der Klang der Familie*, an oral history of Berlin's 1990s club scene edited by Felix Denk and Sven von Thülen. Schwanke had said there that, for him, 'Los Niños Del Parque' by the early 1980s electronic duo Liaisons Dangereuses was *already* techno, and that, contrary to the usual version of events, techno had not seemed new to him and others in West Berlin when the acid house and Detroit wave rolled in.

'That's what I've always really hated about books or TV documentaries or whatever,' he replied. 'They all pretend that, all of a sudden, there was techno.'

'Fallen out of the sky?' I said.

'Yeah, it's so stupid.'

Schwanke was disappointed that *Der Klang der Familie* misinterpreted him as a 'nostalgist' of the Berlin scene. Talking to him, I quickly saw why. He was, in reality, someone who just happened to have a lot of perspective on Berlin's electronic scene, and, while his knowledge was deep, he was at the same time always moving on to the next thing and had little time for the retrograde.

'I was pissed off with Felix,' Schwanke said of that book's editor, 'because it's just not true at all. There were so many people who just only came into the scene when techno was around and they have no other musical background. For me, it was like the eighth step in my evolution of going out and witnessing new styles coming into the mix.'

Schwanke had grown up in West Berlin in the 1980s. At thirteen, he was already going out to clubs, first to Cartoon, then to the main gay club Metropol as well as to Linientreu. He had had a front-row view of how Berlin's club scene developed from then on. His ongoing evolution led Schwanke to help set up the club E-Werk (Berlin's 1990s superclub), work with Depeche Mode, become Coil's tour organizer, found the Internet's first and largest experimental music website Ironflame.org and, more recently, create the successful Back 2 Basics parties, which were predicated not on nostalgia but on exploring the mass of barely discovered, obscure dance music releases dating from the period from 1989 to 1994 or so, a period Schwanke considered more creatively fruitful than our current one.

'There was not even a remarkable shift,' he said of club techno and the electronic music scene in the late 1980s, around the time of the fall of the Berlin Wall, 'because it started at the beginning of the eighties with Hi-NRG and electronic music like

Chris and Cosey, who were in Throbbing Gristle before. They did stuff that you could easily call techno today. They even used a 303 on the B-side of *October Love Song* ['Little Houses'], which is 1983. Then, you had electronic body music, you had Hi-NRG, Italo Disco, etcetera. There were so many styles, and acid house just added to it.'

Ellen Allien, when we spoke, had had a different view. In the 1980s, she said, 'there was EBM, and there was DAF, but there was no techno club. It's completely different – it was a *complete* change.'

'I was in all these West Berlin clubs when I was really young,' she told me, 'and it was more based on funk and soul. It was Black music, like very funky, soul-ish vocals, hip hop.' In contrast to the later techno scene, though, West Berlin's pre-reunification club scene unfortunately had a lot of sexism. 'I hated to go to those clubs, because the guys touched my ass, danced on top of me – really disrespectful.'

For Allien, who had grown up in a progressive household, the experience was jarring. 'It was horrible to go to those clubs as a young girl. I was treated really, really badly by men, in a way I wasn't used to being treated in school or with my friends around me. So I went to the West Berlin clubs because I liked the music, not for the people so much. And when the techno scene later started, I went out to see the people and I didn't like the music at first.'

Schwanke clarified how he first used the term 'techno'. 'We had been used to the term 'techno' since I think 1984, until 1989, and techno meant Yazoo, Front 242, A Split Second, Chris and Cosey, Liaisons Dangereuses, Deutsch-Amerikanische Freundschaft, etcetera,' he said. 'So, everything that was electronic and that was danceable. That was techno. Then, this other movement came along. Some people internationally called it techno; in Germany, it was techno-house.'

The latter comprised the four-to-the-floor music with fewer vocals, such as music coming from Belgium and some tracks by the KLF. 'It was like the danceable electronic music we knew before, but it incorporated other elements that made it much more wild and ecstatic. That was called techno house, and you could easily differentiate it from the techno we were used to in the previous six years. For us it was quite clear.' Over time, the distinction became muddier. This led to confused situations where, say, a DJ booked to play a set of four-to-the-floor instrumental electronic music (techno v.2) would play a set of Yazoo and Front 242 and DAF (techno v.1), to the promoter's chagrin.

The dispute around techno's identity played out in the premier German electronic dance music magazine, *Frontpage*, for which Schwanke wrote in the early 1990s. The term 'techno' eventually meant 'two completely different things, but each section was completely convinced that, of course, *they* were techno, and how could anyone question that – and the others thought that as well'. By 1992, *Frontpage*'s editors Jürgen Laarmann and Armin Johnert 'didn't get along anymore, because one was old techno, one was new techno'. After the magazine relocated from Frankfurt to Berlin, it shifted to fully embrace the newer definition of techno. 'Then, eventually, the old techno was erased from history.' Nonetheless, Schwanke had been excited about the new sound – 'the future of techno', as he said to me. Though typically for his searching ear, by

1995 he felt it had run its course, and he then moved on to more underground music.

I found my conversation with Schwanke illuminating. And Schwanke's view was borne out by what Detroit producers had said in interviews about the appeal for them of early 1980s European synth music. Mike Banks said that when the Detroit radio DJ the Electrifying Mojo began playing Kraftwerk on his show, 'it was our first introduction to techno, or whatever it was called.' When Kraftwerk played Detroit in 1981, the *Michigan Daily* called them the high priests of techno. Kevin Saunderson, who had grown up in New York City going to the disco-dominated Paradise Garage, told the *NME* in 1991 that when he moved to Detroit, 'it was a totally different music scene. Everybody was into Kraftwerk, Depeche Mode, New Order.'

House music productions blew up in Chicago in 1984, later transmitting to Europe, a drum-machine-driven mutation of disco. Musicians in the Chicago scene loaned each other electronic instruments to produce new tracks, creating their music at home without any need for commercial recording studios. The music was disseminated by Ron Hardy at the Music Box and by the Hot Mix 5 on local radio. 'No one knew what we had actually started outside of Chicago in the beginning, let alone what was jumping off in the UK,' said DJ Pierre of Phuture in an interview, referring to how, in 1986, house scored a UK number one single with 'Jack Your Body'.

> So it felt like it was our own little creation for us in Chicago. We had ownership of it as the creators . . . You have to remember that the focus on everything

> we learned in school was always about what some white-American person created, manufactured, discovered, or brought to the forefront. So we were very proud of ourselves.

In developing from disco, Italo, techno pop and R&B, house put the onus on the synthetic (like the Roland TR-808 drum machine) over the live instrumental, an approach followed thereafter by Detroit techno and UK rave. Heard over a club PA system, electronic drums had more punch than instrumental ones. 'House is really a raw, simplified version of disco,' said the DJ David Morales. In that regard, the American house/techno divide, when it appeared in 1988, echoed the disco/techno boogie divide announced in *Sounds* a decade earlier.

Late 1980s Detroit techno was initially considered a local version of house. May and Kevin Saunderson created productions with a view to their being played in the Music Box in Chicago and the Paradise Garage by DJs Ron Hardy or Larry Levan. May's early co-productions 'Nude Photo' (based on material written by Thomas Barnett) and 'Strings of Life' (based on material written by Michael James) were initially termed 'house music', and their instrumental polyphony, while distinct from the house mainstream, wasn't a million miles away from the path-breaking Chicago productions by Larry Heard and Adonis and Phuture.

The separate-genre status for the Detroit house offshoot came about through the UK music industry. The English A&R man Neil Rushton, sniffing around for a potentially lucrative product and making contact with May, got Virgin Records onboard to release a compilation of Detroit-focused house music for the exploding UK rave market, a compilation which, as I've said, they branded with the name techno. Every techno implies an elsewhere, a border crossed; and in Detroit's case, that elsewhere, to which May and Atkins and Saunderson would soon decamp, turned out to be the UK.

A manifesto of Detroit techno (and of all club techno thereafter) appeared in the liner notes of *Techno! The New Dance Sound of Detroit*, penned by journalist Stuart Cosgrove. Distinguishing their music antithetically from Chicago house, May, Atkins and Saunderson – by now commercially mythologized as 'the Belleville Three', supposedly the sole inventors of Detroit techno ('I do not exist?' Rik Davis later commented on Facebook) – stressed their music's experimentalism and European-influenced sleekness. 'Techno is undoubtedly the music of Detroit, but it has none of the latter-day optimism of Motown,' Cosgrove wrote. Befitting this historically singular city – once the bountiful Paris of the West, now America's murder capital, full of decaying ruins – techno was at once cold and soulful, as streamlined as a Ford Mustang. May described the techno aesthetic, by reference to the UK band, as the 'new disorder'. Some further liner-note excerpts:

> Techno music is unashamedly modern in its outlook. It is a mesmerising underground of new music which looks to the future, breaks with the past and blends European industrial pop with Black American garage funk. According to Derrick May, the immensely gifted young producer who works under the pseudonyms Rhythim is Rhythim and Mayday, his music goes 'beyond the beat'. It is not simply dance music but a series of

> sound experiments that often defy the logic of more uncomplicated dance sounds like Chicago house.
>
> The origins of techno date back to the late '70s to the suppressed identity of European synthesiser groups like Kraftwerk and Yello and to British electronic funk groups like Heaven 17, New Order and the Human League. Their music established the synthesiser as the creative core of new music, encouraging a whole generation of young musicians to turn their basements into makeshift studios. Unknown to Europe the ears of Black America were listening with increasing fascination, reversing the age-old flow of musical influence.
>
> Derrick May is undoubtedly the philosopher of techno. He sees the music as post-soul and believes it marks a deliberate break with previous traditions of Black American music. 'The music is just like Detroit' he claims, 'a complete mistake. It's like George Clinton and Kraftwerk are stuck in an elevator with only a sequencer to keep them company' . . .
>
> Techno's sudden shift of tempo and relentless war on familiarity makes it sound like free form jazz for the computer era. It may well be the music of the new disorder but it promises to join George Clinton's Funkadelic and Prince's Minneapolis sound as one of the most experimental forms of music Black America has ever produced.

These musicians were good at self-mythologizing, in every sense. May's image of Kraftwerk and Clinton stuck in an elevator was coined by Brian Eno. ('I would make one group which was a combination of, say, Parliament and Kraftwerk,' Eno said in 1978 to *Interview Magazine*, 'put those two together and say, "Make a record". Something like that would be an extraordinary combination: the weird physical feeling of Parliament, with this strange, rigid, stiff stuff over the top of it.'). Nonetheless, in the 1990s and beyond, as Detroit techno begat hard techno, and hard techno begat minimal techno, and minimal techno begat hypnotic techno and so on, Detroit techno's 1988 manifesto remained potent as club techno's aesthetic programme: *a relentless war on familiarity.*

Certainly, it stuck in my head as I put a full stop on my research for now, closed my laptop lid, replied to the email of a visiting Irish acquaintance, and took a much-needed break for rest and relaxation (well, relaxation at least).

It was late on a frosty Friday night as Adriano, Nick and I shambled back into RSO's concrete yard. We emerged from a cramped cabin in which, at Nick's behest, we'd each just snorted a grainy white line off Nick's cracked iPhone screen, followed immoderately by a punctuating follow-up bump using Adriano's metal spoon. Then, bracing ourselves, trusting in whatever the ketamine might throw at us, we re-entered RSO's main dance floor, a vaulted hall that, for me, immediately took on the aspect of a cosmic stage set.

My first trip was one of temporal dilation.

Blue was the colour: blue of alien encounters, of a Turrell artwork. In my aquatic temporal dilation, to my left, Nick's lanky limbs grew dark and enormous, his thin legs and arms extending into a network of pipes. In counterpoint, three nearby bikini club mermaids started shrinking, becoming astoundingly small. Ecstatic and fearful, I realized I was in an underwater cove. The minimal techno (courtesy of Adriana Lopez, a producer I liked) became emissions of sound bubbles too teeming to grasp. Rather than slipping into a typical Berlin pendular two-step dance, I instead descended into a slower time passage to one side of everyday time, within which my arms became seaweed gently rocked by an oceanic flow. Then, somehow, an hour had passed and the three of us were human again and back out in the bar area with a drink, talking, and I had to pretend to be normal.

'Genius place, Liam!' Adriano said in his northern English accent, slapping his hands on my back. 'We were at a bitter end, but we pulled through.' Earlier in the evening, after we'd been rejected in turn from Sisyphos and the Friday night Berghain party, I had proposed RSO, a new club a bit outside of town. Adriano was a friend of Nick's, and Nick was an old writer acquaintance of mine. The two were in town for a few weeks to unwind and go clubbing. Nick had become interested in Berlin after he had contacted me with a commission, asking me to write a piece for a book he was editing; I'd enthused to him about my experience at Berghain, a place he hadn't heard of, and told him my plan to write a book about it. The ketamine Nick had brought suited this delirious RSO party. From the bar, we went down to the pitch-black basement and indulged again before returning to the smoky dance floor.

My second trip was of dystopian sci-fi.

Having observed Adriano, his thick black hair smoothed back, bodily meditating, hopping from one foot to the other like a warrior monk, and lanky Nick, greying hair spiked, arms aloft like a heterodox Catholic heretic still preaching at the stake, I closed my eyes. I at once entered Detroit of the fake future as in *RoboCop*. The dance floor bodies transformed, in their white visor shades and leather harnesses and leopard print. Burnished and corroded and brown, the RSO club space became a zone of warring electronic tribes on technologically mutated streets. All was silent mystery. Despite our differences, our bodies were sharing in a common, automaton understanding: we knew complicity in this nameless experience, without knowing what it was.

During our next break, his brow sweating, Adriano said the ketamine trips and dancing were therapeutic, helping him work through the strife he had been having with some friends. 'All of it was just meaningless,' he said, miming. 'I was taking it all apart – now this bit, now that bit – now, what next?' Nick looked flushed. 'That was really emotional,' he said, looking down at the floor and almost appearing like he was going to shed a tear from his hawk-like face. 'I went through it all, my life, and my books were in it. I was before God. Mercy,' he said, putting his palms together, gesturing in supplication.

I didn't think at all about techno pop or techno history. I didn't think at all about where the name techno came from. I didn't think at all about the ECC or myself or Ireland. The everyday ceded place to the anonymous. I was just glad not to be lonely, to have company to blow off some mechanical steam.

My third trip was one of overwhelming terror and anxiety.

When I shut my eyes this time, the worries took me off guard. They swept up as a phosphorescent pink and green Leviathan from the oceanic depths: worries about my family, worries about my siblings, worries about my parents, about the discord and animosity I had caused by my waywardness. Into this tapestry, grotesque Day-Glo figures became woven of my failures as a person. My living in Berlin at this age, lapsing into drug-taking, threw into relief my weirdness. Others probably pitied me. The clubbing book I had started to write would fall flat and merely disgrace and embarrass my family. Although I had already made a decision to reject normality when leaving Ireland, I had no frame of reference for judging my life decisions. Maybe I *was* completely mad.

An hour after my intense ordeal, the three of us resurfaced, filled our lungs with cold air and sat silently outside in the yard on the wooden decking. The stars were out and I could hear some other Irish clubbers chatting nearby.

'Epic,' Adriano said, after a while.

'Yes. Tolstoy-like,' Nick answered with his gravelly baritone. 'With all the edits thrown in.'

'And the blooper reels,' I said. 'And the DVD extras.'

There was nothing else to say. I sat staring at the building's industrial facade, crosshatched pipes, silver chutes, graffiti. It seemed like a fake building, a simulacrum like the Centre Pompidou.

It was time to leave.

On the empty train back into the city, the late winter sunrise teased orange filigree on Berlin's unforgiving black skyline. Adriano, his eyes still wide and bright, mentioned having had it in mind earlier, after the repeated bouncer rejections, just to go back to their apartment sublet and watch *Downfall*. 'That would be a reasonable response,' I said. 'And moreover, watch it at half speed, so the experience takes twice as long.'

'Gruelling,' Nick muttered.

Nick and Adriano took a selfie. I realized I had accidentally sat beside a seat where someone had vomited.

The universe is staring at us, I thought.

I wondered how I could write these experiences. All of it must mean something. I had to stay focused. But already my mind was turning towards Sunday evening's assignment.

For weeks, I had been psyched to see Robert Hood at Berghain. Hood was an immense Detroit DJ, the inventor of minimal techno. Sunday evening, too, was Nick and Adriano's final night in Berlin, and after their earlier rejections, they were 100 per cent determined to get in.

Going to Berghain isn't all down-at-heel partying and high-minded aesthetics. If you intend to go with a group, things can get vicious. Battle lines are drawn; enmities surface. Some of you may be more likely to get in than others, and accordingly, before you travel to that hulking fortress of a building to stand at the mercy of the bouncers' swift judgement, each member of your party, outwardly warm and collegial, will have been secretly assessing the others' clothing to decide who is the weak link: to decide who among you will be the reason the rest don't get in.

Nick and Adriano, knowing the stakes, didn't take any risks. They went to one of those trendy Berlin clubwear boutiques and splashed out on extravagantly expensive fetish-styled NAKT clubwear: rubber pants, leather harnesses, an ornate mouth gag. They took pains to wear nothing but black. I warned them off this: it was what the recent wave of weekender Berlin tech yuppies wore. I myself was dressed in a more DIY get-up: a pink bandana, a faux-pearl necklace, a green belly top (across which, in Hood homage, was the legend DETROIT).

As we strode past the Hellweg hardware store in the club's radius, I asked how we should attempt the Berghain door. Nick confidently replied that we would split up: they would be a duo, I would be alone.

It was a sunny afternoon. A frosty breeze blew across the industrial yard and gravel path. A solitary old homeless man collected empty bottles for the meagre cash he'd get from recycling them. At the entrance, there was no queue. Adriano and Nick waltzed right up.

They were bounced right back.

'Give it a couple of hours,' I said, having waited at a nearby kiosk to see the result. By this stage, I knew Berghain's door routine fairly well. 'A new bouncer shift starts in a while. You'll have a better chance with the next crew.'

We waited until the evening, drinking a couple of beers in the adjacent park. Again, the two queued up; again, they were bounced.

They sauntered away, glowering, incensed, along with the other scorned ones. Later Adriano told me they went back to their Friedrichshain apartment sublet, took magic mushrooms, and did indeed watch *Downfall*.

When Adriano messaged me the next day to ask how it was, I lied: 'It was just okay.' In truth, it lived up to everything I wanted and more. I got to experience this Detroit techno master in a prime club setting.

When techno evolved in the early 1990s, with harder, faster, more stripped-back tracks like Marc Trauner's 'We Have Arrived', and European industrial influences from the likes of Belgium's R&S records, the fundamental guiding principle was reduction. 'Jeff Mills's deejaying at Tresor was relentlessly hard from the first day he played there,' Schwanke told me. 'Guess it was what he played like at home but now dared for the first time to play before an audience, too.' (I would later find out more about this when I attended Tresor, the Berlin techno club with which Mills was associated.)

Stripping away melodies, harmonies, verse and chorus meant that, in principle, electronic sound itself might determine its own forms, wild and untamed. Club techno moved far away from YMO's sleek whimsy and Cybotron's poppy funk. As I saw it, this reductionist, *less-than* principle paradoxically created not impoverishment but excess. What we might call constitutional inadequacy – the way in which the stable 'macro' of the musical note becomes incapable of containing the wild teeming 'micro' of frequential noise – opens the ear to a wider reality of sound, beyond the bounds of historically dead models, as natural as corrosion on walls or rust on metal.

After they left UR, it was Robert Hood and Mills who explored reduction in techno with the most inventiveness and influence. 'Rhythms inside of rhythms inside of rhythms . . . that you would perceive only after listening a while,' is how Hood explained to Todd Burns his aim when developing the subgenre called minimal techno. 'Real trance music, hypnotic, drawing you in.' Hood's music was historically significant for Berlin as the main stylistic influence on Berghain's in-house techno artists (under the Ostgut Ton moniker): without Hood's *Minimal Nation* (1994), there would have been no Ben Klock's 'Subzero' or Marcel Dettmann's 'Quicksand' or Len Faki's 'Mekong Delta'.

In the techno of *Minimal Nation*, familiar musical elements are, through *ad nauseum* repetition, defamiliarized.

A well-defined melodic figure will be repeated at length with careful micro-modifications, while, in a polyphonic manner, other figures subtly well up and fade out. In 'Ride', which is based on two simple simultaneous melodic lines, each line's litheness stresses the empty space through which it passes: space is created by the energetic line flashing briefly across it, absence as much the matter as presence. In 'Station Rider E', parsimony is the watchword. Only what is absolutely necessary is included and everything extraneous is rejected. In this music, what at first appears austere through repetition reveals itself as rich. Funk is all.

Hood's most famous solo track is 'Minus' (1994). Over a 4/4 pulse, the placement of a triple-time minor-key ostinato creates an interminable effort to resolve. That constitutional inadequacy is the energetic engine of 'Minus', opening our ear, beyond the surface features, to teeming micro-activity in the shadows. 'Minus' struck me as techno become almost nothing, artistically comparable to the modernist painterly abstraction of Klee and Kandinsky, an auditory canvas reduced to lines and points. (It was notable that, before becoming a professional techno artist, Hood was a graphic designer.)

Hood's was a music whose working and reworking of elementary tonal loops towards an end unforeseeable in advance has kinship with Paul Klee's careful working and reworking in painting of elementary forms (circles, squares). Repetition signals the energetic trace of a point in motion: a dot moving becoming a line, a line ever-expanding, a creative genesis releasing us briefly from the mundane. 'Becoming is more important than being,' Klee wrote, speaking of his conception of the painted canvas in terms of dynamic genesis: 'This fate of boundness should not deter us from knowing that our existence could also be different, that there are regions where other laws are in force, and that we must find new symbols for these laws to reflect their more fluid mobility and more moveable localities.'

Everything was stripped away in a liberating manner to reveal what lay underneath. Plus and minus, a dot and a line: in Hood's minimal techno, in dark club spaces, a mêlée of creative energy sweeps up from reduction to the molecular scale.

The music's reductiveness, too, seemed to be reflected in Berlin's club-goers and how they dressed. Among gays and queers and bohemians and marginalized people, minimal techno affirms not fitting in, affirms constitutional inadequacy, affirms the wild micro over the stable macro. This occurs through immersive darkness and intense repetition, letting you evade the glaring searchlight of the everyday world.

'Now the real Klubnacht begins,' said Xin beside me. Dressed in a pink T-shirt with a tattooed, gym-toned body, the friendly Chinese techno-head was one of the regular Berghain faces I'd gotten to know. He had just noticed Hood entering the DJ box. Through the combination of immense architecture, dim light, ancient-looking grey walls, hundreds of bodies, smoke-filled air and the intense anticipation for this high priest of techno to begin, Berghain's main room assumed the dramatic character of a temple during a sacred festival. Given Hood was an ordained pastor, the comparison wasn't inapt, I thought. Another DJ, Eris Drew, pointed out that Berghain's ecstatic revels and prohibition on photographs was not unlike the principle of the ancient Greek Eleusinian Mysteries: clubbing was archaic revival as much as it was future shock, something I'd later look into more.

From my vantage on a bollard by the dark rooms, I saw a hush fall over the hundreds of expectant faces as this patriarch of Detroit techno appeared in the booth. Then, instantaneously, like flicking a switch, once Hood dropped the beat, the crowd exploded in cries and raised hands and clouds of sweat.

Hood's three-hour set leaned heavily at times towards Floorplan, his gospel house project. Floorplan's other member, Hood's daughter Lyric Hood, sat silent and expressionless behind him through the three hours in the dark of the DJ box. The standout moment (which I made a point of noting happened at precisely 22.17 that Sunday night) was entirely singular, unlike anything else Hood played. It was the track 'Minus' I've already mentioned, one of my favourite techno tracks.

'Minus' at Berghain sounded spectacularly weird. Its appearance was as if, through a clouded cityscape night sky, that urban night of which Cybotron and YMO had sung, a UFO had silently appeared – a triangular UFO, since in the track's relentless motion of three pitches, there was a triadic form. 'Minus' struck me as a bona fide artwork where the other tracks were just music. And, just like a UFO, after three minutes it silently vanished, leaving you bewildered as to what the fuck had just happened.

Surprisingly, 'Minus' was too weird for most of the Berghain crowd. After a couple of minutes of its endless arpeggio, its Klee-like elementary iterations generating an auditory canvas, people around me started talking and checking their phones.

The set rolled on to more conventional territory. Xin and I carried on dancing. But there remained for me a sense of wonder. This is what techno does at its best, I thought – opens up a space for the unrecognizable to pass through. To my right, behind a male gay couple in a tender embrace, was a man wearing a T-shirt on which was written, 'Black Joy is Revolutionary'. Seeing the DETROIT legend on my green belly top, he smiled at me, and I smiled back.

'I think it was impossible to get the whole thing about techno in the formative years without being on the dance floor,' Schwanke had told me. 'Because if you are still standing at the door talking to people and theorizing the whole thing, I think you haven't completely grasped what it was about.' As the drizzle fell the following week on the depressing Weiβensee squat, where afternoons I drank tea in the room of my Syrian neighbours (who spent their mornings at the athletics track, one of the only ways they could pass time with no money), and as my calves still ached from dancing, I reflected on what I'd learnt of techno's historical origins.

Schwanke felt that some Berlin clubs mythologized the Detroit axis in order to hitch Detroit to their own identity. Similarly, the so-called Belleville Three, an epithet for Atkins, May and Saunderson, struck me as a showbiz moniker not unlike one from WWE wrestling. Beyond being a musical experience, techno was a business, and, in a commercial sense, a brand. Musically, Hood always acknowledged the early 1980s iteration of techno, a strand of music that in Detroit he called 'progressive'. In his ears, it synthesized with his father's jazz trumpet (his father was murdered when Hood was six) and the long instrumental intro to 'Papa Was a Rolling Stone' by the Temptations. 'I was deep into new wave growing up as a teenager in the early '80s,' he told *The Guardian*, 'listening to Human

League, Depeche Mode, Gary Numan, Soft Cell, the B-52s, OMD; there was a new wave club I used to go to in Detroit called Club Liedernot.' But this synthesis of influences did nothing to undermine the Black empowerment the music embodied – quite the opposite. Some text on *Minimal Nation*'s vinyl run-out groove reads *music for the progressive*. That was an attitude I had internalized long ago, in my childhood.

Rave New World

What happens when at a young age, the age of dinosaur toys, you're introduced to the most virulent psychedelia? When, alongside cartoons like *The Animals of Farthing Wood*, your television shows kaleidoscopic lights and electronic beats? When, as at school you're mastering your ABCs, elsewhere you're overhearing talk about LSD?

What happens?

I suppose I'm what happens.

Donegal, where I grew up, is a patchwork of bog and beach at the furthest extremity of Europe. My Donegal ancestors were disinherited Irish peasants who clung to the sea. Displacement is my birthright. The memory of the Great Famine, too, lived on in my skinny limbs, and when as a boy I worked with my father and siblings on the bog stacking turf, as the wind whistled across the barren plains, I sometimes wondered about the silent dead multitudes buried under the spongy brown surface.

In rural Ireland, the people are the landscape. Those who fish become fishermen and those who farm become farmers. Those living by mountains become mountains and those who reside in thatched cottages become thatched cottages. This adult is a bale of hay, that child, a stone wall. The landscape has a moral character.

Enter me.

As a child, I used to stare at things a long time without saying anything. I stared, while kicking football with Johnny

Heron, at the grid of grey concrete off which our ball ricocheted. I stared, while working on the bog, at the glistening moisture of the bog hole. I stared at visitors to our family home. And this threatened our common integrity. Staring too long at a jellyfish made you become a jellyfish. Staring too long at something repulsive and alien made you become repulsive and alien. Because your eyes ushered into your community an unsavoury queerness.

Narin Beach was where I flailingly failed to learn how to swim; where with John Quinn I clambered over slimy rocks and threw skipping stones; where with the visiting Northern Irish kids I kicked a football. Narin Beach, too, was where the boy lived who first began bullying me, initially calling me a *space cadet*, because of my spaced-out gazing, then a *freak*, because I freaked everybody out, before at last settling on *Klingon*, because, he laughed, I had a disgusting large forehead. Klingon: through taunts and chanted repetition, the name poured itself onto the snow of my soul.

When as a child you're shy and maligned, you internalize what you're called. Name-calling becomes your insidious narrative, a horrid mirror reflection. You gradually become the queer name as others become the homely landscape. Before long, because of the name-calling, which caught on at school through a clownish English classmate, I came to dread Narin Beach, on whose white sands I was made to feel freakish. Introverted, I retreated into drawing pictures.

At school in Mrs Naughton's class, John Quinn and I had devised an ambitious project. We agreed to draw and catalogue every monster in the entire universe. As well as comics like *X-Force* and arcade games like *Bubble Bobble*, our inspiration came from kids' TV shows like *Sesame Street*, with the furry Mr Snuffleupagus, and *The Magic Roundabout*, with the zany Zebedee. I noticed that my teenage siblings, too, Éamonn, Mairead and Evelyn, were absorbed in such images, but in the videos they watched, *The Magic Roundabout* theme was hopped up over hyper-electronic beats.

Here, boyhood morphs into psychedelia.

I remember one Saturday morning, when my sister Mairead and I were sat on the living-room carpet watching *The Chart Show* on ITV, how a video came on for a new track called 'On' by an artist called Aphex Twin. My brother Éamonn had already told me about him (even though I was only seven). The Aphex Twin video showed a beach like Narin Beach. Aphex Twin himself had long hair and resembled my brother. Aphex Twin, Éamonn had said, was born in Ireland and built his own electronic musical instruments and practised lucid dreaming to create his futuristic music. Maybe he, too, was a species of Klingon, I reflected.

The music video delighted me. It had all the strangeness of a dream. As we watched, the beach transformed into a surreal tableau. Clocks swirled; seaweed came alive and vomited up more seaweed; a deep-sea diver in a huge old-fashioned diving suit ambled about like a spaceman exploring an alien planet. Watching over it all was a towering cardboard figure, the long-haired Richard James himself, the artist as a modern Fionn mac Cumhaill. At the time I didn't reflect on it, but the immediacy of Aphex Twin's 'On' was, I now see, its seaside psychedelia.

John Berger wrote that 'a landscape's "character" determines the imagination of those born there.' Calling this effect 'the address of landscape', Berger gives examples:

> The address of many jungles is fertile, polytheistic, mortal. The address of deserts is unilinear and severe. The address of Western Ireland and Scotland is tidal, recurring, ghost-filled. (This is why it makes sense to talk of a Celtic landscape.) . . . I am suggesting that geography, apart from its obvious effect on the biological, may exercise a cultural influence on how people envision nature – and this influence is a visual one.

In the music video for 'On', the Celtic address (Cornish, Irish) is psychedelic. The beach isn't a place of community banter but a microorganism playpen. Here on TV, it seemed, was our local beach, Narin Beach, but seen otherwise. 'On' proffered a hand of welcome, a vindication of freaks like me.

These childhood events happen before my mind's eye as if I were watching them in a theatre. In our family bungalow, I see myself dressed in red pyjamas. And, stealing into the living room on a Monday night, I am surprised to see an alien. He is dressed head to toe in white. A ski mask and goggles cover his face, and, stooping forward, he less walks than jitters. The alien jitters up and down a leafy country lane in time to explosive electronic music, to a chipmunkish voice screaming, *I'll take your brain to another dimension!* A jittering febrile alien on a leafy lane, like the leafy lane in Cashelgolan, just down the road from us.

The alien is on our small TV screen. But although he's an alien, I'm not scared – quite the opposite. Looking around at my teenage siblings, who are absorbed in the music (the video for 'Out of Space' by the Prodigy), I conclude that this alien is cool – that this alien is benevolent; that, even if I'm being bullied as a Klingon, there does exist a place for such bizarre beings. I guess I feel seen.

Through the lens of our era's cynicism, the video for the Prodigy's 'Out of Space' probably looks naive. But at the time it heralded techno-utopianism. Some will consider ridiculous the idea that the Prodigy and Aphex Twin could ever be a form of pastoral – that rave was about anything other than people getting mashed in warehouses. But in signal transmissions, what matters is less source than receiver. Picked up in rural Ireland by my bullied eyes and ears, rave videos' pastoral scenery romanticized and re-enchanted the world around me.

Initiatives like *Mixmag*'s Blackout have brought an overdue celebration of electronic dance music's African-American sources. Historically, what's important to understand about the Prodigy is their specificity: not from metropolitan London but from a rural backwater in Essex; mixed-race and working class and steeped in underground hip-hop. Melding sped-up breakbeats and rapping, dub reggae samples, acid house arpeggios and UK synthpop melodies, not to mention joyous silly dancing, it was this that rural Irish kids like me related to. I don't think I'd ever seen long-haired boys unselfconsciously dancing before.

Éamonn, Mairead and Evelyn, my brother and sisters, all a year apart, were immediately swept up in the Prodigy's quasi-carnival. They followed the Prodigy's first tour around Ireland, from Castlebar in the west, where the gig was abandoned because of a riot, to Dublin in the east, where the thirteen-year-old Evelyn, as she later told me, was thrown face-first into a cauldron of deranged swivel-eyed dancers. And now here is this seven-year-old boy in red pyjamas, watching androgynous men dancing before yellow and purple skies, then jumping up on the sofa and bouncing up and down on the cushions in a little child-rave of his own.

These days, it pains me to watch the 'Out of Space' video's opening. By the seaside, over lush synthesizer chords, Keith Flint and Maxim Reality stand on a car roof, goofing about. In those carefree scenes I feel wrenching nostalgia: nostalgia for my beachside childhood, nostalgia for those years and that family home forever gone, a loss embodied in rave's golden child Keith Flint, smiling with flowing locks, my beautiful dancing kin, now dead, lost to depression and suicide. The day I heard the news of Flint's suicide, I was devastated. I grieved not only for him but for my youth, replaced by a world where there are no options but normativity and consumerism, no future but nature's conflagration.

And suddenly, in this theatre, the red curtain drops. As it does so, as in some Gaelic folktale, there occurs a freakish reversal. For that youthful boy becomes wizened and old, and at the same time, my adult form becomes boyish. The aged becomes youthful and the youthful becomes aged, a reciprocal process of becoming. The new music has aged; the *new age* has aged.

G. K. Chesterton wrote, in his essay 'A Defence of Nonsense': 'The matters which most thoroughly evoke . . . the abiding childhood of the world are those which are really fresh, abrupt and inventive in any age.' Rave culture was an unconcealment of life's everlasting up-rushing youth. Coinciding as it did with my own childhood, rave culture normalized psychedelia for me, which these days, in this most unenchanted of capitalist worlds, has been a blessing and a curse. A documentary that well captures this is *Rave New World*, which aired one Saturday night in 1994 on Channel 4 and which marked me. Rewatched on YouTube at a distance of decades, it's a time capsule from a different era, by turns illuminating and poignant.

Rave New World documents the early 1990s convergence of youth culture, technology and drugs. 'Pop culture has met the microchip,' the narrator (ex-*Doctor Who* Tom Baker) intones portentously, 'and a strange new creature has emerged.' We see a vast rave in a remote aircraft hangar, all flickering lasers and floppy-hatted teens. We see ecstasy creator Dr Alexander Shulgin attempting to concoct new potions whose psychedelic properties might be vastly greater than the aforementioned drug he helped to synthesize. Naturally, too, we see a man off his gourd at UCLA's Harbor Hospital, having submitted to an experimental 75-milligram MDMA trial, reminding us that there are few things in life more charming than witnessing somebody off their face for the first time on pills ('I'd like to meet the pope right now and share some of my newfound wisdom').

Orbital, interviewed in their studio, link rave culture to the primordial era: we have been doing this since before history, they say, and really that's all we're seeing now – a re-emergence through new technology (echoing Terence McKenna's 'archaic revival' idea, as promulgated by Orbital's peers the Shamen). The brainiac punkish musicians who lead the movement – Orbital, the Future Sound of London – are self-confident, and rightly so, and it's buoying, how full of ideals and answers they are on how the world's about to turn. 'Computers are just generally used in quite boring ways, and we want to use them in more interesting psychedelic ways,' says Matt Black from CGI graphics company Hex. 'The human race needs to evolve its psychic potential in all ways possible.' To me as a young boy, this held wonder. It was also familiar, since it was my brother's world and that of his friends.

If the Prodigy were rave's bright angels, their dark demonic counterparts were the Future Sound of London (FSOL – Garry Cobain and Brian Dougans). Predominantly sample-based, FSOL's music owed as much to experimental '80s UK acts like 23 Skidoo and the Art of Noise as it did to Juan Atkins and Larry Heard. Notable early releases were the 1991 hit dance single 'Papua New Guinea' and the 1994 album *ISDN*, the latter first performed via the then-new Internet (for which they won two Guinness World Records: 'The first world tour by a group without leaving the studio' and 'The first world tour featuring live shows played down telephone wires'; they also hold the record for 'The first internet music download').

The 'Papua New Guinea' video is hauntology to a T, a trip through our lost futures. When I watch it, it *is* my lost boyhood. That track's unlikely commercial success, Cobain later said, was because

> it's familiar but it's also totally exotic . . . If you're going to take somebody on a journey, there should be something familiar, so to a certain degree we were all playing the game of getting something familiar and then warping it . . . that was the revolution of sampling. It was an amazing time.

Interviewed on *Rave New World*, Cobain seems paranoid and megalomaniacal. 'We are masters of the machine, and that's all,' he says from their studio bunker, predicting the coming of a vast societal change, of which FSOL are the harbingers. The group's interplay of madness and familiarity climaxed with the ambitious double album *Lifeforms*, for which they made an accompanying extended video featuring CGI psychedelic visuals that were like nothing else I had ever seen, the florid image of the future in its monstrous beauty (it was broadcast on Channel 4 in 1994 on the same night as *Rave New World*).

A huge ominous alien face composed of a thousand vibrating orbs, its eyes blank and pitiless as the sun, dissolves upwards in a rush; and as the camera follows the face's residue, the pink sky turns into a dark garden of gnarled thorny rose bushes and hovering butterflies; then in turn, all caught up in wild becoming, this garden whirls into a white vortex, and above clouds before a maroon-coloured sky explode into a phalanx of beating orange hearts; finally, FSOL's *Lifeforms* signature object, the 'spike', appears, a shiny poly-tendrilled electronic brain, an oily nodal biomorph.

I see myself sat on the carpet, at seven years old, exposed to it all. I am absorbed in the echoing bird cries, humming Tibetan bowls, synthetic liquid timbres and jumbled sample-tapestry, within which from time to time, my daemon sister, my female alter-ego, a pale young girl appears. The whole effect is of a wild exoticization of my rural surroundings – what the philosophers Deleuze and Guattari would call art as de-territorialization, art as rendering the world outlandish.

I could relate to FSOL's daunting weirdness. My eyes were cat's eyes. My eyes were invertebrate jelly eyes. My eyes were flocks of sparrows passing over treetops; because my eyes always became what they saw. And if my eyes stared too much, it was because somehow they were seeing everything for the first time, regarding everything supposedly familiar as alien. The world was a mutant and so was I.

Beautifully alien, too, with Plastikman's 1994 album *Recycled Plastik*, the CD of which Éamonn owned in a slim white case. *Recycled Plastik* would be a bridge from the open rave music of my youth to the more focused techno of my adulthood. *Recycled Plastik* would be a bridge from hissy cassette tapes to gleaming CDs, a bridge from techno as melodic into techno as avant-garde, a bridge from the organicism of childhood into the plasticity of adulthood, a bridge into that deranged foreign country they call maturity. The tracks 'Krakpot' and 'Elektrostatik' were so taut, so warped, so weirdly beautiful. They were acid-fuelled trips whose vehicle was sparsity, whose destination was oblivion, whose pleasure was sophisticated, whose groove was knowing. The alien logo on the album's cover was my sign. Plastikman's *Recycled Plastik* resembled a giant pill, and it was, indeed, a gateway drug.

Having shown us MDMA research and electronic music and computer-generated visuals, *Rave New World* ends with a preview of a possible future society, at a desert festival where all these elements come together. Here, bathed in the sepia glow of the desert light, we observe the strange new techno tribe being born. 'Rave culture has come a long way from kids dancing in dingy warehouses,' says the narrator. 'Today it boldly proclaims a belief that technology can be psychedelic and even subversive.'

An androgynous DJ in his booth plays techno to a solo, legginged man. A topless woman in a white helmet strides by, and a car transformed into a giant shark replica swerves wildly. These are believers in 'peace, love and the microchip', who on

America's West Coast have merged rave culture with the residue of 1960s counterculture. The techno-utopian entrepreneurial duo Monk state that, connected to new technology – called the Internet – they have become 'pioneers of dashboard publishing'. Monk seem like maverick scientists splitting the atom, using satellite phones to connect with people at home around the world on their computers – 'thanks to the cyber monks of *Monk* magazine,' they say proudly.

Yes, seen now it's not simply poignant but devastating. For as night falls, and as the cheers rise around a towering neon effigy tumbling in flames, you realize that this utopian vision is one of the first small iterations of Burning Man. 'Techno hippies are convinced that, bit by bit, the digital revolution will spread harmony and understanding,' the narrator says, as a topless woman dances before the fire. Watched from the vantage of our twenty-first-century surveillance society, where the techno-utopians have been utterly usurped by dystopian Big Tech capitalists, who have conquered and appropriated everything in our private lives and crushed the countercultural spirit – well, it's not hard to feel mournful.

The blue neon man burns before the night sky, and as the small gathering cheers, we witness a beginning that is also an end. The effigy burning is a stand-in for the very techno-utopian dream itself, immolated by Bezos and Zuckerberg et al., leaving us haunted among the cindery ashes of our retro-futuristic memories. Elon Musk noted, after all, that these days Burning Man '*is* Silicon Valley'. Monk's indie pride thirty years ago, sat in their van beaming images worldwide to dial-up home computers, is depressing to see. 'It's a cultural convergence that – really, you can't name and claim it yet because we're in the middle of it,' they say with optimism of rave culture. 'We'll know what it is when it's over.'

Decades down the line, how do we avoid forgetting what rave culture originally meant? In a now highly corporatized electronic music scene, how do we keep alive that native weirdness, the vitality rather than the shell, the shock of the new rather than the commercial efflux? Is it possible to stay forever fresh and young? Are we mad to yearn for those days, their self-confidence?

Around this time, I had a chance to chat with Eris Drew. A Chicago native, a regular, at the time of writing, at Panorama Bar, and a label head, along with her partner Octo Octa, of T4T LUV NRG, Drew is for many one of the most inspiring people in electronic dance music. As well as her DJ sets and productions, which hearken back to the exciting openness of 1990s rave, Drew is known for her activism, public speaking and empowerment of other trans artists. On her Substack, she often writes essays exploring rave's connections to the archaic, psychedelia and liberation, and to what she calls the Motherbeat.

'Motherbeat is a name for something in nature which is always there,' Drew told me when I asked her about this metaphysical idea. 'It is the rhythm in all things. She is essentially a goddess because she represents something important that humans too easily try to forget: that we are part of nature; even our machines speak in the same voice as Mother Earth. Nothing we do can challenge her and we forget her at our own peril.'

As a recovering James Joyce obsessive, I appreciated the resonance with the Anna Livia Plurabelle archetype in *Finnegans*

Wake. It confirmed for me how rave culture reprises aspects of earlier artistic modernism.

The Motherbeat was revealed to Drew after, at a rave at the age of eighteen, she experienced a disruptive spiritual awakening. She became aware of what she has referred to as a 'phase transition in the psychosphere', marking something's arrival. Thereafter, the Motherbeat helped Drew to heal and guided her artistic path, both individually and in the wider community. 'I am 48 years old,' Drew said, 'so embodying her means simply doing maternal good things for others in the scene: for example, hosting workshops, teaching others to DJ, taking care of people having a hard time at events, organizing psychedelic safer spaces. Mama stuff. High priestess stuff.'

On a recent Sunday evening, I caught a powerful set by Drew in Panorama Bar. I had just come back from a trip to Dublin that left me sad and confused, and when I arrived in the humid Panorama Bar, the lighting was purple and dreamy, and the crowd queer, and dancing beside Drew were her partner, the DJ Octo Octa, and their friend Cormac, the queer Irish Panorama Bar resident.

Drew was spinning all vinyl as usual and looked like she was concentrating intensely (she later said she had taken psychedelics for the set in a ritualistic way). As she hit her groove, there was an intensely colourful atmosphere, and I found myself soberly tripping out with my eyes closed. It felt healing. My body became transported, and I ached somewhere inside for my dead childhood – or undead really, since I still feel myself to be that child, one whose world no longer exists.

I mentioned to Drew how I felt that those avatars of my childhood such as Aphex Twin were almost faery-like. Drew agreed that there was a return there to the otherworld of Celtic myth. 'Motherbeat is here to remind us that some myths are true,' she said, 'and that we need stories to explore the mysteries of being that science can't computationally reduce.'

Tied with this, the club experience itself is not always pleasurable; it can also be an ordeal, a necessary one which we invite unto us so that we can change. 'So much of the dominant cultural mode is meant to make us comfortable but it doesn't,' Drew said. 'We need to get uncomfortable to really find some sense of peace in this life and to reach deeper understandings.'

Ordeal, she said, is one technique in the raver's toolkit, as important as mind-altering substances. Examples included sleep cycle disruption, fasting and overexposure to sound. 'Ordeal opens us to the power of subjective experience. It helps us to quiet the rational routine operation of our minds so we can focus on other energies, thoughts and realizations.'

What I experienced as the sad extinction of rave's early utopian spirit, and the loss of my childhood identity, was, then, more a case of dulling. The Motherbeat was always still there inside. In experiencing Drew's sets, I knew she was right.

'So much of the language regarding these experiences is filtered through the entertainment industry,' she pointed out. 'We need to create a lexicon for clubbing which bypasses that every chance we get. And we need to stay at it, because they'll take the language we used last cycle and turn it into commerce.' She pointed out how the language of 'healing' and 'transcendence' even gets used by festivals these days to sell their tickets. 'That language solely came from artists and ravers a few years ago.'

Given how twenty-first-century tech capitalism subsumed 1990s techno-utopianism, we might wonder whether anything remains of rave culture's promise. Back in the 1950s, Adorno wrote of progressive music by saying that, although to 'speak of the aging of the New Music seems paradoxical', precisely this futuristic music (in his case, avant-garde classical music) 'has begun to show symptoms of false satisfaction'. What Adorno saw creep in over time was amnesia: amnesia for why one was making these weird sounds, for what the original impulse was, so that eventually one was simply making pseudo-'futuristic' music in a mindlessly rote way. Adorno noted: 'The aging of the New Music means nothing else than that this critical impulse is ebbing away. It is falling into contradiction with its own idea, the price of which is its own aesthetic substance.'

Drew took issue with this when I brought it up. 'So much of the conversation in this scene is about what is the "good music" versus the "bad music". Instead, we should focus on what is the "meaningful experience" versus the "less meaningful" . . . We need to focus on the power of people's subjective experiences *now*, rather than casting the values of the scene in terms of memory alone.'

For trans people like Drew, and for all those who refute gender conformity, dancing in clubs, around other queer people, is a way of moving beyond the binary's colonial control mechanism. 'We are not new,' she wrote once on Twitter. 'We are old. As old as old can be. As old as the oldest. The first of the first. The last of the last. We permeate the ancient myths. We shape new culture as it moves forward. Humanity is 4everGNC.'

Drew pointed out to me again the connection between transness and the archaic revival. On the subject of futurism, she said, 'so much of the cultural pushback against trans visibility is anxiety caused by a reflection of the future that everyone knows is coming. In so much as transgender can be thought of as an ability to make choices about body and identity (*that* is a thorny and complex set of assumptions), the choices humans will soon have about their own bodies and the bodies of their children goes far beyond gender/sex, and this terrifies people very deeply.'

Her closing words to me, typically, were inspiring. 'Remember that the world around us is alive and we are part of this mama matrix. As much horror as there is in this world, it is still a truly amazing thing to be alive.'

Wordsworth famously said that the child is the father of the man. The genderedness of that statement aside, I realize now that that child I was then, drenched like a sponge in psychedelia, gave birth to the person I became, this alien exiled in East Berlin.

It was heavenly to experience as a child that rave era, when the faery beings seemed to hold out once more a hand of radiance. In psychedelia, I found a home. If my actual home was a rural bungalow by a hazel forest in an Irish community where I was bullied as a monstrous Klingon, a virtual home had come into being, the dizzying and dreadful techno sublime (my bully and I later patched it up, incidentally, and these days get on well). As far as being an adult alien goes, I take inspiration from the famous remark by Diana Vreeland, former editor-in-chief of *Vogue*, that people shouldn't conceal their supposed faults but rather brandish them with pride.

> If they have a gap between their teeth, make it the most beautiful thing about them . . . Make an asset of your faults. If you're tall, be taller – wear high-heeled shoes.

> If you have a long neck, be proud of it, don't try to hunch over. If you have a long nose, hold it up and make it your trademark.

Along these lines, I have learned to lean into my weirdness – to embrace and take pride in it. Which, at queer parties in Berlin, is really the prescription.

The Art of the Dance Floor

'Berlin is a brand,' Dimitri Hegemann remarked. The grey-haired grandfather of Berlin's techno scene was sitting onstage beside UR's Mike Banks and Basic Channel's Mark Ernestus. They were gathered at a Kreuzberg venue as part of a Detroit/Berlin panel to discuss techno and investment and the night-time economy. Hegemann, co-founder of the festival Atonal in the 1980s and of the club Tresor in the 1990s, was clear-eyed enough to say this, though it didn't stop a feminist punk from standing up and, at the top of her lungs, denouncing him before the bewildered audience as a capitalist stooge for daring to use the word 'economy'.

Anyone who's half-read Jacques Lacan knows that the surest way to excite desire is to present something while keeping it hidden. The mainstream exposure of the *Berlin* brand – Berlin as youth culture capital, city of techno and graffiti and GDR ruin porn – ironically owes directly to the underground scene's ethics of concealment. Berghain is emblem of this. Alongside the club's music, architecture, debauched environment and marathon opening hours, two core factors that have ensured Berghain's renown are its Fort Knox door policy and the ban on all photography.

Every Saturday night, dressed as they think they're supposed to dress, steadying their nerves with a beer, hordes of tourists descend, easy to spot in the queue. You could even happen upon them in the club's darker recesses – that ponytailed girl and her boyfriend having an experience of profound erotic abandon while also, Ben Lerner-style, self-consciously experiencing themselves having *an experience of profound erotic abandon*, fucking clumsily, then, post-coitus, more clumsily still turning on an iPhone torch to scour the sodden floor for a set of dropped keys, as, in the surrounding darkness, gay men watched on like tribal natives curiously observing some loggers.

This was Berlin clubbing in the age of the experience economy.

Writing in the *Harvard Business Review*, B. Joseph Pine II and James H. Gilmore described the experience economy as a market in which 'a company intentionally uses services as the stage, and goods as props, to engage individual customers in a way that creates a memorable event'. In other words, paying for an experience specifically because it's clandestine and gives you a *You'll never believe what I did* story to tell Charlie from HR at the water cooler. This is escape rooms, immersive theatre, secret cinema, dark dining, corporate Burning Man packages, ayahuasca retreats, Instagramming yourself walking on the wild side in Berlin – and, these days, Berghain and other brand-name clubs.

This covert incursion of appropriative capitalism into the club scene, and the paradoxical role photography has – how Berlin clubs' ban on photography at once conserves and excites outside interest in this subculture – made me wonder about how, as an artist, you could represent the club experience without ruining it. Being a writer, I was of course caught up in this. To think it through, I began exploring how visual artists represented techno and Berlin's clubs.

A good opportunity was the exhibition *No Photos on the Dance Floor! Berlin 1989–Today* at the C/O gallery, which I attended with my art critic friend Rebecca. *No Photos on the Dance Floor!* presented photographs of Berlin's club scene by the likes of Wolfgang Tillmans, Sven Marquardt and Camille Blake, and the coffee table book published to accompany it contains interviews and essays by authoritative critics like Thilo Schneider and Philip Sherburne.* Leafing through the book's pages was, for the initiate, like looking at a family album, with shots of our adoptive families. For those who wanted to flick straight to a specific club, the front of the book had a handy index. Seventy-seven clubs were listed in all, from ://about blank (2010 to today) to WTF (*c.* 1994–9), pointedly including their lifespan. Conspicuously absent, though, was the at times wonderfully flamboyant fashion characteristic of queer parties like Homopatik and Buttons.

Martin Eberle's architectural photography series *Temporary Spaces* (2001), shot over a decade, documents buildings that hosted club nights. Subjects range from the famous (the old Tresor on Leipziger Straße) to the obscure (Dirt). Eberle shoots interiors and exteriors and the images are always devoid of people, focusing on the architecture. Outdoors in a concrete wall under green leaves, we see a closed orange door. In the corner of a room that's lit up orange and scarlet, where two tiny glitterballs hang over a prefabricated wooden counter, sits a battered armchair. In a street shot, a nondescript grey facade stares at the viewer with dirty wooden window frames and an iron cage over the door. For anyone who's spent time among Berliners,

*Interviews with those noted above and quoted in this section are from this book.

there's something familiar about this restrained style and dry humour, letting the spaces speak for themselves.

'For those of us who were around,' Eberle writes of the post-reunification period in Berlin, 'the club and the city are conflated in our memory; we recall the sense of emptiness, the abandoned spaces, the as-yet-unformed quality, the new ruins alongside the destroyed spaces that had remained unnoticed and untouched for decades – the feverish, hallucinatory possibilities of the present.' In observing this counterculture that emerged in the cracks, it's hard not to recall the French May '68 slogan, 'Sous les pavés, la plage'. Looking over the best club photos made me feel that there's a link between ethics and aesthetics: a photo's aesthetic power is, I felt, proportionate to the photographer's respect for and understanding of the clubbing subculture's ethics.

A recurring theme is the difficulty of representing transience, and the artistic spur this provides. That difficulty is partly to do with the club's environment. 'Flashing lights in front of a black background, fast movements with little light, which do not record what the eye perceives on the film,' as Tillmans says. Curator Heiko Hoffmann, in the exhibition book, observes that 'a busy dance floor on a club night could hardly offer worse photographic conditions: a dark space, flashing lights, fast movements. Capturing what the eye sees is almost impossible.' For proof of this, look no further than the near-ubiquitous shittiness of club scenes in cinema, from *RoboCop* to the German thriller *Victoria* (2015) and beyond. Far from capturing the exhilarating feeling of a nightclub, club scenes in cinema are invariably like videos of people dancing at a wedding. True artists thrive on such challenges, though, as director Patric Chiha showed in *La bête dans la jungle* (The Beast in the Jungle; 2023), wherein the dancing is deliberately slow, inventively elongated, stylized and exaggerated.

George Nebieridze is, alongside Spyros Rennt, one of my favourite contemporary scene photographers. His photographs document the recent Berlin underground, with club nights centred on the LGBTQ+ community. Punkish concealment is centre stage. One page spread in *No Photos* features, on the left, a photo of a mirror clouded with speed, and, on the opposite page, three male figures outdoors in jackets striding away from the camera. The speed on the mirror obscures the reflection; a face can sort of be made out but there are no distinguishing

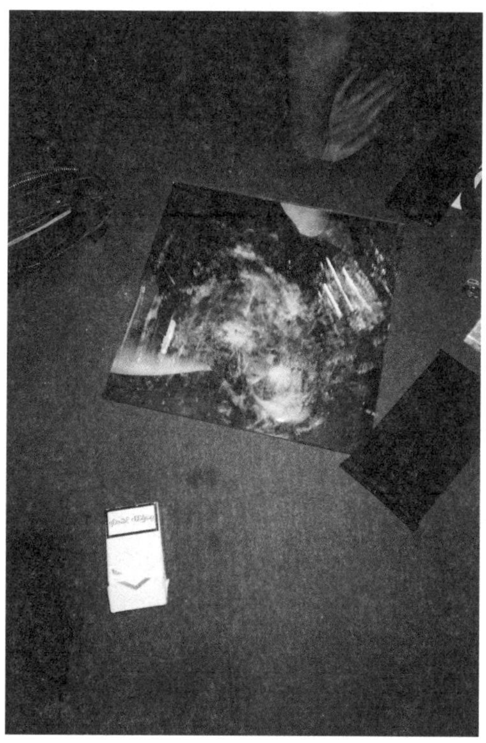

features. Similarly, the three figures in jackets and hoodies embroidered with Herrensauna patches are somehow both self-conscious and incognito. Playing at once insider and bouncer, Nebieridze here coaxes the viewer while keeping her out of the pictured scene. We're shown what we're missing yet, in keeping with the underground ethos, we're not included.

These days, Berghain bouncer Sven Marquardt's celebrity in Berlin is such that there's a mural of his tattooed face in Schöneberg. Marquardt's first career as a young GDR punk was as a fashion photographer, and his photos in *No Photos* are from the immersive C/O installation *Black Box*, where, in a darkened room, they were accompanied by Ostgut Ton (Berghain's record label and booking agency) artist Marcel Dettmann's techno. The portraits are in a neo-noir style, and as always for Marquardt, the photos are analogue and black and white. None are of clubbing per se, but his subjects are associated with the scene.

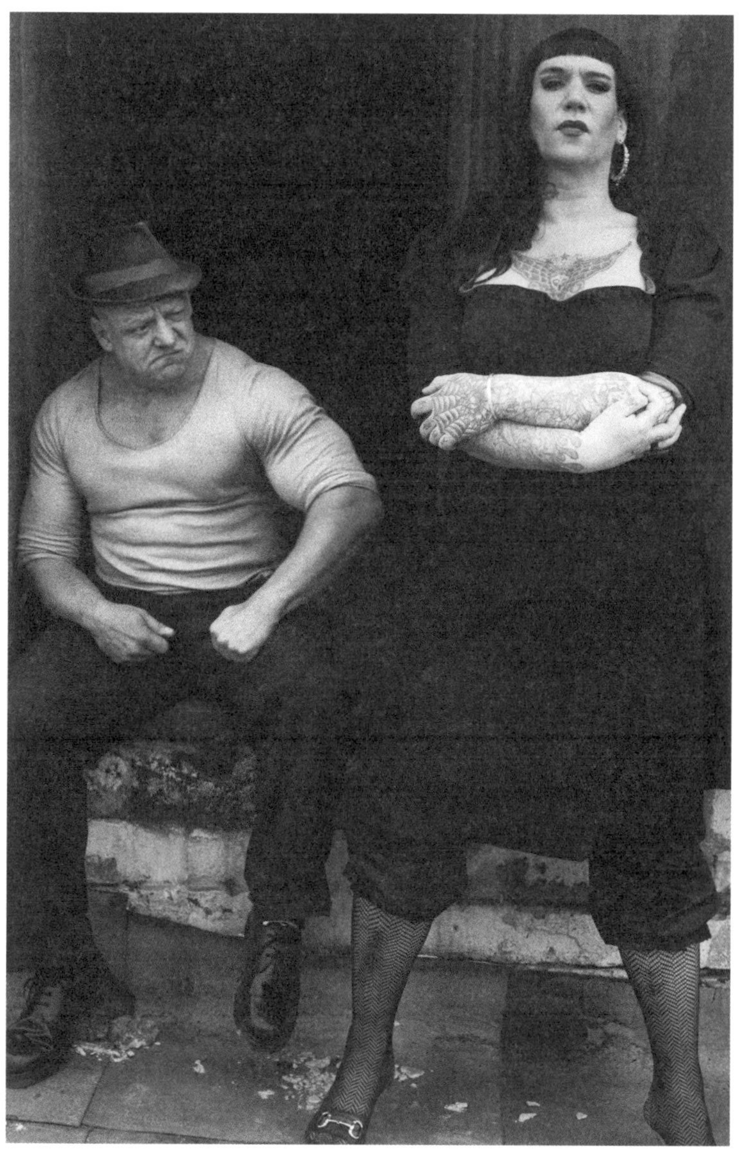

A square-jawed stubbled man stares at the camera with a cigarette in his mouth. A stocky bald man in a fedora and fitted t-shirt crouches on some steps beside his scowling brunette moll. A suited man with an eyepatch broods beside a long-haired grizzled type wearing a headband. Berghain figures are there: one of the bouncers with a bare chest; ex-barmaid Shambhu Leroux; Dettmann. 'My photographs always captured a staged moment; they still do,' Marquardt said. 'I am not a documentary photographer . . . I do think some of my photos are theatrical. But then again, so am I sometimes.'

Marquardt's images, under the guise of gritty authenticity, present a stylized image of masculinity (only one woman features here, the above-mentioned trans musician Leroux). A cursory look shows raw images of Berlin underworld types; a closer look shows images as stylized as shots of James Dean from the 1950s. (Dettmann can't help but look wholesome, though, like your cousin from the countryside who plays in a metal band.) *Black Box*, says Marquardt, is 'our attempt to use sound and images to communicate something that comes from Berlin'. When we went to the c/o exhibition, my friend Rebecca wasn't so keen on Marquardt's photos, and they are polarizing (as he himself, Berghain's gatekeeper, is). But I like them. When you accept that the portraits are exaggerated and their 'authenticity' is deliberately contrived, and when you see that Marquardt has generally shot friends and acquaintances, they appear as the photographer's mythologization of his friendship group – an artistic act with a rich heritage. It reminded me of Yukio Mishima's gay novel *Confessions of a Mask*, where the young protagonist recalls realizing 'that what people regarded as a pose on my part was actually an expression of my need to assert my true nature, and that it was precisely what people regarded as my true self which was a masquerade'.

Other photographers give different perspectives. Marco Microbi's photos document live music gear: tangled cables, a Roland TB-303, a Focusrite interface, yellow headphones, a Korg synth, an orange Boss distortion pedal. Carolin Saage's photos of the defunct club Bar25 chart its carnivalesque mayhem. With its tree-fringed outdoor space of wooden decking and sand, Bar25 informed the aesthetic of subsequent Berlin clubs like :// about blank and Sisyphos, and, as the club's resident photographer, Saage had a privileged view. A stern-faced female staff member in a straw hat holds the tattered guest list for a woman whose name is missing. Legs disappear into a huge rabbit hole flanked by leaves and wood. Glitter and sequins and feathers explode around myriad dance floor bodies under hovering orb-like glitterballs. A wide shot from a boat shows Bar25's entire perimeter at night along the shore of the Spree: between trees,

lit up pink and orange and yellow, it's part Arcadia, part *Apocalypse Now*.

As would impress me again when I later met him, Ben de Biel's canonical photos show the post-reunification period and the freedom of the clubbing subculture's beginnings. De Biel's series *Berlin 1990–1995* also shows how drastically Berlin has changed. East German Trabi cars parked on the street outside the Bunker club; burned-out vehicles buried in the wasteland behind the squat Tacheles; and Sven Väth at the Love Parade in 1992, heroic and bare-chested, wearing arm gauntlets, holding a super-soaker and looking like a retro-futuristic comic book character. Monochrome lends these images historical gravity.

Tilman Brembs's photo of dancers at the 1990s club E-Werk is one of my favourite Berlin club images. In tone and scale, it's like one of those nineteenth-century romantic canvases such as Courbet's *The Diligence in the Snow*, wherein human forms

are dwarfed by nature's daunting vastness. Here, in an expansive space, a cluster of dancers are lit by a sole spotlight, like a comet's tail. Their bodies are silhouettes within boundless darkness, a dark that is as much a character as the dancers. Anyone who has been at Tresor or Berghain knows that darkness, and Brembs conveys its romance. Brembs's other photos of the 1990s, from the series *Analog Rave/Zeitmaschine, Stempelhände*, show, among other things, how much Berlin club fashion has changed. Where in the 1990s the fashion was often similar to UK raves (Day-Glo, hi-vis vests, white gloves), by the 2000s Berlin club fashion fully embraced more fetish, punk and goth elements.

Victor Luque's photographs of the party Cocktail d'Amore faithfully convey the feeling of being in the club Griessmuehle. The triptych *The Way to the Cosmic Hole* shows three images of the same stretch of grotty corridor. Bodies, mostly men's, walk towards the exit; a couple of women pause for a chat at the proscenium overlooking a small dance floor out of shot. But you can't identify anyone: they're anonymous bodies. Luque uses the technique of *contre-jour* – when the camera faces a light source with a body in the way – pointing his camera to the open doorway to animate the club's interior. Within the darkness, a beam of blue dawn light cascades in from the door, through the striking bodily silhouettes, making the air palpable. 'Were it not for shadows, there would be no beauty,' Jun'ichirō Tanizaki writes in the 1933 essay 'In Praise of Shadows'. The male torsos are in shadow not by accident but essentially.

There are tons of talented club photographers you could talk about, but one who's unavoidable is Wolfgang Tillmans. The Turner Prize-winner in 2000, Tillmans started photographing in the late 1980s, covering the rave scene. 'This music so inspired me that I wanted not simply to capture this feeling in images but also to share the joyful message of house music,' he said (his gallery declined to let me reproduce one of his photos in this book, as they had insisted that he be allowed to vet the text and layout). Tillmans's photos of Snax are the only photos of that men's sex party ever published, as far as I know, and they're how I remember Berghain's main dance floor when I first went to the club in 2006. Since then, he's kept an association with Berlin club culture, with two of his large-scale *Freischwimmer* photo prints mounted in Panorama Bar (another in the series, *Freischwimmer #84*, was auctioned in 2017 in London, selling for a measly £605,000).

Despite the disingenuous simplicity of Christopher Isherwood's Berlin credo – 'I am a camera with its shutter open, quite passive, recording, not thinking' – representation is always involved, always artificial, never innocent. Tillmans's photos are those of a participant rather than a colonist, which is why they're effective, and they show transient moments rather than stable identity. In a way, they seek to capture transience itself. The photos' cheap resolution is apt, related to 'the poor image', as Hito Steyerl defines it. Tillmans's photos aren't some transparent glass; they *look* like photos, often like ones you yourself might have taken of friends on a night out. This isn't just down to the unvarnished quality or inexpensive print: it's tacit in the relation within the image between photographer and subject.

Tillmans looks for beauty in the unglamorous everyday. Of Tillmans's club photos, my favourites are those of after-hours scenes, as in 1992's *We Haven't Stopped Dancing Yet*. One photo shows three men slouched on the ground outside a Berlin club.

It's the next morning and the party continues. The central figure wears a baseball cap, green sports jacket, tracksuit bottoms and Doc Martens. He has an arm casually around his friend, who, in sunglasses, is worse for wear. You feel the warmth of the morning sun on your dirty skin and smell the stale tobacco. You feel the intimacy. From the photographer, there is complicity, and from the subjects consent. The group are friends; there is empathy. The moment we see is not so much captured as re-expressed. The aesthetic and the ethical are for the artist bound together in this injunction towards fidelity: that the image remain faithful to its subject. It's an injunction maintained, too, by Ema Discordant, the in-house photographer for the queer party

Buttons, who sadly died while I was writing this book, not long before I met the artist Viron Erol Vert to talk about his striking artwork for flyers and record covers.

Interlude

Inside Berghain's main room, the darkness is palpable. There's a flickering red strobe. And it's almost viscous, the redness, the dark, the heat. Many inside are topless or near naked.

Rene Wise is playing four hours of relentless grooving techno and it's exactly what I need – no lulls or melodies, just cascading pulses. Eventually, absorbed in one particular track – I think it's his 'Primal Fever' – I close my eyes and become the music. I mean, I become the music's visual sensation – a shimmering square, inside which there's a circle and a vertical line. That's why I come here: through my body, through sensory deprivation, through high weirdness to become something other than myself.

You come here to escape the obligation to correspond to yourself.

I feel a tap on my shoulder; it's Andreas. Bald and bestubbled, a head over me in his navy tank top, he stares intently at the DJ box. I like that Andreas is analytical about the music; he really listens. Over time, I've gotten to know more people at Berghain, and it's curious how a lot of them are like me, aging introverts who don't need company to go dancing. Andreas will later become a friend, appearing every now and again like one of Kerouac's bodhisattvas.

On recent Sundays, there have been more young professionals here. Today, thankfully, it's getting freakier, and beside me there's a butch lesbian in a yellow cycling vest, tottering. There's a topless redhead dancing like a drunk spider. There's a short woman with thick black glasses, smoking. And there's a tattoo-plastered woman with pearls, who I will later help off the dance floor after she takes a turn.

Overhead, through the dry ice and the blue strobe, the air turns a thick deep-sea shade of blue. Through this, flickering green horizontal strobes spread, like shoals of fish. I dance harder in response.

Then, far off above, through the blue, I see an obscure body. The body's totally in darkness except for a radiant white crown; it gestures regally to the dancers below. I stare up at her, transfixed – all I can see are the glowing crown and silhouetted body. It's so bizarre, like a dream, the crown of white light, this queen overlooking the writhing dance floor as a vocal refrain sings, 'Work . . . work . . . work this pussy' (a track by one of my favourite producers, Truncate).

Later, I will see her up in Panorama Bar during Avalon Emerson's set – a beautiful Black trans woman, wearing a bikini and amulets and beads, eyes closed, lost in the music.

The club as an immersive artwork, I think – the club as an *auto-generated* artwork – though of course that's too hifalutin', too cerebral.

☾☾☾

Berghain's foyer, during the club's first decade, housed a huge artwork by the artist Piotr Nathan, spanning the entire ground-floor wall facing the *Garderobe*. Comprising 171 square aluminium panels and measuring 25 metres by 5 metres, Nathan's artwork was entitled *Rituals of Disappearance*. Its neo-romantic vista showed, in monochrome, a coastal maritime scene in which stormy seas and tornados, the elemental forces of nature, wreaked havoc. This sublime scene was deliberately intended to be the last thing clubbers saw before they entered the void of the club. The choice of imagery, Nathan said in a statement quoted by *Resident Advisor*, was inspired by his view (not unproblematic) that partying at Berghain re-enacted in the context of modern industrial society the cultic celebrations of Indigenous tribes:

> I believe it is not too farfetched to describe this form of celebration as a ritual, a mystery in the sense of a cultic officiating, during which the innermost element remains a secret. In the context of the music and aura of Berghain, the terms 'cult' and 'secret' receive a nonverbal reading. The mural *Rituals of Disappearance* provides the first visual impression, appearing as a gateway to the entrance area of the club. It is inviting to enter the mystical ambiguity, to marvel at the enigmatic nature and explore the secret behind this massive mural.

Although the artwork was no longer there, replaced by myriad small paintings by the same artist, I had the club's artworks on my mind as, on a cold afternoon in Kreuzberg, I went to meet Viron Erol Vert, a contemporary artist whose ebulliently imaginative work I had long admired, and who for many years worked at Berghain, including helping with the power station ruin's renovations.

Born to migrant parents, Vert grew up in northern Germany and also spent some of his childhood in Istanbul and Athens. After moving to Berlin to study art, he met Michael Teufele at a party, who told him he was planning to open a club and invited Vert to work there. 'I said, "Yeah, I need the job,"' Vert told me when we met at a smoky Kreuzberg café. 'I could work at the weekend and study during the week.' In early 1999 he began working at Ostgut and Lab.oratory, as a bouncer and at the cash desk. Thereafter, he had spent half his life working at the club. If at times in the early years, surrounded by hedonism and fun, Vert regretted having to work rather than party there, his simultaneous proximity and distance, being both inside the experience and outside it, allowed him to absorb the club environment for later re-enactment. 'I transformed it into something else,' he remarked of the club's influence on his art.

When Berghain opened, Vert began contributing art to the club's flyers. As with all his work, his flyers and record covers are richly imaginative. Conveying the felt experience of being in the club, they are often characterized by animal and plant elements, brilliant colour and intricate geometries. Some of Vert's best-known club artworks are for Luke Slater's Planetary Assault Systems and L. B. Dub Corp releases on Ostgut Ton. His cover for Planetary Assault Systems' *Plantae*, at once composed and delirious, shows human heads connected to tubes and machinery in a quasi-factory that, when you follow its surfaces, evolves into flowers and plants. The struck-dumb human expressions on the bald heads present a queer – as in weird – sight indeed. The art is in synergy with the music, complimenting Slater's psychedelia with a studied animism, as if the space itself had a life.

I was curious to know if, when Vert created figurative flyer art, he had a narrative in mind that he wanted to convey to the viewer. 'It depends on the piece,' he replied. 'Every time it's different.' Because he draws and creates work non-stop, he said, 'I don't have to think about [the visual presentation] as right to left or up and down. I try actually to look from all perspectives.'

In images like Vert's December 2016 Berghain flyer, there was a simultaneous centredness and absence of a centre. This related, in my mind, to the immersive quality of a club night, which can feel like a disorienting experience with neither beginning nor end. 'I think that there is, for sure, a middle,' Vert said of these images. 'But there is not a finish, in the end – or not in a classic way.' To always be in the middle, I suggested, meant a kind of freedom, freedom from causes or origins or ownerships. 'We're always in the middle in a way,' he replied, 'and it's also good to know that. That it's possible to be in the middle, and that you don't have to focus on an entrance and an outside, let's say.'

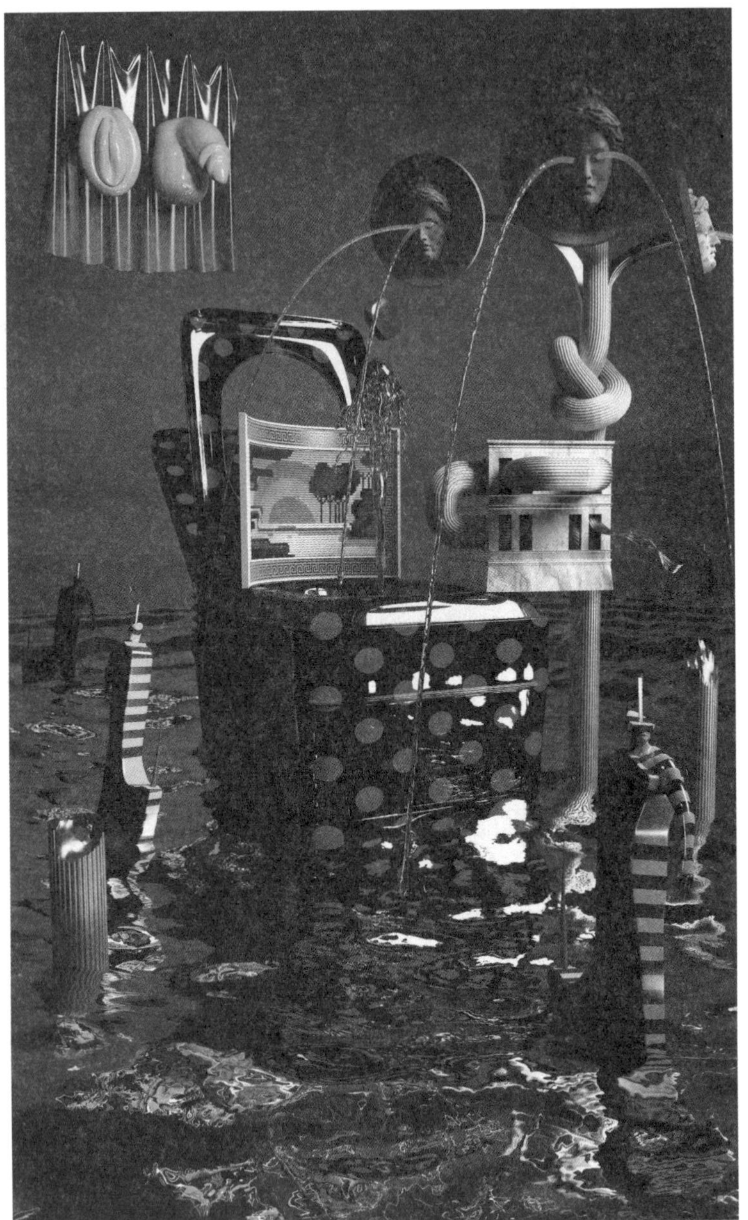

Vert connected his interest in the club experience to his migrant background: the 'aspect of transition, of entering one world, then the other', he said; 'this migration element some people describe when they go to Berghain. It feels also at the door a little bit like that.' I told him he was, for me, one of the visual artists who, more than anyone else, faithfully and imaginatively conveyed the club experience, in a kind of non-linear way. 'I'm happy that you have the feeling,' he said. These images drew on the vibe, he said, from his 'endless nights working at the club; I worked there for 25 years.' Such visions enact the sensations generated in the club, sensations that can affect change in the one experiencing them. 'It is for sure a different place,' Vert said of the queer club space as an experience. A modernist artist with whom Vert feels some affinity is the Greek composer/architect Iannis Xenakis. Xenakis's story also involved migration, and some of his later artworks, like Vert's recent work, were immersive multisensory environments (in Xenakis's case, the so-called polytopes, which combined laser lights and electronic sound much like techno clubs would later do).

These days, Vert exhibits internationally in various media. His recent work has been largely site-specific. Vert was fascinated by the types of human experience he witnessed at Berghain, Ostgut and Lab.oratory, many based on intimacy, and this influenced his creation, in installation works, of 'spaces where people can meet and hang out together, or share a moment together'. One of these, commissioned by Bonaventure Soh Bejeng Ndikung for Galerie Wedding, was called *Dreamatory*; for it, Vert installed beds and invited visitors to stay overnight in the carefully designed dream space. Another, at the Kunsthalle Baden-Baden, was *Garden of Ornaments*, where, through use of colour and form, Vert created an immersive, alternate perspective on the entrance hall of this august building. Through this, he highlighted the multicultural history of what is too often assumed by some conservative Germans to be a monoculture; predictably, some of said guests responded with outrage to Vert's work.

Working carefully with colour and form, and attuned to spatial experiences that unimaginative architecture may have neutralized, Vert engaged with and queered these environments, introducing an artistic kink that defamiliarized and unsettled them. 'There is a little bit of a parallel universe there, in my opinion,' he said of the queer club space. 'It is linked to the outside, but it also folds up something totally else, with other rules.' When you're inside such a space, you have to relearn 'how to behave, rules, what is right and wrong – or whether there is something right and wrong. This is what is fascinating also, and maybe what kept me there so long.' The immersive darkness of a club can defamiliarize you from yourself and generate new types of identity, both personal and interpersonal. This is something I saw in Vert's installation works, too.

As our conversation drew to a close, I reflected on what we had discussed. Clear for me in Vert's art was how a queer club space like Berghain, through shocking our senses, allows us to think anew about the everyday mystery of simply being alive. Animals regularly appeared on Vert's drawings and illustrations for the club. This becoming-animal, he said, related to some of the intense experiences he saw at fetish events. Alongside brutishness, there was revealed in such experiences, he thought, a sensitivity, and this informed the animals he drew. 'The animal element was fundamental for me,' he said, related not only to 'sexual acts, but also heart to hearts; showing yourself, sharing

this moment together'. There was an innate otherworldly romance in this, he said, 'like a fairy tale or something'.

The artist, too, is like an animal: an animal whose offspring, artworks, take flight into the world, sensory butterflies emerging from the gooey grubs of experience.

Biomorphism

> The effort to fathom the giant mechanism is in itself a move towards the abyss, a beginning of madness: for every lure seems an expanding vortex, which soon takes full possession of the unfortunate and carries him away through a night of terrors.
>
> NOVALIS

Deep down I know I am becoming a bird.

Deep down, under red spotlights in Berghain's darkness, as I dance on the podium within the techno's clamour, I realize that, although still humanoid – a human with disappearing fingers – I am *becoming a bird*.

I look down at my fingers; they no longer look like they're mine. Weirdly, they look like a painted portrait's fingers. Extended, my painted fingers drip Pollock-like onto the podium floor. Arched out, my elbows are becoming feathery wings.

I gaze up into Berghain's vault, that abysmal height. Spreading in tridents, blue lasers flicker, inscribing and erasing blue lines. Far away in the distance, two large green dots hang motion-less: a pair of monstrous green eyes.

My heart thumps and my shoulders swing. The venue is colossal, a world unto itself. And at the mercy of this dark cave, which, saturated by Rrose's techno, is insatiably exploring me, I am becoming avian.

Rrose's music changes. From the surrounding speakers, deafeningly loud, comes a chorus of high-pitched shrieking. This tinny noise shifts my perspective.

All around, as if we've suddenly been thrown into the greenest forest, the high-pitched shrieking and whirring – of cicadas, crickets, kingfishers – intensifies Berghain's strange environment, intensifies my process of *unbecoming*.

Terror and excitement grip me. My fishnet top, a grid spanning my torso, curves in and twists like a vortex. My chest throbs; my fingers drool; feebly, I try to keep dancing.

Beside me on the podium, also lit in the red spotlight, a tall trans woman in a white bikini with a blonde ponytail dances with exaggerated grace. As she pirouettes elegantly before Rrose in the DJ box, I self-detach; I see myself quivering. *I am beside myself, watching this happen.*

I am no longer dancing but flapping, befitting the bird that I am becoming. An image flashes in my mind's eye: the Max Ernst painting I used to see at Tate Modern, *Forest and Dove*: a meek helpless bird scratched onto a forbidding dark background, a little dove drowning within a nightmarish forest.

I come to Berghain these days not only prepared for unbecoming but dying for unbecoming. I'm dying to be explored by Berghain's night, dying to burst from myself, dying to die while remaining alive. It's an eminently philosophical urge, I tell myself flatteringly. Wasn't it the German Romantic poet Novalis – a veritable Berghain patron saint – who said that philosophy begins with self-annihilation (*Selbsttötung*)?

For me, 'unbecoming' and 'becoming' signify the same thing: sloughing off your habitual self, your *without-door form*, through the force of influence exerted on you by a nearby body or thing. Thus, through exposure to a forest, becoming-forest; to an ocean, becoming-ocean; to techno, becoming-techno.

The word 'unbecoming', however, has the advantage of stressing two important aspects of the process: first, that in becoming other, we are unbecoming ourselves; and second, that such an event cannot but be utterly unseemly, often embarrassingly so. Becoming-other is always completely *unbecoming of you*; it flies in the face of all that's proper, all shared standards of taste and reason, all social mores. What self-respecting person would want to invite to their home for dinner a giant jellyfish or mollusc?

Under the red spotlights, in Berghain's heat, my mouth is dry. I open it wide – impossibly wide – and feel from my throat begin to emerge a beak. From my thick bare legs come two thin stalks. The stalks penetrate the paint-sodden podium. My painted fingers have by now oozed off completely.

I look over at Rrose in the DJ box. Rrose's pale face and dark fringe and black lipstick are impassive; focused, she conjures from the black void of Berghain's vault a torrential forest, all febrile shrieks and skittering pulses. This is techno at its most ecstatically amorphous.

Below us on the gloomy dance floor, hundreds of bodies shift their slow thighs.

On this red-spotlit podium, my mind gushes with inky darkness. Into me pours the immersive forest; into me, the clamour of mosquitos, crickets, bees; into me, woodpeckers, nightingales, larks, kingfishers. They enter my body through my ears and eyes; they shriek and whir and flutter there, rupturing Berghain's arboreal silence. Within me they flutter and whir and shriek and scream until all becomes dizzying.

It dawns on me: I'm not in fact becoming a bird; no, I'm becoming something else. But what?

A few days earlier, I was sitting in the sun outside Ostkreutz station eating ice cream with Delphine, with whom I was doing a French–English conversation exchange. Delphine is a pragmatic woman with a neat fringe who works in spiritual therapy. I said that, for me, when the conditions are right in Berghain, I *become the music*. This confused her. Delphine goes to silent discos in the woods at Müggelsee, where sometimes she and her friends put on their headphones, strip off their clothes and dance.

'It's therapeutic,' she said.

Delphine gave up drugs and alcohol recently after an acid flashback by the work photocopier unspooled her sense of self.

In the Berghain main room, when the music fills the space absolutely, you enter a non-semantic zone. In the smoke and sporadic flashes, everything becomes pantomime. The visual is hieroglyphic. And in the dance floor silence created by this immersive music, you can overflow your bounds, slip from your body, slip from yourself, become a beam of light or a column of air or whatever.

When you lose yourself in this way and become something else, Delphine asked, how can you relax? Isn't it dangerous? How can you know who you still are? How can you be sure you will return to yourself?

My melting blue ice cream dripped on the concrete.

'I just trust in it and submit completely,' I said.

Deep down I know I am mutating. As the high-pitched shrieking streams through my ears into my body, it dawns on me that I am, in fact, *becoming-insect*.

My mouth is not a beak but a mandible.

My wings are not feathered but translucent.

My wings are four, not two.

My legs are not two but six.

Exploding on an arborescent drone, Rrose's forest clamour shrieks all around as I shrink, past the bird scale and down into the insect scale, into the nervous twitching of a dragonfly.

I crane my insect head. Above in Berghain's vault, a bright plane of blue has appeared. Tints of intense Klein blue thickly mat the vaulted gloom; it is an ecstasy of blue.

My agape dragonfly mouth becomes a blue void. I try to cry out; my voice is just ecstatic blue space.

I am afraid. I tremble.

Exposed as an insect on the podium, I am now prey for the swirling kingfishers, sparrows and ravens, whose heads spin round and round me, pointed beaks pecking.

Everything becomes urgent.

Whatever its effect on me, whatever the hazards of unbecoming, I absolutely had to experience Rrose's Sunday afternoon set at Berghain. Rrose is not simply one of today's pre-eminent techno producers, adventurously exploring techno's potential as artists like Steve Bicknell and Basic Channel did in the 1990s. And Rrose isn't simply an excellent DJ, conjuring dense forests of sound. Rrose's invented persona puts into play the conceit of personal identity. That persona: dark hair, lipstick, painted nails; an allusion to Marcel Duchamp, who created a female alter ego, Rrose Sélavy (a French homonym for 'Eros is life').

Experiencing Rrose at Berghain is particularly fitting. As I've said, what Berghain's founders, Michael Teufele and Norbert Thormann, wanted to create in this boundless ex-GDR power station was a club as a work of art. Berghain is a safe space – albeit an insanely intense safe space – in which you should be free to do what you want and express yourself however you wish without constriction or persecution or shame. When you enter Berghain, passing under the Dionysian colossus, stepping onto the iron stairwell surrounded by fathomless concrete, your outside self is free to undergo *Selbsttötung*. Crossing the threshold involves shedding that mask, a liberation.

Underground techno has always involved personas. Richard D. James is Aphex Twin; he's also The Tuss, Polygon Window, AFX. Mike Banks is behind not only Underground Resistance but

The Martian and X-101. On a mundane level, the play of personas is not unlike a rock band and its members' side projects. But with some artists, like Rrose, it's artistically instrumentalized. The self's cryptic instability – the fact that we're always obscure to ourselves – gives birth in techno to other selves, night-time selves.

There's no such thing as being there neutrally, I told Delphine. Everyone in the club affects the environment simply through being there. Everyone contributes. So, when I'm dancing in the main room I get off on exposure to all the strange faces and personas and costumes around me. You become intimate with those faces and personas and costumes, existing in each other's zone for an hour, communicating non-semantically simply through being in a field of vision. And in that situation inevitably you have to ask yourself: what am I contributing?

The maritime-themed cover of Rrose's EP *Beware of Shells* (2018) shows a crown of shells and pearls and coral set in front of a peach-beige orb on a white background. In the centre of the crown, above beaded rows of pearls, rests prominently a pink scallop shell inset with three crystals. At the top of the crown, five cerithium shells protrude upwards, their bases encrusted with silver balls, their whorls tapering in spirals towards pointed ends. The maritime crown's colours – beige, purple, pink – enter your eyes as sickly sweet and unreal. There is something disturbing about this sea crown. It's a coronation of the human; but it injects the human with the mermaid strangeness of subaqueous minerals. It's a becoming-inhuman of the human, achieved at the point of the human's coronation. Like the music, it's an exposure. By exposure I mean: a positing-forth by which your inner self is mutated.

Beware of Shells's music is highly refined in terms of production and composition. On the title track a sound that at first seems industrial in character – a semi-quaver pulsation, its frequency envelope gradually filtered over background buzzing – at a certain point perceptually morphs into a sound biomorphic in character, the signal emitted by a living invertebrate. This is techno as expression of post-industrial ruin; this is also techno as the sound environment of maritime life relentlessly proliferating. Eventually the music's manifold layers, throbbing and clicking and pulsating, rise to a crescendo of collective excitement – a natural polyphony, free of any tonal centre – many-stranded seaweed and coral entangling in myriad patterns.

Within Rrose's aesthetic, music and visuals align: quickening, outlandish, *unbecoming*. Techno and visual aesthetic and drag are consistent. RuPaul, when quizzed on his 'real' identity, says that regardless of whether he dresses male or female it's all drag. Nor does he limit his identity to the human: 'I am everything and nothing,' he says, notably (not everyone and no one). Delphine said she hates techno because of how, in contrast to house music, which has emotion and soul, techno is anonymous and inhuman. I replied that I like techno precisely *because* it is anonymous and inhuman. For me it allows a radicalized Romanticism, re-arising in our Anthropocene conflagration: the recognition of, and desire for, something beyond the industrial everyday, which alienates us from boundless nature.

Exposed under red spotlights, the night in my veins, shrieking in my ears, I have slid right past becoming-bird into becoming-dragonfly. It couldn't be more unbecoming.

The surrounding wildlife reacts. In this oleaginous gloom, the kingfishers, cicadas and crickets, the bullfrogs, nightingales, larks and crows, hover, shriek, whir, flap, stab, spin and circle around my panicking becoming-dragonfly body.

Heartbeat racing, I am in danger. Nonetheless, although in this grotesque spectacle, I am freaked and my four germinal wings twitch, what *glamour!*

Exposed to the Klein blue square far overhead, I feel a need to beat my four wings. But I'm paralysed. Assailed by these lark and crow and kingfisher heads, I feel the sweat drip into my enormous bug eyes.

By the DJ box, I notice the bikini woman. Now, she has a massive orange beak. She is *becoming-toucan*. Proudly she fluffs her wings, dwarfing me, and she dances nimbly, slipping forwards and back to the beat. I tremble beneath that fearful symmetry: the white toucan face, black toucan eye, protruding toucan beak seesawing and gesturing in mounting avian delirium. Is she readying to swoop?

No: she is dancing to acclimatize to her terrain, awaiting a mate. The toucan in her bikini is becoming one with her new habitat. Her padding feet rattle the empty glass bottles by the wall.

My four legs cling to the floor and my abdomen shoots far out behind me; my eyes become bulging and compound; my legs become multiplied and my diaphanous wings, viscid, unfurl, readying for flight.

My dragonfly mind knows I need to fly, to leave. It can't be a coincidence that the dark vault overhead is brilliant with Klein blue. That blue is what I must seek. As the kingfishers and sparrows whirl around, as the toucan pads her feet, I focus my attention on the music. Rrose's music is a collective alarm, a solar beat, a sloshing seashore within the forest.

A serene delirium, the high-pitched shrieking continues. The beat pounds, carrying with it in my chest my anxious dragonfly heartbeat. Sweat stings my globular eyes. But now, as I enter the sound more and more, other sound figures appear. The insectoid shrieking, granular flow and insistent pulse affect each other. They are inaudible forces wearing masks.

Now, as I listen, the insectoid swarm liquidates. The insistent pulse sweeps downwards: from the treble, where it was clacking pebbles, it sweeps down to the bass, where it becomes dull pounding on a loosely bound animal skin. Within a second the insectoid shrieking drowns in filtered scummy tidal flow.

The music shifts on.

The spell breaks.

Facing me, the toucan woman puts one hand on my shoulder. My six legs and four wings withdraw. My ears ring. She smiles a toucan smile and asks, 'Is this yours?'

She holds a Rubik's cube: the accessory I brought to the club. I always accessorize when I'm clubbing (rosary beads, action figures, juggling balls); I must have let the cube fall to the floor earlier.

I start coming back to myself. She smiles, slowly becoming a woman again.

All I can manage, kneeling on the podium, is to nod slowly.

Techno is traditionally associated with dystopian urban environments and ruins. But in the music of some contemporary techno artists – like that of Rrose, or of Polygonia on her EPs such as *Living Patterns*, and on the two artists' collaborative album *Dermatology* – the vision is of abundant nature and rich ecology. I thought of this techno as biomorphic techno. Biomorphic techno reminds us of our connection to the natural world. This makes it an ideal medium to remind ourselves that every techno city, no matter how seductively futuristic, is ultimately destined to collapse and give way to a jungle.

'Each time I visit nature,' Polygonia told me, 'I feel that our society strongly moved away from the fundamental human connection to nature. As this makes me deeply sad, I see it as my mission to remind people of their roots.' Polygonia – a multimedia artist who also works in the visual domain, as well as in experimental music and jazz – considers techno to be an empty canvas on which one can potentially explore any thought or concept. 'As techno is so often linked to industrial contexts,' she said, 'it sticks out even more if this genre is approached in the opposite way.'

Rrose first appeared in 2011 with two EPs on the Sandwell District label, one of which featured her now-classic track 'Waterfall'. Thereafter came a slew of EPs on their own Eaux label and the albums *Hymn to Moisture* and *Please Touch*. She is inspired, in part, by spectral music, a compositional attitude that views sound as a quasi-living organism and treats pitches like frequencies; and on a remarkable central triptych on *Please Touch* – the sequence of tracks 'Spore', 'Feeding Time', and 'Spines' – the music conveys a process of becoming, with electronic sound objects mutating one into the other. In this vision, techno manifests an exhilarating audio environment full of teeming micro-features.

I asked Rrose about how nature inspires their singular techno productions. 'It's just an intuitive link,' they said. 'The things that inspire wonder and curiosity in me tend to relate to natural forms, shapes, textures and things like that. I think I'm searching for a similar sensation when I make sound. And I often think of it more as a process of discovery than composition.'

The older subgenre out of which this aesthetic developed is called hypnotic techno. Its founder is Mike Parker, and the epithet 'hypnotic' that people use for his music (such as 2001's seminal album *Dispatches*) was meant to express that aspect of the music that seemed designed to evade our categories. In terms of metre and rhythm, tracks by Parker (and those of producers like Takaaki Itoh, Rrose, Donato Dozzy and Oscar Mulero, who all followed him) often aren't in your usual 4/4 metre, but are instead in, say, 6/4 or 5/4; or, if they are in 4/4, their main repeated arpeggio motif will sound triplets over the four, creating undulating textures – as in Takaaki Itoh's track 'Warbler'. 'By reducing the number of sounds used to create a track,' Parker told me when I interviewed him, 'I attempt to make each element significant.'

Rrose combines this with concepts and techniques from contemporary classical music. 'The composers that are directly inspiring to me are people like James Tenney and Éliane Radigue,' they said, 'who often had ideas that were in some way simple but who applied them in a very profound way. Then, the listening experience that would arise from that I personally find very profound. I think I'm trying to do something similar with techno.' Gérard Grisey, founder of spectral music, spoke of musical composition as an ecology of sounds. Every sound ought to be treated as unique in itself, within a network of such unique sounds, each interdependent. Composing music according to this principle means escaping outworn historical models such as major/minor tonality. The result could be psychedelic (or 'chronotropic', as Grisey once said).

I asked Polygonia if psychedelia was one of her artistic focuses. 'I love psychedelic experiences as they have mind-opening and healing effects,' she replied. 'With my music I want to enable the listeners to reflect beyond their regular thoughts. Each time when people approach me after my sets and tell me that they tripped hard without any influence of substances, I feel that I reached one of my highest goals.' She said her tracks should feel like living organisms. 'The complex structures of nature are extremely psychedelic to observe and understand,' she said. 'Therefore, it's the perfect inspiration in order to create such experiences for my listeners.'

Parker also stressed the kinship between techno, in its club context, and the natural sublime. 'Working in techno is a way for a single person to orchestrate a really big, immersive time-based experience using only a small amount of equipment,' he said. 'I agree that listening to it on a proper sound system can make it a catalyst for liberation, like standing at the edge of the Grand Canyon. At least, I hope that my music invokes scale and an experience of transcendence.'

In *The Big Reveal*, the drag queen Sasha Velour – one of my favourites – points out that the roots of the art of drag are more ancient than the word 'drag' itself. 'After all, identities like "queer," "trans," "cis," "gay," "straight" are modern,' Velour writes, while drag is from time immemorial. I asked Rrose if she uses her drag in a club setting, in combination with her music, to evoke something archaic.

'Initially it was kind of an experiment,' Rrose told me of her drag persona. 'I wasn't sure how I would react to it and how the project would develop or how long it would last. But different meanings have become important over the years.' She said it functions on a few different levels. 'There's the personal, which I try not to talk about too much, but it has led to pretty intense personal reflection on my own gender identity. But also, what it does in the space of performance, this is something really important to me.'

Rrose said, of the way people looked at them and experienced their music when in a club space, 'you do get a sense that this is a kind of magical, alchemical situation, where the music involves material transforming, and this is also a person who has transformed themselves somehow. I think of it as an invitation to the audience, to say, "This is no longer the normal space of your life. This is a space where different things can happen."'

At the time of our interview, Parker's house in Buffalo had just been damaged in a catastrophic blizzard. 'The Anthropocene has created some really bad environmental problems,' he said when I asked whether techno retained any utopian force, 'and I wish I had the foresight to answer your question in a meaningful way. Techno as an art form is still evolving. If not utopian, it still has the potential to be otherworldly.'

Up in the Panorama Bar toilets, metallic doors clang. Reverberant voices echo. Snorts explode like gunpowder.

Sitting on a leather bench before the metal cubicle doors, I hold the Rubik's cube. I warm my arm in a solitary shaft of sunlight entering the toilets through a window behind me. It is a hot day outside.

Before me the cubicle door bursts open and a man and woman tumble out. The girl is American, has blue hair and is dressed in a green bathing suit with red socks and purple trainers. She steps into the beam of light and I withdraw my arm.

This light, where did it come from? Let me recharge. Jesus is real. *Jesus is real.*

Below her blue fringe, her sleepless eyes close. She holds a yoga pose in the light for all of five seconds before her eyes reopen and her mouth submits to amphetamine babble.

I have this place near my flat in Baumschulenweg – but wait, you've never been to my flat, have you? What's your name again? Julian? *Julio*, right, I'm Ocean Breeze. Yeah, *Ocean Breeze*. Look at the colours I'm wearing, red and purple and green, I love matching. And look at my shoes, I spent too long in the sun and my blue shoes turned purple! And this lipstick, you know what it feels like? *Blow jobs.*

Around the corner, under the urinal trough, the pee slave hunkers. Topless and dressed in jeans, he looks up and pleads with his eyes. Eventually a man in a leather gimp mask obliges him. Behind them I see an enormous amorphous lime-green blob. The lime-green blob turns its solitary lidless eye to me as, before it, the pee slave gratefully takes the gimp's watery stream in his mouth.

How could you talk or write about this? How could you write these, at one with their nature and habitat, without violating or exploiting them? How could you relate this environment to others without becoming a male beast trampling the undergrowth, marking his territory?

Finished, the gimp zips up. The pee slave smiles, child-like in gratitude.

Danke dir!

Bitte sehr.

Party Like It's 1999 BCE

In the late 1980s, when Hamburg-based Ben de Biel, a photographer by profession, first crossed the border checkpoint into East Berlin at Chausseestraße, he and a friend found that, presumably due to energy shortages, the centre of the East was just as dark as was Kreuzberg in West Berlin. 'All of the houses were empty,' de Biel told me, speaking in fluent German-accented English, as I sat opposite him outside a café on Auguststraße. 'It looked a bit demolished. It looked like the war had stopped yesterday, and this was what was left over.'

An artist-entrepreneur with the debonair air proper to one who founded one of Berlin's most successful clubs (Maria, where Peaches cut her teeth), de Biel was dressed in a beige Kangol flatcap and large tinted eyeglasses, and he smoked while drinking a glass of Chardonnay. I had deliberately arranged a meeting *en plein air* at the junction of Auguststraße and Tucholskystraße in Mitte in the city's east, a stone's throw from where Berlin's most famous squat, Tacheles, used to be – recently reopened as bland luxury condos and an artwashing gallery. 'Tacheles, we don't talk about it,' de Biel said wistfully.

Jean Baudrillard wrote that 'something in all men profoundly rejoices at seeing a car burn.' As de Biel told me of his first forays into this abandoned eastern city centre, some of it barely touched since the war, I imagined the tingling excitement the young artists and squatters must have felt.

'The entire area between Friedrichstraße, Torstraße, Rosenthaler Straße and Oranienburger Straße was a designated demolition zone and already to a large extent vacated,' de Biel told Felix Denk. But since the GDR couldn't afford to offer citizens new living spaces, 'Anarchy reigned back then . . . If we didn't see light at a place for three days, we opened the apartment.' West Berlin's 1980s squatting heritage – during the Cold War, West Berlin, as an island within the GDR, became a bohemian colony, with many going there to escape conscription – meant that, post-1989, countercultural *Wessis* had the know-how to renovate and rewire buildings.

In Germany, a historical reset of this kind is often called a *Stunde Null*, a 'zero hour'. When I asked de Biel about whether Berlin's club scene grew out of a *Stunde Null*, he frowned and shook his head, too matter-of-fact for that idealism. He went on to explain how, initially, he had actually been reluctant to move to Berlin because of how grotty it was. 'Honestly, it was a fucking poor city except for a few districts like Charlottenburg and far West.' A layer of dirt from the coal smoke covered everything. 'Always if you touched a lamp post, you would look at your fingers and they were completely dirty. You needed a complete wash to get it away. So, we tried not to touch anything on our way, and especially not to put your fingers in your mouth afterwards.' I remarked that that must be why, in Berlin, everyone dressed in black.

Although the apartments in West Berlin were bigger than in the East, initially this wasn't enough of a draw for de Biel. Then, after the Wall came down, things changed. 'When my friends started to squat, the house where I lived later in Kleine Hamburger Straße, I realized, okay, this is absolutely in history a special situation,' he said. 'Because I came from a capitalistic country, and we all lived in capitalistic countries insofar as we didn't live in the East[ern Block], which were socialistic countries. The capitalistic system means private property. So, this is normally prohibited for everybody who has not been invited.'

Residential buildings in East Berlin were open for anyone to walk into, owing to the Socialist government's laws around property. 'The practice was to leave everything open, because you didn't have a telephone,' de Biel said. 'So, if you wanted to meet someone, you went up to the third floor. There was a roll of paper and normally, like, a pen on the door hanging. So you leave a message: "I was there, we can meet then and there." And then we met there.'

Nonetheless, de Biel and his friends knew that this situation wouldn't last forever; the question was for how long. After the initial bureaucratic headache of fusing two different systems together, next came the reorganization of property. 'And normally, that should be easier,' de Biel told me. 'Except here was a situation where a lot of [stolen] Jewish property was in the conversation.' One such building was the old Wertheim department store, which would house Berlin's most famous post-reunification club.

Ellen Allien also told me about the techno scene's emergence in the early 1990s, stressing that one had to see things with a longer view.

'I think it's more about the history of Berlin,' she said. '*Everything* was bombed. And my generation is the generation from the parents born during the Second World War, or growing up after the Second World War.' Allien benefitted from the strong women who were her forebears. 'Women are respected in Berlin, since we were building up Berlin,' she said, referring to the post-war period.

When the Wall came down, Allien explored East Berlin with gusto. 'It was crazy, you know. For us, it was like being freed from prison, with the Wall. Finally, I could take my bike and cycle and cycle and cycle. Okay, it was getting darker and darker the further you went into the East, no lights, no advertising, no shops! Everything black, the walls full of rust from heating during the winters.'

The clubs were where hitherto separated people could mingle. 'It was like an environment in which to meet,' she said. 'All the Eastern people and Western people came together, along with people who moved to Berlin to express themselves.' At first, the electronic music was too fast for Allien and strobe lights made her uncomfortable. 'I never liked white stroboscope,' she told me. 'It always made me nervous. There was a lot of strobe, and techno, and smoke.'

Then, she went to the club Planet for the first time. The experience changed her life: there, she met people who were like her. 'These were *my* people in this club. Good conversations, good social skins, I would say.' She learned to dance to techno, growing obsessed with the music. 'I had for the first time on the dance floor my first eight hours, without drugs. On the dance floor, I closed my eyes, and I could dance for the first time in my life eight hours. And then it clicked.'

As things went on, Allien worked at Tresor on the door and at the bar. There, she came under the influence of the club's co-founder Dimitri Hegemann, who became a friend and who encouraged her to DJ. It didn't take long for Allien's talent to become apparent, and her career took off. 'He's a visionary and one of the most important people in Berlin,' Allien told me of Hegemann. 'In the techno world, he's the most important person from the first generation of techno in Berlin.'

Tresor was founded in 1991 in the former Wertheim bank's subterranean vault. 'If there was a definition in the dictionary of "underground",' Juan Atkins once said, 'there would be a picture of Tresor in it.' Jeff Mills, for his part, considered Tresor 'the first true techno club'. As a record label, Tresor became the European base of illustrious Detroit techno producers such as Atkins, Blake Baxter, Underground Resistance, Kelli Hand, Drexciya and others.

I'd noticed that when you read about Tresor the word 'legendary' crops up a lot. After Tresor's legendary founding, its original Leipziger Straße location became legendary, as was the club's legendary connection with those legendary Detroit techno artists it promoted with so many legendary releases on its legendary Tresor record label, which isn't even getting started on the legendary nights so many absolute legends spent partying in that legendarily dark basement.

After my meeting with de Biel, I was reflecting on this on a grey afternoon in late summer as I strode into the exhibition 'Techno, Berlin and the Great Freedom', held in Kreuzberg's enormous Kraftwerk building, the former hydroelectric plant in whose complex Tresor now resided. Curated by Adriano Rosselli, the multi-storey exhibition celebrated the history of Berlin's first techno club. I was soon planning to visit the club itself for the first time to see Oscar Mulero, a master of multilayered hypnotic techno sets, so I was keen to do my homework.

Every good music scene has an origin myth, and on the exhibition's ground floor, documentaries projected on screens told that of Berlin's techno scene. One day in 1991, three young German men were stuck in traffic a stone's throw from the sandy wasteland of Potsdamer Platz (Dimitri Hegemann, Achim Kohlenberger and Johnnie Stieler, who told the tale as I've recounted it here in the book *Der Klang der Familie*). In the interwar years, Potsdamer Platz had been Berlin's metropolitan centre. Dense with bodies, intercut by trams, it was home to the bohemian café culture and seedy cabaret nightlife that inspired modernist art like Isherwood's tales, Jeanne Mammen's lesbian *Revue Girls* and Otto Dix's lurid street scenes. Potsdamer Platz, Europe's Times Square, was where urban modernity presented its neon-lit face. 'Berlin in the 1920s was way ahead of everything that called itself "new",' Marlene Dietrich later recalled. Now, it was an eerie wasteland.

Aware of the derelict buildings dotted around the former East Berlin district of Mitte, and hunting one they could potentially use as a club venue, the three men spotted from their car a dark facade that piqued their curiosity. Having gone away and procured the building's key from a Stasi superintendent, the three men eventually returned and explored the musty ground floor. The building the men entered had been part of a department store that was in the Weimar era one of Potsdamer Platz's grandest attractions, bedecked in the drapes and banisters and accoutrements of high consumerism. Since the war it had lain ruined and untouched, cast outside history.

They explored the dusty ground floor. After some time in the gloom, as if in a mystery novel, they discovered behind a bookcase a door; it had been painted over, and beyond it a staircase led underground into the midnight-dark basement. 'We went down into this slippery stalactite cave without lighters,' Stieler recalled, 'and after fumbling around in the dark for a bit, we eventually found the door to the vault.' The vault was that of the department store's bank, and inside it, the air they breathed was fifty years old. 'That must be what it feels like to find an Aztec treasure,' Stieler recalled. 'None of us said a word.'

Having already been involved in running the small nightclub Ufo in Kreuzberg and Schöneberg, the men were struck by the space's potential. 'It was magic,' Hegemann said, 'like the walls were talking to me.' Those dark walls, the myth goes ('for the first two months it was strange and scary to be there,' DJ Rok said of the club), conjured forth the techno club the way, in myths and legends, a temple calls into being a particular people. 'As I entered I could instantly feel the magic present in that cellar,' Hegemann said of its discovery. 'It had this unfinished quality I really liked, which corresponded with a time of emergence of a new music style.'

Where a promoter from Frankfurt or Ibiza or London would have painted the walls, hung a glitterball or two, fit some tasteful coloured lighting, Tresor's founders more or less kept the building as it was, dark and unsafe and austere, clearing away the rubble and rust but leaving the ruined bank's safety deposit boxes. Enlisting friends, the trio renovated the building, which had no electricity or water. They arranged a sham licence for an art gallery with a bar. Above, the ground-floor space was designated for milder house music; underneath, the basement had concrete walls a metre and a half thick, a DJ behind metal bars, smoke and a solitary intense strobe. The club's name came easily: Tresor. Which in typically literal German fashion means 'vault'.

The club's logo – three concentric circles – was copied from a leftover door bolt.

West Berlin's post-punk scene had been all about the anaemic and the angular. Einstürzende Neubauten's industrial music involved using power drills onstage with sheet metal percussion and dissonant guitars, and bands with names like Malaria! speak for themselves. Hegemann had programmed these bands at his experimental Atonal music festival, alongside the likes of UK visitors Coil and Psychic TV and Deutsch Amerikanische Freundschaft (DAF)'s electronic body music (EBM). That general aesthetic carried over into the 1990s to make Berlin's techno scene darker and more intense than in other countries, as if historical trauma were being purged. One electronic musician whom Hegemann had booked for Atonal in the 1980s, Jeff Mills, proved particularly influential.

Mills and Mike Banks's outfit Underground Resistance came to play at Tresor following a tip from Joey Beltram, producer of 'Energy Flash'. One day, out of the blue, Mills recalled, Beltram phoned them to say that, when he'd played their track 'Eliminator' in Germany, the crowd had gone crazy – they had to get over there. UR sent Hegemann and Co. their new X-101 EP; the Berliners promptly asked if they could release the EP and booked them to come over for a live UR performance and Mills DJ set. 'The performance was a pivotal moment,' Hegemann recalled. 'It was something special. An incredible intensity. For me the way forward was totally clear after that. We were purists then. Detroit – that was the orientation.' Thereafter Tresor became the European home for many Detroit techno artists, and Mills went back to Berlin much impressed with the intensity of the club's dark basement. Eventually, following a stint in New York City as resident DJ at the Limelight, Mills would move to Berlin.

I was fascinated by how Mills's musical style evolved in response to the ruined underground space of Tresor. 'Jeff's whole sound had changed,' the Detroit techno DJ Alan Oldham said of Mills's return to Detroit after his exposure to Tresor. Where UR had retained some conventional pop elements, like lush chord progressions and song forms, the solo music Mills laid out on his *Waveform Transmission* albums was raw and avant-garde. It adhered in this way to what Beltram had said of techno in 1991. '[House DJ] Frankie Knuckles' music is the same today as it will be ten years from now and as it was ten years ago,' Beltram told *Melody Maker*. 'To me it's old farty music.' Citing his love for heavy music like 1970s hard rock, Beltram added, 'I like psychedelia, but I like computerized psychedelia. The clubs here in Europe are cool – there's a real futuristic tone to the music and people.'

The salient aesthetic characteristic of Mills's club sets is shock, emitting a torrent of relentlessly weird electronic sounds. In this, his music reminds me of some of the ideas set forth in Alvin Toffler's *Future Shock* (1970), a book that had influenced Detroit techno founders Rik Davis and Juan Atkins. *Future Shock* describes a shift in art away from the classical towards immersive multi-sensory experiences: 'Artists also have begun to create whole "environments" – works of art into which the audience may actually walk, and inside which things happen . . . The artists who produce these are really "experiential engineers".' This art evinced a new era, which we could know through it. Mills's sets, and those of the many who copied his style, give the listener a little bit of the future in a pure state.

When the influential Berlin duo Basic Channel took up Mills's corroded template, they shifted techno elsewhere. Basic Channel's music incorporates hiss and crackle: analogue artefacts, the worn sound of the medium. In this way, it evokes the same sense of melancholy yearning we feel before urban ruins. As with architectural ruins, it elicits nostalgia for a time you never experienced. It can feel like the aural equivalent of Gerhard Richter's candle, manifesting the dream-like quality of the everyday, or of Anselm Kiefer's spectral grey corrosion. The flanging effect lightly applied near the end of 'Phylyps Trak' makes the music's rhythmic pattern gently ebb and flow away from the listener. The music sounds how Berlin looks in black-and-white photographs: emotionally, you feel as one would among urban ruins.

At the wonderful Tresor exhibition 'Techno, Berlin and the Great Freedom', the club's unusual discovery – ruin, anachronism, splitting linear time – elicited various artistic responses. On one of the gritty power plant walls were daubed silhouettes of children, recalling prehistoric cave paintings. Elsewhere, black-and-white photographs of early Tresor clubbers included one of a woman with a mohawk looking like a warrior from a pre-industrial tribe. Most spectacularly, on the second floor, opening onto the huge ceiling, Anne de Vries had made a scale-model replica in sand of parts of the original club – sand being, in Brandenburg, everywhere, and thus the main substance your dancing feet abuse.

Reflecting on Tresor's discovery, the detail that fired me wasn't the swashbuckling Romanticism of these three young men discovering an ancient tomb. Nor was it the Situationist

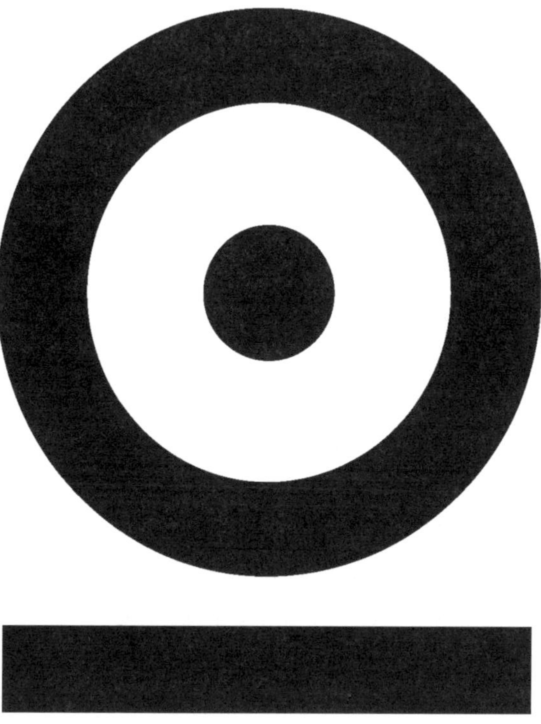

détournement, whereby a former commercial hub is repurposed into a countercultural space. No, it was that Stieler cadged the club's logo from an old inscription on a piece of metal. In this elementary graphic form – a circle inside a circle inside a circle – found in a zone abandoned by history, I couldn't help but see a primordial drawing on a cave wall.

Artistic modernism was long aware of how industrial-age art fractures linear chronology. Brassaï made this connection in his 1933 article 'Du mur des cavernes au mur d'usine' ('From Cavern Walls to Factory Walls'), wherein he described how, in modern-day Paris, 'two steps from the Opera, signs resembling those of the Dordogne caves, of the Nile Valley or the Euphrates, emerged on the walls.' Picasso, like the Dadaists, sometimes made artworks from found objects with minimal retouching. Painter Françoise Gilot recalled how one of these came from a metal oven.

> In the old gas stoves, there was a burner that looks like a sculpture of a woman by Picasso. To make this obvious, Pablo mounted one on a wooden base and named it *Venus of Gas*. 'In three or four thousand years, one might say that in our time we worshipped Venus in this form, just as we declare with confidence about an Egyptian object: Oh! It is a votive vase used for worshipping the gods.'*

'Day is dawning,' Giorgio de Chirico wrote of the modern era. 'It is the hour of the enigma. It is also the hour of prehistory.'

At Berghain, I'd often experienced anachronistic encounters. One evening, breaking from Honey Dijon's sweltering Panorama Bar set, I went to the first-floor toilets, beyond the Vulcan forge bar with its charred black walls and ripped brutish men, and at the stainless steel urinal trough, as harsh orange light shone through the stained-glass window, I found myself standing over a supine man on the dirty floor. His brow was flushed; in his hands he held a funnel connected to a transparent tube inserted into his ass. As my brain tried to make sense of this man's kink – he continued fidgeting on the floor with his urine enema device – a stately figure stood at my shoulder: a muscular man, chest breathing deeply, in a huge jackal helmet.

---

* All quotes in this paragraph are taken from *Préhistoire, Une énigme moderne*, listed in the Bibliography.

The jackal likeness, over the man's exposed chest and leather harness, masked his entire head. For the rest of the evening, that hulking speechless jackal man stayed in my mind like – there's no other way to describe it – an ancient Egyptian atavism. František Kupka's 1903 Symbolist painting *The Way of Silence* shows much the same seductive irrationality.

The Romantics were the first artists to voice our alienation in the industrialized West. 'To be one with all that lives,' wrote Hölderlin, 'to return in blessed self-forgetfulness into the All of Nature – this is the pinnacle of thoughts and joys, this the sacred mountain peak, the place of eternal rest.' But universal knowledge was already erasing anything irreducible to objective representation, leaving behind shock and hauntedness. 'Nature closes her arms, and I stand like an alien before her and do not understand her,' Hölderlin said, who ended his days alone in a tower after a mental breakdown.

Hölderlin's words express our wider incredulity, the sense of being thrown into a history we can't understand and barely believe in – yearning for the romance of a distant past or future, another era onto which we project our fantasies of escape. In light of all this, it seemed fair to link Caspar David Friedrich's ruined Attic temple at dusk, rising from an undulating valley, with the ruined ballrooms of Detroit, with their filigree smithereens, and the abandoned industrial yards of East Berlin, through whose concrete weeds sprout. Was this the appeal I found in the story of Tresor's founding – the romance of decay?

'Ruin porn' is the term often used for photos and videos of de-industrialized architecture. Edward Burtynsky's landscape photographs, for example, show nature reclaiming the West's detritus, shedding doubt on our progress-based historical narratives. 'Part of the romance of these images is getting there to capture them, wherever "there" is,' notes Ryan Madson in a discussion of one of the signal works of the genre, Andrei Tarkovsky's film *Stalker* (1979). I once accidentally came across an entire ruined barracks in the countryside near my squat. The experience was deeply eerie. As I trundled back into the city afterwards, I reflected that the essence of the ruined barracks' strangeness was the feeling it gave me that I had briefly stepped outside of history, that risible everyday narrative in which I had always felt so alien.

'This is like a piece of performance art,' my friend Barry said as we lugged my sofa into the elevator shaft and from there up into the sky. I could see his point. I'd been feeling not a little desolate as I'd endured my elongated sojourn in the hulking ruin-cum-squat on the edge of town, and after a while, the residents on my corridor had dwindled down to just the Syrians and me. But mercifully, as summer came in and light and colour returned to the world, I managed to wangle an escape.

My new abode was a studio flat on the twentieth floor of an East German *Plattenbau* or high-rise building. Some would consider that living arrangement weird. But, stood amid boxes on the decades-old lino floor, as I looked out the window at the green treetops and *Plattenbauten* stretching away to the horizon, I didn't care. Living here, I was free: no flatmates, no squatmates, no noise. The man from whom I was subletting was a German translator who'd moved for the foreseeable future to Senegal. For the rest of the year, I would settle into a routine of working at home during the week, doing mindless copywriting while squeezing in my own writing time, and at weekends, cycling down to the nearby Friedrichshain district, where Barry lived, to go clubbing.

'Any interest in hitting Tresor this weekend?' I asked Barry, handing him a cup of tea. He shook his bald head. 'Band rehearsal Sunday. But gonna meet Davey on Friday evening, if you wanna come along?' My old friend from the squat, David, was in Berlin for an academic event. 'Already arranged to catch up with him in the afternoon,' I said, starting to unbox my stuff, 'so might see you after.' Later, as the city lit up outside my window, I flicked through a book I'd come across that was keeping me focused, Annie Dillard's *The Writing Life*, a second-hand book I'd bought at Saint George's Bookshop in Prenzlauer Berg. Slim and elegantly written, the book was full of homespun wisdom. Reading it, I pen-marked a passage:

> Why do you never find anything written about that idiosyncratic thought you advert to, about your fascination with something no-one else understands? Because it is up to you. There is something you find interesting, for a reason hard to explain. It is hard to explain because you have never read it on any page; there you begin. You were made and set here to give voice to this, your own astonishment.

In place of my having any writing mentors or even writer friends in Berlin, Dillard's words felt part motivational pep talk, part philosophical challenge.

I was still mulling them over at Kottbusser Tor as, having passed by the drug dealers, I went up the steps to Kotti Cafe. The radio was playing George Michael as the Turkish- German waiter with long curly hair wearing a string vest came over to us, smiling. I ordered a mint tea and David ordered a beer. We chatted about Berlin and about my writing. I said how one thing I'd noticed in writings on club culture, even in the best articles, was a lack of engagement with the music itself: the central element of dance music clubs was always conspicuously absent. 'Keep going anyway,' he replied. 'The clubs want legitimation. For them it is about the music above all, which is something I think people forget. Because of all the sensationalism.'

'There's a good line-up at Tresor on Saturday, if you're up for joining?'

David blew out some cigarette smoke and smiled. 'Let's see how the night goes.'

We ended up meeting Barry down in Neukölln along with Frederick, a debonair Swedish historian with whom David was developing an academic project. At the Bierbaum Zwei on Sonnenallee, a 24-hour local bar yet to be invaded by the hipster class that had colonized the district, the four of us stayed up all night playing pool in the back room and drinking cheap beer, then at five in the morning, still full of energy, Barry, David and I jumped in a taxi to the club ://about blank, where, at a party called poly|motion that specialized in slow dance music, we ended our night the following afternoon in the club garden, sat on wooden decking under a blue sky. A redheaded Irishman with pale skin chewed my ear off about how he took LSD with his biker mother. Barry and David were off dancing. 'That's fascinating,' I said, making my escape past bodies wearing denim hot pants under pierced faces.

Stumbling down a leafy avenue, where posters advertised a midweek talk at the club about Pierre Bourdieu's book *Distinction* (://about blank was run by a left-wing so-called

Antideutsch crew, who, I later learned, in a distinctly German cognitive dissonance, combined anarchistic anti-capitalism with strident Zionism), I entered the toilets and saw a vision in the darkness of two reptilian human faces, all red and yellow blotches. I stumbled and peed on my leg. Komodo dragons could smell blood at a distance: what of these two?

For whatever reason, night was the zone of experience to which I'd been banished: night, even in daytime; night of excess and madness; night of lostness and foundness and disorientation; night of romance; night of which you couldn't speak, and which demanded expression.

You were made and set here to give voice to this, your own astonishment.

Reporting on the Berlin club scene in *i-D* magazine in 1991 – the first such report in the anglophone press – Matthew Collin described a north German version of rave that was intense and austere. Where Britain's rave scene was all whistles and Day-Glo, Berlin was 'so dark . . . claustrophobic blackness . . . lost amidst the fuzz of smoke and signal'. Wolfgang Tillmans, who photographed the scene for the *i-D* feature, considered this techno subculture to be the emergence of a new avant-garde full of outré visions and inscrutable music. 'The techno event is a type of popular art,' wrote a 1998 editorial along these lines in the German art journal *Icons: Localizer 1.3*.

> The degree of immersion (the degree of emotional participation and the feeling of entering an artificially-generated space) is crucial, as in an interactive environment. The dancers enter a physical and psychological

> space which has severed its links with everyday conceptions of time and space. Sound waves and light form a technically simple but effective interface which makes entering imaginary worlds possible.

Within this darkness, you could lose yourself. More than that, bombarded by the electronic repetitions, disoriented as in a cave, catching glimpses of barely-there faces, you found yourself in a space into which, freed from the everyday, your imagination could overflow, giving rise to hidden versions of yourself.

What a disappointment, then, when, after all that, my night at Tresor turned out to be such a damp squib. Or should I say a damp squib inside a damp squib – since, for this aging clubber, different levels of annoyingness looped maddeningly around each other.

What was wrong? Well, first, Tresor that night seemed to have no door policy. Pretty much everyone got in. So, when I finally reached the legendary Tresor basement – to access which you pass down a very long subterranean corridor – I was confronted by masses of young dudes, many topless, bumping into people. Shoulder-to-shoulder, drinking beers, they were out of place in this iconic space and oblivious to the techno. At one point, a group of ten young lads beside me on the dance floor, all dressed in cookie-cut black T-shirts, started chanting a football song. Inadvertently, I burst out laughing.

Tresor's basement dance floor architecturally was atmospheric. But for this old-timer, it became like a cruel prison. It was pitch black and had a low ceiling. I couldn't walk half a metre in any direction without banging my shin off a concrete block or having some invisible teenager barge into me in the gloom. Take one step forward: bump. Take one step to the side: bump. Stay in one spot and try to dance: bump . . . bump . . . bump. The dance floor entrants, all dressed in black, like clones, flailed in the matte darkness straight into me. I felt like I was in an amateur dress rehearsal for a newly discovered late Samuel Beckett play.

Oscar Mulero, as ever, played a fine hypnotic techno set. And at the front of the dance floor, I finally found some proper heads to vibe with. But, by then, I was no longer vibing. I realized that Tresor's sister club Ohm, one of my favourite Berlin spaces, was more my kind of place. On the Tresor dance floor tonight, I felt positively geriatric.

After three hours, I was done. I went home.

De Biel, a brilliant documentary photographer, chronicled the emerging subculture in classic black and white with his Nikon F2. Through his photographs, we share in the free-spirited optimism of these young artists making their homes within the ruins, inventing what would eventually become Berlin's electronic dance music scene.

'There were so many free spaces, spaces with no houses,' he said. 'So, here's a house, there's a house. Especially in Chausseestraße, every second house was *there* and the other houses *weren't there* – there was nothing, just free space between houses. And the other houses, they still had like these shooting holes from the past War.'

One thing de Biel said had been new to me, running counter to Berlin's Tresor-as-techno origin story. At the time of Tresor's founding, de Biel lived in the squats Eimer and Tacheles, and in the latter, he said, the squatters founded what was in fact East

Berlin's *real* first techno club, the less-snappily-titled Ständige Vertretung.

'It was honestly the first techno club in East Berlin,' de Biel said of the short-lived space. 'It opened up before Tresor.' I told de Biel I was surprised to hear this, since Tresor was always described in international media as Berlin's first techno club. 'That's okay,' de Biel replied with a smile. 'I love Dimitri, we're friends. I think we have no problem about that. He is a nice guy. He is a visionary.' With this, I had no trouble agreeing: regardless of my experience that night at Tresor, Hegemann remained for me Berlin techno's primary figurehead.

I got to meet Hegemann myself when, at the invitation of its Dean, the sociologist Martin Fuller, I visited Tresor's new Subcultural Academy. This was an institute for training the next generation of club culture professionals, situated above Kraftwerk.

Surrounded by the dials and levers of the former GDR power plant's control room, Hegemann spoke of his career and of how, at a young age, the Woodstock Festival had inspired him to seek an alternative way of living. 'There was lots of space,' he said of the years after the Berlin Wall fell, 'and space is the first thing you need if you want to change the world.' The clubs he and others formed weren't just spaces for hedonism: 'For me, the clubs were incubators,' he said, harnessing 'the power of the night' towards positive social change. Fuller noted that sites such as these for ecstatic experience have existed in societies around the world throughout history. 'Clubs are spaces where new stories can be told,' he said.

From my meeting with Hegemann I came away with a sense of how compelling it is when someone has a positive social vision, the basis of any community. People like Hegemann remind us that we should always (as the painter de Chirico wrote in one of his notebooks) 'Live in the world as if in an immense museum of strangeness.'

Mills dedicated his debut album *Waveform Transmission vol. 1*, released in 1992 on the Tresor label, 'to those who realize it is never safe to look into the future with eyes of fear. It is what we make it out to be! FUTURE = REALITY.' The effect of this futurism can be, paradoxically, to return us to a prehistoric standpoint. In this, there was a crossover with the inhabiting of ruins, zones outside of history. The temporal paradox is evinced in the *Waveform Transmission* logo, which recalls the Tresor logo. On the grainy black-and-white cover there's a cryptic icon, concentric circles notched with smaller circles and nodes. It looks like a symbol from some alien race, and at the same time, like a stone etching from primeval man. This suggested to me that Mills's music, as modernist sound art, was as much about undoing as it was about doing: about wiping away a false historical narrative. Still, I found it hard to get how (as someone who witnessed it told me) Mills arrived at the Tresor anniversary exhibition in a chauffeured limousine, flanked by bodyguards. That kind of celebrity act felt a bit distant from the Berlin underground.

Now, as I write these lines by the window of my twentieth-floor apartment, opening onto the unreal city – grey tower blocks, green treetops, pink sky – I realize that I don't fully buy Toffler's 'future shock' idea. It's not that I don't think future shock is a thing. It's more that, by contrast with Toffler's trepidation about the strange future rushing into us, it's really the tyranny of the everyday – of being a human at all in the first place – that I find bewildering. In this way, I'm not so much a past person being forced to adapt to a strange environment from the future. I'm more like a *future person* being forced to adapt to a strange environment from the past.

I have *past* shock.

Club Oblivion

When, after weeks of prevarication, I finally decide that, yes, I *will* go to the weekend-long closing party of one of Berlin's most beloved nightclubs, Griessmuehle, the first thing I wonder is what I should wear. Should I daub my lips purple again and rock up in my black and white stripes? Or, since I'll be going with my new girlfriend, Indrani, should I instead wear the bandana she bought me, orange and green, with a string vest and silk floral shirt? An outlier is my fetish gear – mesh, dog collar – but although it's a queer party, fetish isn't Cocktail d'Amore's vibe, and although you want to be unique as you dance in the abandoned industrial units, you also want to fit in.

Like the butterfly effect, where a red admiral's wing-flap in the Caribbean invariably causes a devastating hurricane in the Outer Hebrides, one incorrect item of clothing at Griessmuehle's Cocktail d'Amore closing party might destroy my whole weekend. And Griessmuehle's closing party isn't just any party; it's an historical event, so you want to be dressed right. In our images of history, fashion's the unsung hero; without fashion, Napoleon at the Brandenburg Gate would have ruined his Prussian conquest by wearing fluffy pink galoshes; and had JFK, rather than a tailored suit, worn an Aran jumper and sandals with socks, his famous 'Ich bin ein Berliner' speech would be long forgotten, remembered if at all as an embarrassing low point for our species. Such are my wild thoughts as, having confirmed, after depressed months laid up ill, that I will indeed have one last dance at Griessmuehle, I think about what to wear.

Perhaps Oscar Wilde's quip in *The Picture of Dorian Gray*, 'It is only shallow people who do not judge by appearances. The true mystery of the world is the visible, not the invisible,' is for you just that, a pretentious quip. But in the endless midnight of a party like Cocktail d'Amore, the deepest can truly become the skin.

A gay nightlife staple, Cocktail d'Amore was founded in 2009 by the Italian DJ and production duo Giacomo Garavelloni and Giovanni Turco (AKA Discodromo) with Berghain resident DJ Boris. 'Our taste was Italo, disco, house, and in general music that would create some emotional reaction,' Discodromo told me. 'No other queer clubs or parties were offering this music. So together with Boris, we decided to start our own night, mainly for us and our friends, who felt the same way about the music offerings from the club dance scene.'

Cocktail started off in a basement on Ritterstraße in Kreuzberg, before subsequent peregrinations around Berlin took in, writes Daniel Wang, 'a former brewery in Rollbergstrasse . . . Chez Jacki on the Spree river bank . . . a trashy, non-descript storefront hidden between '60s Plattenbau apartments and the Kino International; and an odd farmhouse-like structure behind the Hamburger Bahnhof'. Having arrived at Griessmuehle, a former factory in which Garavelloni and Turco installed a high-end sound system, the monthly party seemed able to end its wandering, finding a lasting home.

Cocktail's musical aesthetic is hybrid, open, playful, filthy, intense, self-subversive: in a word, queer. In the wintergarten, you might hear Alex from Tokyo blasting out 'Relight My Fire'; in the main room, Discodromo spinning some indefinable psychedelic melange; in the smoky cosmic hole, Trent playing slow, narcotic crunk; then, in the garden, as dawn's rays glimmer through the branches, Daniel Wang spinning as an *aubade* Tomita's kitsch electronic synthesizer arrangement of Ravel's *Boléro*. 'We still book unknown talents we get excited about and try to create a unique yet very varied sound that some by now call the "Cocktail sound", unable to put it into a specific genre or defined box,' Garavelloni and Turco said.

Psychedelic-cum-pornographic graphics courtesy of Pindar Andriopoulos have been there since Cocktail's first flyer – a bouquet of roses made of cocks. Cocktail d'Amore's record label hosts productions by the likes of Discodromo and Sfire (Jeffrey Sfire and SOPHIE). For me, the track that distils Cocktail's vibe is 'Sfire 1', a sweet and driving party track with vocals by Marcela, electroclash meets Italo, light-headed and wistful and child-like, a track that, after SOPHIE's death, I would find almost unbearably bittersweet.

When Saturday night enfolds us in its mysterious embrace, it's wet and dark and grim as only East Berlin in deep winter can be. On the tram to Indrani's flat in Moabit, West Berlin, as I pass the hulking *Plattenbauten* at the Platz der Vereinten Nationen, I pass the time reading about Griessmuehle online. Located in the district of Neukölln, Griessmuehle is housed in a former grain mill (hence the name). Industrial units, railway lines and a canal insulate it from the outer world. Grain silos stand erect in rows or lie prone with revellers having climbed inside them. Wooden decking stretches away through sparse trees, which people climb up for shenanigans. Campfires are started; heart-to-hearts happen. The canal flanks the site like a moat, a ballast against reality – until now.

Griessmuehle's eviction is an example of what Germans call *Clubsterben*, 'club death'. There isn't much you need to know about it. Briefly: the club was on a lease; the property developer owner decided it was time to kick the shabby clubbers out to give way to the predictable generic hotel/office spaces/*exciting retail opportunities*. Berlin's Club Commission and politicians stepped in as mediators, and after 45,000 people signed a petition and Neukölln's mayor spoke out, a compromise was reached: the site is to be bulldozed, but the mooted *exciting retail opportunities* are to become instead an *exciting cultural opportunity* (corporate sleight of hand); meanwhile, Berlin's politicians will help to find Griessmuehle a new home, supposedly (says the rumour mill) a site in the austere eastern district of Lichtenberg, the district where I live, in my modest apartment on the top floor of a GDR tower block with decades-old lino floors, a knackered sofa and a dizzying view of other Soviet high-rises stretching away to the horizon.

Janelle Monáe sings from the speakers and anticipation clasps my stomach as, in the bedroom of her flatshare, Indrani tells me about the performance art piece she's writing. It's a spoken essay about her Indian grandfather, she says, the stern paterfamilias who during the Partition moved the family from India to New Jersey. Indrani's performance piece is about how in his patriarchal shadow the ties between his three daughters came undone; it's about how patriarchy sets women against each other.

Indrani was raised by her white father's family in North Carolina. She sometimes got to visit her mom in the Detroit projects.

'Two thousand words. Now I have to memorize it. But I have my B2 German exam the same week, and I'm worried I'm putting too much pressure on myself.'

I watch her apply blue lipstick at the mirror. We met months ago at a club night at Panke in Wedding and grew attached, two migrant artists with de rigueur precarious freelance work. That night was Indrani's birthday and on the dance floor she was impossible to miss, laughing in an elegant white gown and gold earrings. We danced and hooked up and spent a weekend together during which we listened to Princess Nokia and she told me about her *Fifty Dates of Grey* Internet art and Cindy Sherman and the Berlin Diaspora Society she was trying to get going, a support network for Brown artists. Tonight she's opted for a silver space-age dress with blue lipstick; on her forehead is a jewelled bindi. Meanwhile, I'm on the floor rooting around in my suitcase like a dog.

Indrani pops the cap on her lipstick and purses her lips. 'What do you think?'

I look at this retro-futuristic space diva in Indian jewellery.

'Gorgeous. But lose the fake septum ring, babe, you don't need it.'

My answer makes us both self-conscious; I feel my cheeks glowing and I go back to looking through my clothes. 'At least I got us on the guest list tonight,' I say, changing the topic.

If at their least imaginative clubs are four walls and a ceiling for people to get fucked in, at their best clubs are stages in which new personas aren't simply possible but demanded. So, while

I'm drawn to the music and only sporadically take in what's around me, Indrani spends her time looking at the hats and belts and shawls and wigs, absorbing the inventive looks in what is effectively an art space just as much as is some sterile Mitte commercial gallery.

Baudelaire described fashion as 'a symptom of the taste for the ideal which floats on the surface of all the crude, terrestrial and loathsome bric-a-brac that the natural life accumulates in the human brain'. Fashion, he said, was 'a sublime deformation of Nature, or rather a permanent and repeated attempt at her reformation'. I can get with this idea of dressing up as an insouciant act of freedom in a degraded world that always falls short of our ideals. A person dressed stylishly shows *esprit*, truth through artifice, as I'd learnt from my Galway girl friends years ago. And through style you can express your gender however you want.

Now, I lift from my suitcase the porcelain harlequin face I found in a bargain bin in Humana. I attach the enigmatic smiling face to a lanyard and hang it round my neck. Yes, this'll do; Complicious, I'll call her, this harlequin who looks like Kraftwerk's niece cross-bred with Ornacia from the sixth season of *RuPaul's Drag Race*. As if creating a collage, I stumble upon my outfit by accident: after Complicious, I dress myself harlequinesque.

I enjoy the lipstick's taste as my lips turn red and black. I enjoy my red-and-black chequerboard blouse with the lumpen shoulder pads. I enjoy my knee-high socks in red and black stripes, my black shorts, my leather bumbag, my face that, below my red bandana, I powder matte white. As if virginal, free of vulgar identity, untainted, my face emerges anew: daubed white blotches, dragged black lines, a surrealistic white under a thick black X. But in inventing my face I erase myself, erase my face while retaining it spectrally. In clubbing at Griessmuehle, in making myself art, isn't that ultimately the freedom I desire – death?

I've always felt alien to myself. Yet that ridiculous existential scenario – *always driven to seek and fail finally to become identical with yourself* – can be flipped into a liberation. Your self becomes the open portal through which you step to find the unknown, clasping for it in the darkness of your insides, the darkness of the club space, this sealed-closed world. Yes, it's hard to disagree with Baudelaire when he writes that, deep within such night-time spaces, the clubber is 'quite within her rights, indeed she is even accomplishing a kind of duty, when she devotes herself to appearing magical and supernatural'.

I come back to myself. Indrani's yuppie downstairs neighbours are banging the floor with a broom. 'Ignore it,' she says, picking up her keys. By now it's well past midnight, but before leaving her apartment we take a couple of photos. The last time we went to Cocktail was on Halloween, and we took photos of Indrani in elaborate Marie Antoinette garb with a thick bouffant, pink gown and guillotine-marked neck, and me in a furry waistcoat and bandana. This time, scanning my photo, Indrani looks uncomfortable. I look over her shoulder.

Yes, I look ludicrously camp.

Not being overly blessed with queer friends in Berlin, the first time I went to Cocktail, having heard about it by word of mouth, I went alone. And I gabbed to randomers and had fun. I still remember the feeling, down the line, at Cocktail's tenth birthday party, when in a dark and teeming main room, Boris dropped

Patrick Cowley's 'I Feel Love' remix. Sweat-scented and balmy with body heat, the room lifted off. As Cowley's synthesizer solo grew ever more ludicrous, hands threw silhouettes on the rainbow lights; two men made love; a hand-standing Italian woman tried not to topple over; the state of play was friendly, gay, delirious, and I felt like I'd been transported back in time to NYC's Paradise Garage circa 1980.

'It's a disco that absolutely blew my mind,' the artist Keith Haring said of the Paradise Garage, adding that it was 'nothing like other gay discos . . . It's the closest thing to being at a Grateful Dead concert, except that it wasn't this hippie thing, but taking place in a totally urban, contemporary setting. The whole experience was very communal, very spiritual.'* That sense of quasi-spiritual freedom – in style, behaviour, gender, music – gets at Cocktail's appeal. An Englishman spending a year in Berlin told me that Sundays at Cocktail had become his 'church'. You could be whoever you wanted to be without giving a shit what anyone might think. Turco, the party's co-founder, said that, looking back, 'my life in Italy seems like a previous life. We both share this feeling, actually. When we moved to Berlin, it felt like being reborn. Completely. Sometimes I look back and I feel like I never had a life before Berlin. I was asleep, kind of.' Except now Griessmuehle is being demolished, it's winter and my bones are degenerating, and everything feels uncertain again.

Shimmering Alexanderplatz appears outside the window as Indrani and I sit on the train heading west. As per my standard

*Quoted in Lawrence, *Life and Death on the New York Dance Floor*, listed in the Bibliography.

transit routine, honed over years of gruelling bus journeys to Donegal, I have ambient music on my headphones, *All Lanes of Lilac Evening* by Siavash Amini and Saåad. Now, reading online again about Griessmuehle's closure, the music inadvertently imbues everything with a mournful, almost melodramatically tragic air, all tape hiss and synth pads and arpeggiated minor chords – a growing sense of *ennui*, regret and carsickness. For light relief I switch to the Facebook event page and scroll the comments. There's a post from co-organizer Giacomo: *Fun game: post a sneak peek of your ultimate outfit(s) for the weekend! (we know many of you have been working on it since the announcement of the last cocktail emerge eheh)*. As in the Bayeux Tapestry, the figures unfurl: a bearded man in a tiger costume; a bespectacled nerd sporting a full-body condom à la *The Naked Gun*; a Barbie doll, naked, tied to a pole by her heel-length blonde hair; a paunched bearded man modelling a pink bikini. But a palpable sense of unease has seeped into the fun: as with the bereaved woman in black drapes and a thick veil ('I'll be the grieving widow all in black lace whispering "amore . . ." between sobs'). I take off my headphones – the train is edging into Sonnenallee, our stop – and I show Indrani how the most reactions are for a humorous stock photo of an East Asian man wearing a medical face mask. 'Thank God you got us on the guest list,' she says, as we step out into the rain.

'The guest list's been frozen,' announces the party's gatekeeper, a swarthy man in white robes; he delivers his harsh judgement with a bizarrely quavering voice. 'There's absolutely no space left in the club,' he tells us and the other disappointed guest-list hopefuls gathered in the rain before him, 'so you'll have to wait for people to leave.' 'How long?' I ask. Behind his handsome face and shrill Aussie accent, I remark the light-headed look of someone coming up on a pill. 'Minimum three hours. Join the guest-list queue back there,' he concludes, pointing a hundred lamentable yards back down the long alley.

How proud we were, and now how crestfallen we feel, trudging back along the queue's multitudes of gay men in colourful outfits and women with piercings, every further footstep a humiliating slap in the face, taking us away from this party of parties! Eventually we end up behind an Irish group sharing a bottle of rum, among whom I pretend not to notice the redheaded Limerick woman who once Airbnb'ed a room in my Alt-Treptow flatshare and who brought all manner of druggy chancers back to our apartment from Griessmuehle, having noisy sex while I lay cooped up and miserable in the neighbouring box room.

'What'll we do?' I ask Indrani. Her narrow eyes are dimming. 'I dunno babe, not feeling so good. Think I'm getting a cold.' 'Will we go to that other place for a while where Ashanti ran the karaoke night?' 'The one at Richardplatz? That closes at two thirty,' she says, looking at her phone. 'In ten minutes. Sorry babe. I know you wanted to go dancing for your birthday. We tried. What about another club? Is there one nearby?' The mere thought of going to some lesser club when the last Cocktail is on is rancid, like going to the cinema to see a new print of *The Bitter Tears of Petra von Kant* and, finding it sold out, having to settle instead for *Leap Year*.

I get down on my hunkers. The alleyway is wet and dirty and voices babble from both queues – the long guest-list queue and the infinite queue for normal punters. A woman emerges from the club, staggering boldly. 'Does anybody have a lighter?'

she asks the queue. 'Do you have a lighter?' I shake my head. A man leans over the steel barrier with a lighter and she pushes back his hand: 'Just because you are good-looking, doesn't mean I must talk to you.'

Everything becomes messy.

I drift.

In my mind a dream image flashes up: bodies in plumed Venetian masks, queuing in an alleyway; queueing not for a club but for soup. It's the video for David Bowie's song 'Fashion'. In a New York City dance studio, an African-American woman in a leotard directs people to imitate Bowie's gormless gestures, before snippets interrupt from fake TV ads for amphetamines. The video is a collage of nonsense, lacks any semblance of narrative and snatches victory from the maw of defeat. Reduced to attitude and pose, Bowie generates a sense from his material that couldn't pre-exist that material. This is exactly what I love in club style: *the unforeseen made necessary*, the liberating trust in surfing the wave of one's imagination; life not as a set pattern but as an open experiment.

My reverie breaks.

'Time for evasive action. Stay here, I'm going to blag it.' I stride purposefully to the top of the queue, where the burly Turkish-German bouncer is letting people in who already have a wrist-stamp. I gesture to the Asian-Australian gatekeeper in his white robes. Brandishing my phone, I explain that I'm a writer and, look here, I wrote this piece about Cocktail d'Amore for *The Guardian* and, you know, I might write about tonight's party, but I'm not able to stay on the whole night, just a few hours and – 'Oh, why didn't you say so . . . You're not *guest list*, you're *press list*.' With relief, I dash back and grab Indrani. 'Busy night,'

I say cheerily to the robed man when we return, who looks like he's trying to stay on top of his jackhammer heartbeat. He smiles weakly and nods – 'One last time' – then, giddy with excitement, we're inside under red lights.

At this point you might have to bear with me, reader, because it's later in the night, and everything's blotchily cartoonish.

I can't take my eyes off this lanky, haughty woman. She's dancing on a platform near the DJ box and she's yellow-skinned and femme. She's wearing an airy Twiggy dress and Holly Golightly sunglasses and she sets one platformed shoe before the other, one platformed shoe before the other, foursquare, rhythmic limbs, right-angled elbows, while dancing beside her, his toady squatness ridiculously complimenting her lank pout, there's a headless monster. He has a shrivelled green face set in his tummy and he jives and jives, a carefree Blemmyes, waving a pair of white rave gloves – quite touching!

Below the disco femme and the monster there's a gay couple in the early stages of an encounter. A smiling boy in a string vest and blue shorts reaches one arm towards the older bearded man's crotch. Then, out of nowhere, the boy's arm merges with the bearded man's penis. Their joint penis-arm extends, a writhing trunk, a rippling waveform, an autonomous third entity, in time to the music.

And here, hand in hand, stumble space-age Indrani and harlequin me, half-mad, as my little smiling amulet Complicious dangles from my neck. Cocktail's main room is a throbbing shadow, a flickering scrum pounding with Hi-NRG music. The dark is interspersed with halogen strip-lights. A huge pile of empty bottles lies in the corner. And it's buoyant. Most of the men are topless, a virtual-reality gay club painted by Breughel, wet paint oozing in the heat. Cocktail's main room is like a laboratory for masculinities. Men experiment with masculinity, push at its contours, rearrange their gender in perceptual shards. Military epaulettes and leather jockstraps, drag and butch, animal and vegetal – through fashion's doorway, all wind in dance.

The dance music fascinates. My over-analytic mind characteristically flies into action trying to figure out what genre it is. Techno? Too many motifs. House? Too lacking in melody and harmony. Psychedelic, anyway – hybrid, the sonic correlative of the paint on my cheeks, of the necklace's geometrical relationship with Indrani's left shoe, multiplied by the hour of the clock, divided by the inverse square root of my heartbeat's bpm . . . But wait, that screaming – is it? – yes, Suicide, Alan Vega mixed over these beats – so surprising and unsettling!

I tug at Indrani's warm hand and we slip through the ranks down to the back of the room. From the ceiling, angry orange lichen droops and blue bananas grow. Two men embrace in hi-vis vests. Viscid like glue, a membrane of an enormous eyelid unfurls across the ceiling for several metres, a biomorphic banner, ebbing towards that teeming pile of empty glass beer bottles underneath the speakers, glinting in the flashing disco lights like an insect's compound eye.

Now before me there's a punk with blue skin and a green mohawk. His single head has multiplied into three heads, and each head is stacked upon the other. The blue punk leaps into the air, three mouths agape, and in his topmost head's mouth, I now see, this blue freak catches wonderfully a dazzling pink laser beam that's shooting from a huge bust in the corner, a statue of a green-skinned bearded bear.

'It's like a sauna,' Indrani says, disrobing her silver dress. Dizzy and sweating, I hang its flying saucer sheen over some exposed piping on the back wall, as drops of cold water drip on me from a ceiling crack. 'Much better.' She smiles.

At the top of the room, flashing red and blue lights trace broken geometries. Past them flies a huge pair of hairy balls. The balls are autonomous from any phallus and body. The airborne balls shoot out billowing dry ice on the dancers below, a cordial emission.

Happy birthday baby, Indrani's smirking blue lips mouth as, her hand clasping my gloved fingers, my eyes flick open. Two green femme cone-head aliens are beside her, conjoined twins in yellow lace knickers. Pulling me through the darkness towards her bra and jewelled bindi, Indrani presses my waist against hers, and I feel her warmth, and in my skimpy shorts, shorts through which she so crudely groped me earlier, I feel myself getting hard. Happily my white face and lipstick aren't a turn-off. Happily she's forgotten . . .

Languorously kissing Indrani's warm blue lips under the bellowing speaker, I disappear out of my body through her mouth, at the back of this teeming squirming dance floor, sluiced altogether from existence, vanishing in stars and nebulae, disappearing in comets through our bodily congruence, which I've so much missed this mentally ill winter, disappearing from my white face, my red-and-black painted lips and red headpiece until, brought back to myself again through a hard object under my shoe, I realize Indrani's not here. I'm standing on a man's foot and in dumb apology I gesture to his scowling boyfriend, like a pantomime.

The stronger the cut that a club effects with the outside world, the better the club is. Industrial ruins and non-functional architecture are best: they seclude, shelter, create exclusivity; and, when there are no windows, no sign of the sun rising or falling, they can allow clubbers to forget absolutely the outside world, the oppressive ferule of ever-ticking clock hands; to submit to play and glamour.

'Either the well was very deep,' Lewis Carroll writes, 'or [Alice] fell very slowly, for she had plenty of time as she went down to look about her and to wonder what was going to happen next . . . Down, down, down. Would the fall never come to an end?' It can feel like this entering Griessmuehle. Having passed under a railway bridge and turned left onto a long alley, you walk for an age towards Griessmuehle's entrance along a kilometre-long stretch of concrete, Alice's well having rotated 90 degrees to become a dirty inner-city catwalk. As you transition, you're granted at least a preparatory sideshow. Dishevelled club kids walk in the opposite direction, tender from their sleepless adventures, distraught or smiling crookedly.

So as Indrani and I, at 2 a.m. on the rainy night of Griessmuehle's closing party, walked down the long alleyway towards the club, a shadowy woman and man appeared enigmatically in the distance. They were like emissaries of a foreign land. The woman in particular, a drag queen in a crumpled cocktail dress, with blonde curls and a tiara, projected a regal air, all the more effectively seductive because of the exposed catwalk of her approach. Her wrangled regal head seemed a pre-taste of Cocktail: *you are entering an altogether different place*. Indrani and I approached the drag queen and her courtier-companion, and I thought of how Proust's narrator describes, from the Paris opera stalls, gazing up in wonder at the spectacle of the Duchesse and Princess de Guermantes making their entrance:

> I had no doubt that their manner of dressing was peculiar to themselves, not merely in the sense that livery with red collar or blue lapels had once been peculiar to the houses of Guermantes and Condé, but rather as for a bird, where its plumage is not some added adornment of its beauty but an extension of its body. The way the two women dressed seemed to me like the snow-white or the many-coloured materialization of their inner worlds.

Inner worlds that exploded with wild gentleness in this Griessmuehle queen's dilated pupil, exploding to envelop us.

A plump bird woman with yellow plumage has fashioned a mask from a glitterball, and she pushes past us as we lean on Griessmuehle's main bar, as the distant music pulses over babbling voices. I'm still waiting at the bar to get served. How long has it been?

Bodies bustle in the red light. Across the bar there's the bald lesbian anarchist from Berghain chatting to the bulbous man with a goatee who always wears a rubber suit. A huge bouquet of fragrant white lilies dominates the bar, lending to the impression of a canteen on an alien planet.

The barman with a black hood over his face and hardware chains around his neck has ignored me for twenty minutes, doling out shots and long drinks to every other fucked face.

What's the problem? He's currently light-heartedly chit-chatting to two men to my right. Indrani wraps her arms round me.

'I feel like the music was better last time,' she says.

'I felt like we were in a film in there,' I reply.

'You already said that, babe.'

The man with a handlebar moustache whom I spotted outside in the queue wearing a dinosaur hat (an elaborate home-made hat fashioned from a child's 3D dinosaur jigsaw) pushes past us. In my left hand I clutch Complicious's porcelain. Finally, through his hood the barman stares me in the eye, and, after in German I greet him and ask for two vodka Mates, with faultless *Schnauz* (a distinctively Berliner show of contempt) he takes my money and throws the too-generous tip in the jar, deliberately without comment.

'Heterophobe,' I mutter grumpily as I hand Indrani her vodka Mate. 'He just sees you as one thing.'

'Well, the . . . he doesn't know your . . . your persuasion,' Indrani stutters hesitantly.

There's awkward silence. Indrani avoids eye contact. Yes, of course we will have to discuss this. But why the fuck now?

The bar's redness, Grosz red – my mind's redness.

'Look,' Indrani says, switching topic, pointing at nearby graffiti. '1UP. Remember their mural by your Treptower Park flat?' Around the white trail of the 1UP crew's tag, too impatient to await the club's imminent destruction, grubby patches of moss have already begun sprouting, encircled by red admiral butterflies, which seem to be visibly multiplying.

'Butterfly effect.'

'I have to go pee upstairs,' Indrani says, turning and walking.

As I follow her, a lingerie-clad man almost falls down the stairs on top of me, embarrassed as I catch his arm. Briefly we chat. When I look up, Indrani is gone.

Walter Benjamin spent years writing his endless Paris Arcades project. The modern discotheque concept, an immersive social space with artificial lights and a disc jockey, arose in Paris in the 1950s, spreading to the USA in the early 1960s. To the extent that the discotheque is French in origin, and that its spread demonstrates capitalism's standardization of urban space, it's a kind of twentieth-century cousin of the nineteenth-century arcades. Benjamin quotes a contemporary *Illustrated Paris Guide* on that urban novelty of the 1830s–40s: 'a new contrivance of industrial luxury . . . glass-covered, marble-floored passages', lit by gas lamps, linking shops on either side, 'so that such an arcade is a city, indeed a world, in miniature'. Not dissimilar to club spaces at their most ambitious; especially when, as in Berlin, they're literally housed in the ruins of commerce and industry.

The Parisian arcades for Benjamin showed how capitalist reality acts: instituting an artifice as if it were natural. 'With construction in iron, architecture began to outgrow art,' Benjamin wrote. Architecture here isn't innocuous and neutral, simply a passage you walk through. Architecture in fact articulates you as a subject; it insidiously tells you who you are, a capitalist consumer and little else. Here is the birth of our modern world. These miniature environments, so aesthetically dazzling, induce narcotic forgetfulness, and in doing so, they erase other possible worlds, until you altogether forget who you might otherwise have been. Eventually, there is no longer any outside. Alongside the nineteenth-century standardization of public space came a concomitant, no less contrived domestic interior: 'The private citizen who in the counting-house took reality into account, required of the interior that it should maintain him in his illusions,' Benjamin notes.

As time has gone on, from radio to TV to 5G, information technology has taken up and exploded what we might call the immersive arcades principle. The local Parisian prototype was projected wholesale onto our global sensory environment. Actual (IRL) and virtual (online) alike, our mass media world, as Marshall McLuhan said, exists recursively, ceaselessly iterating, propagating itself as a spectacle, a de facto work of art. (Nietzsche in his notebooks: 'the world as a work of art that gives birth to itself'.) 'Phantasmagoria' (*Phantasmagorie*) is the word Benjamin used to describe this homogeneous society and how we experience its alienating pseudo-reality. The resonance with Freudian phantasy isn't accidental: to call the everyday a de facto artwork is basically to say we're in a waking dream.

Phantasmagoria: doesn't that suggest the surreal environment of a night-club space?

I think of the club as a play-within-a-play, a phantasmagoria-within-a-phantasmagoria. A Berlin club can be like a deconstructed arcade.

Embroiled in the everyday weave, the stream of dead concepts and dead images, of faded ideas and bland repetitions, all of which stage-manage us unbeknownst to ourselves, we might come to realize one night that, although there is no outside, we have the power within us to work the weave. With an artistic eye, at special times we can embody fashion, say, in a way that gently tears apart the dream-fabric smothering us. In such cases, as with the butch queen in lingerie I just bumped into on the stairs, dressing up positively expresses a more real selfhood.

That club culture should owe so much to queer movements is no coincidence. In Berlin in the early twentieth century, the sexologist Magnus Hirschfeld initiated progressive attitudes and safe spaces for people of queer and trans identity. Judith Butler, following later, talked about critical gender consciousness as 'how to work the trap that one is inevitably in'. Butler shows how, at a deep structural level, gender and sex norms generate and organize us as conscious subjects. Gender identity is preconscious: it's wed to architecture and fashion as the texture of our collective dream. 'Fashion,' Benjamin wrote, 'like architecture, inheres in the darkness of the lived moment, belongs to the dream consciousness of the collective.' Queer club people reformulate and refashion the world. Their club world simulacrum shows that the outer world was always already a simulacrum. No wonder at Cocktail I instinctively started wearing peculiar outfits: those outfits, I realized, put me in touch with a more real self.

For now, as I pass along Griessmuehle's charred black corridors amid bedlam, dressed in my harlequin gear, it's as if I'm in a Brechtian version of the capitalist phantasmagoria: the stage set is broken; the lights, flickering; the general apparatus, exposed and about to collapse.

I wait for Indrani in the narrow upstairs corridor. Bodies and heads move in every direction. Duos and trios go about their night, eyes bulging; I hold Complicious. This morning – could it be true? – I felt suicidal; hard to believe, I think, clutching Complicious tighter. After all my drama about what to wear, most of the other men here are semi-naked, wearing leather harnesses, pearl necklaces. And after my weeks laid up depressed, how mad it is to be in this carnival atmosphere. Beside me, passing out on his feet, a fucked man props himself up against the wall while his boyfriend asks him what he took (he can't remember). From over the archway leading back downstairs, someone tears away the green fire escape sign, which is less concerning when you remember that the whole building is going to be destroyed in a few days anyway. The proximity to extinction gives everything a preternatural clarity.

I dash inside the dank room of urinals, which, as in all Berlin clubs, is plastered in fly-posters; I pee beside two men who have joined forces to enable the semi-conscious one to piss. A gymnastic woman, pants around her ankles, backs up and tries to piss in the urinal, spreading her legs in an arch, bending down to the ground and doing a half-splits. At Berlin club nights women suffer from the fact that the cubicles are always clogged with groups doing drugs.

I leave the urinals and go into the bigger toilets to seek my silver-dressed girlfriend. But I don't see her queuing there, and she doesn't answer when I call.

'I need a new life,' says a woman beside me in the queue in denim jeans, à propos of nothing.

I've taken off my headpiece and feel all floppy-fringed frazzled Manila Luzon as I take in the woman's freckles and bulbous pupils.

'What's wrong with your life, dear?'

Shaking her head, she deflates me with a literal German reply. 'I am just joking.'

The filthy toilets resound with white noise babble. Where's Indrani? A woman behind me in the toilet queue says that she was standing outside Griessmuehle for four hours, so I let her go in ahead of me. And soon I've been waiting at least thirty minutes for Indrani, or waiting for one of the drug clusters to vacate a cubicle, and chatting is the only thing passing the time.

From her jeans pocket the freckled coquette produces a pink tube. 'This stick is my only treat. Wanna see?'

'My lips already have lipstick, babe. But sure.'

I turn the lip-balm over in my fingers, not entirely sure of what I'm meant to be seeing.

'That,' she says, 'is my only make-up. (She's wearing eye-shadow.) It costs forty euros for this one stick. It does not colour your lips in an artificial way but . . . helps the colour that your lips are already.' I look at her moist round pink lips.

I nod. 'An enhancer.'

She grabs it back and turns to a stoned-looking Hispanic guy to her left. 'He is no good. You wanna try?' He smiles lazily and she begins dragging the stick across his lips.

An oblique connection strikes me. Of course! All those pink faces I was seeing on the dance floor, and now this pink embellishment . . . Weird . . . Does it mean something? . . . That I should – put some on?

Two muscular American men dressed in black are leaning against the closed cubicle doors. '*Deine Tätowierungen sind wirklich cool*,' the coquette says to one of them.

'Thank you,' he drawls, then looks at his toned bare chest. 'Yeah, let's see . . . Boston . . . London . . . Tokyo . . . and this one here I got in Berlin.'

'That one is best,' she confirms, touching his right bicep, on which is tattooed a tacky pseudo-South Asian frieze, a horribly crude pseudo-Kama Sutra scene showing Ganesh fondling a woman's bare breasts. 'But stay it like this,' she adds, 'do not overdo them. The blank spaces are just as important, so stay it like this.'

Am I just being mad or is something clandestine being communicated here?

'Isn't that sorta cultural appropriation?'

The coquette looks at me, then sneers at her new pal. 'Virtue signalling!'

Instinctively, for comfort, I reach for the plaster mask round my neck.

Ah! It's gone.

'Fuck!'

'What's wrong?'

I clutch at my hair and look in vain at the filthy ground. 'I've lost something.' This is great. Now not only have I lost Indrani, I've lost Complicious. That mask isn't just a straightforward accessory: the white harlequin face, the red and black lips smiling, is my miniature, my homunculus, my ideal. With Indrani nowhere to be found, this second loss really makes me anxious . . . I feel exposed, like Dolly Parton losing her wig.

Everything's out of kilter, like a doctor's waiting room. A door swings open and a man in Day-Glo yellow underwear strides past holding his phone, talking exuberantly on Facetime – he must have gotten a good report . . .

On the floor I see the coquette's chapstick in a puddle. As soon as I notice the pink stick, the puddle starts turning pink. A rippling mouth coalesces – two yellow eyes.

The freckled woman turns her slim green irises towards me. Her warm arm touches mine. 'Come, you need a shot?'

No small part of my *Drag Race* infatuation is the joy in seeing people invent themselves: naming themselves, pouring themselves out, the joyous paradox of Willow Pill exaggerating and exaggerating that hair and eyeshadow artifice to reveal her authentic truth. Benjamin thought that, through dialectical analysis of modern Paris at its dreamworld's inception, he could show the roots of our modern alienation. But doesn't camp do the same thing – and with brio? For queer people, parodying gendered fashion norms – whether the outfit in question is a police officer's uniform or a prom dress and moustache – works the trap, tears the map.

Really, Clarice Lispector speaks for me when, in rhapsodic mode in *Água Viva*, she writes: 'I, anonymous work of an anonymous reality only justifiable as long as my life lasts . . . I'm still not ready to talk about "he" or "she". I demonstrate "that" . . . I am pure *it* that was pulsing rhythmically.' Yes, Lispector's androgyny is the ideal. I mean, she's so femme, yet so butch; she's butch *inasmuch* as she's femme. How couldn't you want that freedom? Likewise, in the club's dark box, somehow I realize my masculinity to its maximum extent – that which I am – through becoming-woman. And that's no paradox.

> Nothing is so ephemeral as a theatrical performance – it even differs from night to night – and, in an age when songs, concerts, films, books, the explosion of the Challenger, the inauguration of a president, can be reproduced over and over again, hoarded and stored, what Ludlam did on his little stage is remembered solely by people who happened to see him.

This is Andrew Holleran in his essay on Charles Ludlam's early 1970s Theatre of the Ridiculous. For me it just as well describes a night out at Cocktail d'Amore or Buttons.

Camp and wild, the Theatre of the Ridiculous arose in New York City in the same post-Stonewall moment as gave birth to our dance music culture, which, prior to disco's mainstreaming, initially kicked off at places like the Loft and Gallery, and later at the Paradise Garage, with Black and Latino gay men at its core. At these parties, the line between gay and straight could blur. 'As David Rodriguez would say, "Straight to the next man!" or "He's bisexual: he likes men and boys!"' said Michael Gomes, as Tim Lawrence reports in his history of the NYC scene, *Love Saves the Day*; and, as Lawrence reports the DJ Nicky Siano saying, 'There were so many people who were just *sexual*. A lot of black men would have sex with other men but didn't consider it gay sex . . . It wasn't about gay or straight. It was about, "Hey, let's party!"' Sexually we're actualized on a spectrum, which though it has gravitational poles of greater or lesser probability is nonetheless as inexhaustible as timbre or colour. How liberating, then, to throw your shabby inherited hang-ups out the window – and how nerve-wracking too.

On the Berlin dance floor I gravitated towards queer people. They were more attractive and more interesting. In contrast to the straights – on autopilot in a breeding-based society – queer people, I thought, had had to work to become who they were, and I supposed that that was why on dance floors they usually felt more open and respectful. Yes, in Berlin's clubs it was the homos who were hetero (multifarious) and the heteros who were homo (homogeneous). That's why, as well as the intense music, and although truthfully I didn't know many people there, I felt at home at Cocktail – in blue fishnets or ludicrous epaulettes or whatever – I felt free. In this ludicrous *mise en scène* – this industrial ruin that worked the trap – I felt free. And at some point a strange thought dawned on me: *this is a fabrication to which you go to get a dose of reality.*

In the aforementioned essay on Charles Ludlam's Theatre of the Ridiculous, a heartfelt homage to drag and camp, Holleran writes:

> Ludlam was comprehensive – pure theater. Which we were starved for – driven to his little group by the staleness of Broadway, the fatuities of a mass-produced, television-dominated, film-and-book-soaked century that gave equal time to the fall of Beirut and the fire in Michael Jackson's hair started by a commercial for Pepsi Cola. Drowning in what Godard said the West had simply too much of – Culture; on the lam from history, novels, films, the *New York Review of Books* – and none of them any FUN!

All of which captures the ridiculous theatre of clubbing, Saturday night's essential oblivion – the oblivion of this club Griessmuehle, the homely oblivion that shelters us all.

The dance floor below is a far-off fug of darkness, a dingy aquatic pool. From a rickety platform above, we watch the bodies moving, only faintly visible through their dancing motion, a shoal of fish intermingling below the water's dank surface, the etiolated strings of a Giacometti canvas.

The music is slowed-down electronic crunk. Its *largo* effect is as if, after an ambitious bump of ketamine, reality had lost track of itself – had, in clumsy slow motion, dissociated and was trying in vain to grasp and catch itself. Below us, the costumed bodies enact a languorous pleasurable pantomime.

This is the Cosmic Hole. It's the second of Cocktail's three dance floors, hidden away at the back of the factory building. Its vibe is spacier than the main room. Overhead, a solitary red light bulb is set in the high wall, a distant red dot emitting terminal cosmic pulses, rendering everything red, rhythmic, as the industrial space stretches away into night-time black.

'It's like we're in a movie,' Indrani says.

She looks at me, pensively. I finally found her here five minutes ago, leaning alone on the unsteady proscenium rail.

I don't know what to say. I remain silent.

Through the mist I'm watching the two men behind the decks, the tall, bearded Trent smoking a joint and the fresh-faced Dama spinning a record. The track's a slowed-down early '80s electro jam in which, on every off beat, the snare strikes in cavernous reverberation, slam . . . slam . . . slam . . . buildings exploding . . . towers tumbling. (Later I'll learn that Trent and Dama DJed back-to-back in the Cosmic Hole for 24 hours continuously . . . a legendary set.)

A straight couple in matching rhinestone policeman's hats, pink and blue, elbow past us, descending the stairs down into the Hole. I feel woozy, the combination of music and heat and lighting perfectly expressing, like a living canvas, that tension, impossible to quell, of being here, embodied within the interior of an old building that, so familiar from these parties, the Sunday mornings of my recent life, will imminently never again exist, its corridors and rooms and darknesses poised only for the void, a veritable world that will soon be nothing, less than nothing, giving all our actions and fashions here – this eye contact, that thought, my glance at that lapel – a sense of . . . not profundity, but rather the opposite . . . that vertiginous sense, as in Paul Valéry's *cimetière marin*, of being more identical with themselves than ever before:

> I no longer have any importance. Now I'm the present itself. My personality is completely wedded to my presence, in perfect harmony with whatever may occur. Nothing more. No further depths. The infinite has been defined . . .

I remove my cheap white gloves. Against the darkness my hands, fingers extended, become flowers blossoming, petals unfurling.

'Let's go down,' I say. I take Indrani's hand and we descend the staircase.

On the basement dance floor I glance back. Indrani smiles.

No need to explain yourself. She knows.

A tall man in leather and amulets, a Bronze Age warrior, is fanning Indrani's face, while at the edge of the dance floor there's a man and woman making love. The heat down here is brutal. Being in a milieu, a hazy middle, through dance eventually leaves you unsure of where exactly you are: the distinction between outside and inside is surreally melting in this soon-to-be-destroyed building.

'I feel like we are in a film in here,' I shout.

'You already said that, babe.'

'Did I?'

Kraftwerk's 'The Model' comes on, slowed way down, and one or two people cheer (I hear myself among them), and Indrani moves her head to and fro. And Indrani's bindi resonates with the rhinestone police hats. And we entwine hands, then she lets go, and the electro emits spirals, and my ears become spirals, and the distant red bulb's dot stretches out into a thick red line, and my eyes, following that line, become stretched into red lines, and my mouth becomes stretched into a red caricature of my mouth, and here in the middle of the dance floor, reality stretches and is wildly exaggerated, more truly itself than it's ever been before or ever will be again. And on the ground before my harlequin striped socks, for some reason there's a furry hobby horse, mute and inexplicable. And intensely, the hobby horse regards me. And now, as in a painting, a burnished late Rembrandt, wherein the force of condensation and focus brings us back to the reality of, say, that pair of thick black shoes, paradoxically through making those black shoes vividly strange, or as in a poem, wherein the vortical condensation of language, away from everyday utility, brings us back to the polymorphousness of reality itself, so too now on this dance floor the absurd parade of fashion and play and pantomime, set to synthetic electronic pulses, brings us back, through collective estrangement, to whatever it is that underlies our waking life and which is usually occluded. And as soon as I think this absurdly grandiose thought, I go to type it in my phone, in my notes app, but my phone screen's a humid blur and after a few squint-eyed seconds I give up. And it doesn't take long for the night, too, to become a humid blur, a lurid smearing of pink into red, of blue into yellow, each colour intermixing to beget some new mulch, red and white making pink, and yellow and blue making green, and pink and green making blue, and so on, wonderfully dirty and wonderfully fecund, and wonderfully destructive, too, smearing Saturday night into Sunday morning till somehow Indrani and I, in the harsh daylight, are sitting on a bench beside the pink furry rocking horse, and of course Indrani, who enjoys herself until her body fails and we've collapsed together on the S-Bahn platform, collapsing a few metres from a bearded uniformed cop who may or may not actually be a bearded uniformed cop, ultimately doesn't really care that much, since she and I are drawn to each other for who we are rather than who we're not.

In Praise of Filth

When Indrani and I jokingly chatted about our next visit to the KitKat Club, she set me two conditions: that I be her slave for the night, and that I be naked except for a leash and Union Jack underwear. Now, you don't need to know much about Irish history (colonization, famine) to understand the ignominy for an Irish person of being on a leash in Union Jack underwear. Which is why I agreed. For if our night at KitKat wasn't going to be flamboyantly perverse, what would be the point?

But then COVID-19 came, and the club closures came, and the global misery came, and our pervy plans were shelved.

When the next visit did come, I was alone on a grey Saturday afternoon, standing in KitKat's courtyard, waiting to have a gun pointed at my head – a temperature gun, that is. Above me, a sign said 'Life is a Circus'. Under my coat, I wore ragtag clubbing gear: a red-and-black chequerboard harlequin top, leather wrist bands, black boots. Turning the corner onto Brükenstraße, heading towards KitKat's wicker fence, I had worried I might be overdressed. It turned out I wasn't overdressed enough. Around me in the babbling courtyard it was all svelte tartan kilts, lacy lingerie and studded dog collars. At KitKat, one overdressed by wearing barely anything.

I was at KitKat for Club Culture Day, a day of support organized by the Berlin Club Commission for Berlin's COVID-devastated nightclub sector. I was happy to hand over €15 to attend an art exhibition in a temporarily reopened club space; I wanted to give something back.

Does anyone need an introduction to KitKat? Presumably you've heard of this club, this Berlin nightlife institution, the horny satyr to Tresor's Hyperion, the club whose keystone is sex positivity. Presumably every Berliner at one time or another, dazed or exhilarated, has wandered lonely as a clown in the wee hours through KitKat's labyrinthine underground corridors, surrounded by obscene Day-Glo murals, Psy Trance waveforms, animalesque eyes, red velvet drapes, gynaecology chairs and humping asses, burlesque and bondage. Wild though it may be, Kitkat is as humdrum in Berlin as double-decker buses are in London.

Born in 1994 in the echo of Berlin's club explosion, KitKat Club's founding concept was the fusion of electronic dance music with sex positivity. And that fusion makes perfect sense. Because doesn't all music aspire towards the condition of sex? Whatever the case, there's no denying that KitKat gives a different spin to that Hollywood adage, *If you build it, they will come*.

KitKat's brand is permissiveness. It feels like an enchanted cave, or, if you prefer, an adult playground. There's a swimming pool and a room decked out in medical equipment: anatomy posters, IV drips, a hospital bed. Here, play is taken seriously. KitKat takes at his word the German luminary Friedrich Schiller (along with Goethe, a leader of classical humanism), who wrote, in his 1794 *Letters on the Aesthetic Education of Man*: 'Man only plays when he is human in the fullest sense of the word, and he is only fully human when he plays.' Though presumably, when Schiller wrote this, he didn't have in mind a genderqueer crowd in leather bodices gazing at a woman bound by ropes suspended from the ceiling.

If I dwell on clothing in relation to this kink club, it's because in many ways KitKat is like immersive theatre – or better, a circus. 'We were a circus family of tightrope walkers who never for one moment allowed themselves to get off the rope,' Thomas Bernhard writes metaphorically of his difficult, bohemian-tinged childhood; 'below us lay normality, but we dared not plunge into it, because this, we knew, would have meant certain death.' Normality means death for many of us tightrope walkers who end up at this club, where for the night we join a band of bearded ladies, lion tamers, jugglers and clowns, fire-breathers, whip-lashing ringmasters, assorted freaks, dancing, disrobing, erotic. Eroticism means role-play, role-play means drama, and drama means making a show of yourself – in power plays like doctor/patient or mistress/slave.

RuPaul famously said that we're all born naked and the rest is drag. And indeed, KitKat's costumes for the most part are created not by putting clothes on but by taking them off. Nakedness at KitKat, the club's co-founder Kirsten Krüger said (in the short film *The Dissidents*), acts 'to overcome social distinctions, as there are no longer any conventional indicators. At the same time, with every item of clothing you hand over you also hand over part of your conventional behaviour.' Often as you queue on a Saturday night, Krüger can be seen sat on a high stool at the club's entrance, smoking a cigarette, scrutinizing the hopefuls, admitting or turning people away (with or without her trademark taxidermied cat).

As is the way with Berlin clubs, people speculate about what Krüger looks for: whether she discriminates, say, against brunette men or blonde men. She insisted the club's policy is anti-elitist. 'At this location you can meet people whom you might never have encountered otherwise,' she said. And it's true. More than at any other major Berlin club, I've whiled away the early hours at KitKat talking shit and exchanging life lessons with all sorts of bon vivants and philosophers and randomers, hanging out by the swimming pool and sauna. KitKat's favoured music – unfashionable trance – serves, I suppose, pre-emptively to defuse potential techno snobbery.

KitKat's other founder is musician and pornographer Simon Thaur. 'In the year 2007 I stopped my porn productions because my interests went strongly towards an intellectual direction and research about what life is all about,' Thaur tells us on his website. 'In the last 10 years I worked upon a system which is able to proove [*sic*] connections between planetary influences and the hormonal axis. During this time I managed to write down around 3000 pages material upon this matter which will be published soon.' Thaur is a tall, bald, charismatic man about town. His artistic CV is varied enough to take in pop-up guerrilla porn shoots on Berlin's streets ('suddenly your perception of reality seems to shift and you experience a scene just like in those movies') and an ornate musical setting of Blake's *Songs of Innocence and Experience*. Watching him in a videoed interview, I found his whole shtick creepy rather than playful.

It's no exaggeration to call Krüger and Thaur sex-positivity pioneers. In the early 1990s, they were inspired to create the KitKat Club by their twin interests in BDSM and Goa trance parties. If you've ever attended a full-moon party on Ko Phangan, you'll feel at home at KitKat. Whatever you think about the music – and I'll admit, with the exception of the Gegen party, I find it pretty awful, ditto the weak sound system

– KitKat's erotic ethos was remarkably ahead of the curve. Recent sex-positive Berlin parties like Pornceptual followed decades behind. Sex positivity here involves embracing rather than rejecting the weird. 'You no longer behave the way you normally would,' Krüger said of KitKat's vast cave, a friendly play and fetish environment. 'People lose their inhibitions and find themselves in a new world.'

All of which applied, needless to say, to pre-plague times.

The masked security guard pressed his temperature gun to my forehead. I got the all-clear, and in I went – down the steps, through a long tunnel, past flickering candles and exposed brickwork. Ambient electronic music washed over me. There appeared the first in a series of photos: a semi-naked brunette Madonna, her limbs bound by white ropes, exposed before black velvet drapes. In being enslaved, there's gleeful power – power not least over normality: for when you're outside its jurisdiction, normality can do nothing to reclaim you. That tone-setting photograph was by Andrea Galad. Other artists' work followed, most of it platforming queer identities (Michelle Gutiérrez Fernández, Rory Midhani, Miron Zownir).

This Club Culture Day exhibition was organized by Gegen, a queer sex-positive night at KitKat and RSO. 'When people do not recognise themselves in the new people they meet at Gegen,' Fabio Boxikus (the party's founder) told *Attack*,

> you create in them, first of all, a moment of disorientation, which becomes the golden door to the unknown. Through music, this terrain of exploration unites what was divided before. The component of music unites them

> and creates a magnificent moment of liberation where even sexuality is freed from the chains of prejudice, inhibition and shame.

In Gegen's ethos, I was reminded of what Audre Lorde said of the erotic: in inviting absolute otherness to enter us, the erotic encounter implies beyond ecstasy an ethics of care.

As I navigated the narrow catacombs, memories arose. I remembered the dragon statue belching fire over a dance floor teeming with leather-clad bodies. I remembered the obscene Day-Glo murals and Indrani and me making love in a booth decorated like a stagecoach (into which Thaur poked his head). I remembered a musician friend playing a wild gig while a Japanese woman in a sailor outfit cracked eggs over her body. I remembered a teacher friend, fuzzy-haired, disrobing and leaping naked into the swimming pool. And I remembered being frog-marched through the crowd by a bouncer, almost thrown out for inexplicably forgetting to leave my phone at the cloakroom.

In the medical room, I saw the spot by one of the hospital beds where one night we watched a petite East Asian woman pouring hot wax on her naked body. She was on her knees with her vagina exposed. The wax was pink, green, purple, and as she held a candle's flame to her skin, she writhed and rolled her eyes back in ecstasy – or mock-ecstasy, since it was all theatre, a bravura performance demanding a viewer. My English friend Lucien complied, and committed what I suppose you might call a faux pas by getting down on all fours and staring directly at her cunt. An East Asian woman sat beside me in black lingerie was quick to chastise him. 'You should not do that!'

'I'm sorry,' he said getting up, hair unkempt, face flushed. 'You're right, I was invading her space.'

I told the woman Lucien was high tonight on MDMA for the first time and totally uninhibited. She was Korean, with a tall body and haggard face. She asked me what my kinks were. 'Nothing weird – you know, dominating, exhibitionism.'

She yanked at my metal ring. 'Why do you wear this dog collar if you're not a sub?'

'The look. With the chains and bandana, it makes me feel like I'm in a 1980s New York gang.'

'So, you're a top?'

'I can switch.'

She scoffed with disdain. 'There is no such thing as *switch*.'

'I take it you're into domination, then. Would you walk all over me in those?' I asked, pointing to her high heels.

'Oh, yes!'

'On my balls?'

She mulled it over. 'If you wanted me to.'

'No. Though I know some men are into that.'

I mentioned my girlfriend, then joked about a typewriter fetish (a couple were using a nearby typewriter), by which point, rolling her eyes, she had gotten up to search for a real man. Two men passed by wearing baby hats and nappies.

The French thinker Georges Bataille (who literally wrote the book on *Erotism*) thought it 'very important to realize the infantile character of eroticism in general'. Bataille had in mind how sex relates to prohibitions: the illicit, the threat of punishment. Sure enough, one of my earliest vaguely sexual memories is when, on a summer holiday as a boy, I was made to strip naked along with a friend and dance before the laughing eyes of some older girls. I remember giggling along stupidly at my own expense, too young to know what was going on. I don't doubt it planted a seed for exhibitionism.

Many years later, in Dublin, I stumbled into sex play with a writer woman named Tracy. We met on Tinder. In the afternoon light in Tracy's garret, we were naked on her sofa, talking dirty. As I pressed down her wrists, she was being brattish. Looking up, she taunted me.

'Would you fuck me with that broom handle?'

'Yes.'

'What else would you do to me?'

'I would come to your office, bend you over your desk, and fuck you in front of your colleagues.'

'Oh, that would be hot . . . But seriously, you're such a fucking sissy, you wouldn't even be able to get it up, ha!'

She laughed with wild derision in her eyes, and she loved the feel of her skin tingling after I lightly slapped her face. Our brief liaison made me realize that what in my early twenties had come from drugs, by my late twenties now came from sex. Sex play wasn't just about sensual pleasure: on a deeper level, it meant undoing the unitary self. Play was a doorway to a zone where different versions of you could appear, conjured from your body – unfamiliar selves coming into surreal naked play.

I passed further into the Club Culture Day exhibition. For a while, I stood looking at Gegen's posters, designed by artist Stefan Fähler. Fähler's style highlights obscene body metamorphosis. A bald man, his dome that of a penis, drools from two mouths, one above the other. A wide-eyed woman has bulbous breast-and-ass appendages emerging from her face.

A red-faced man in a white shirt, smooth skin where his eyes should be, has a penis growing from his forehead, which his mouth sucks. Where LSD is mental psychedelia, erotic play is bodily psychedelia.

William Burroughs pointed out that, in wet dreams, banality and eroticism go hand in hand. Dreams with nudity are often bland, while a dream about, say, being at the supermarket buying a packet of red lentils can require you to have to wash your bedsheets. In fetishes, I'm particularly drawn to aesthetic bizarreness. Beyond women in full-body shiny latex, beyond men dressed as babies, more marginal still, you have people who stand on toy trains, people who completely cover their heads with whipped cream, people simply getting their hair cut, a couple painted and costumed like Milhouse and Bart; or more specific still, a woman sat at a Singer sewing machine, wearing a pink wig and silver halter top, using a green telephone to dial a prescribed sequence of numbers: extremely specific: the inexplicable kaleidoscope of kink's palette.

Probably, as Bataille says, such weirdness stems from random childhood events. But the whole process of entering and enduring a night at an underground club like KitKat – a subterranean network of dark chambers – adds to kink a metaphysical dimension beyond the psychoanalytic.

In primitive cultures, the cave through ritual could become the portal to the spirit realm. The exquisite Palaeolithic cave paintings at Lascaux in southern France (dating from circa 15,000 BCE) feature bulls and deer. They also feature an enigmatic figure: before a huge bison, a bird-headed man. It's speculated that he represents the figure of the shaman; that, as in ancient Egypt, where priests wore jackal masks, the Palaeolithic shaman during rituals wore an avian mask. The Lascaux bird-headed man also has an impressive, erect cock. James David Lewis-Williams, author of *The Mind in the Cave*, notes that 'male erections are common in altered states and in sleep, and it is a peculiarly Western notion that the motif always stands for virility and fertility.' Is it a stretch to think of KitKat and Gegen as tapping back into this? It's no secret that, hungover from the Judaeo-Christian epoch, we're still recovering from sexuality's erasure.

A millennium after the Palaeolithic era, in ancient Greece, Dionysus was the god of metamorphosis, wine, frenzy and fertility. Liberty was the watchword (in Rome, Dionysus was called Liber). One myth, recounted by Ovid and retold by Ezra Pound, tells of Dionysus, in the guise of a pretty boy, being abducted by Tyrrhenian pirates, who intend to rape him and sell him into slavery. Instead, with innocent violence, Dionysus wreaks havoc on their ship, making vines sprout from wood, conjuring lynxes and turning the pirate crew into dolphins.

> And where was gunwale, there now was vine-trunk,
> And tenthril where cordage had been,
>   grape-leaves on the rowlocks,
> Heavy vine on the oarshafts,
> And, out of nothing, a breathing,
>   hot breath on my ankles,
> Beasts like shadows in glass,
>   a furred tail upon nothingness . . .
> Fish-scales over groin muscles,
> lynx-purr amid sea

Dionysus stands for the anarchy of fecundity, the subversion of metamorphosis, the queerness of nature. The pirates stand for capitalistic appropriation.

Writing in the nineteenth century, in the nihilistic industrialized West, Nietzsche argued that we should reclaim the Dionysian attitude.

> The word 'Dionysian' means: an urge to unity, a reaching out beyond personality, the everyday, society, reality, across the abyss of transience: a passionate–painful overflowing into darker, fuller, more floating states; an ecstatic affirmation of the total character of life as that which remains the same, just as powerful, just as blissful, through all change; the great pantheistic sharing of joy and sorrow that sanctifies and calls good even the most terrible and questionable qualities of life; the eternal will to procreation, to fruitfulness, to recurrence; the feeling of the necessary unity of creation and destruction.

Of course, in play, there's always a danger of this attitude lurching into mere hedonism or even sadistic cruelty. Consent is all.

With consent, within the club, you are immersed in warmth and darkness. People become dream animals. The music becomes a continuous low hum. The club, the modern cave, returns us perhaps to the womb, to the time before time, to the time before the loathsome horror of individuation.

Lewis-Williams writes about how a 'shaman's activities as a sorcerer, or his own conscious act of entry into the supernatural world, were a kind of "killing"' – in other words, sacrificing the everyday self. That we should want to sacrifice the ordinary self is hardly a wonder. In a *Der Tagesspiegel* interview with KitKat's founders, Kirsten Krüger put it well. She pointed out that 'in day-to-day life, full of necessities, there is a reason for everything. At night, there isn't necessarily a reason for what you do.' At night, we can embrace unreason.

Capitalism requires of you many things. The most basic and most challenging for me is that you be a person, an individual (never a multitude; never more nor less than one). You have to be either straight or gay, man or woman, adult or child. You cannot be everything at once or nothing at all. Everything you do has to have a meaning, a *use*. The theorist Jenny Edkins writes:

> Pinned down like a specimen insect . . . the person is immobilised and made present, available to the gaze of a bureaucracy, an administration . . . It does not allow for the being as such, human or not, a being never fully present, displaced, always arriving too late or too early, escaping categorization, unknowable – a being who is always missing, never fully grasped even by themselves.

Life in the so-called normal world, let's face it, is bizarre. Walking the streets at dusk in this unreal city, you have to go along with the fact that you are this strange unreal person. Waking up, you have to accept that you are this person who is supposedly waking up. It is incomprehensible that any of it is happening, yet you are obliged to take it seriously. You are expected to take life seriously, when in reality life is ridiculous, and being a person is beyond ridiculous.

I started unravelling in depersonalization when I was in my mid-twenties. I remember one evening sitting on a bench in

Russell Square in London literally not knowing who I was. It was profoundly disturbing. I felt like my insides were on fire. Some succour came from philosophy (Bataille, Butler, Derrida). It came from going to the National Gallery and bathing in the beautiful blue canvas of Titian's *Bacchus and Ariadne*. And it came from the squat raves I went to near the reservoirs in south Tottenham, at one of which grapes and LIBER were painted on the wall. My flatmate at the time used to attend the fetish party AntiChrist, but I was still ignorant of that world. I bought him a copy of Nietzsche's *The Gay Science*. Though he had no problem dressing as a latex slave at AntiChrist, he was too embarrassed to read *The Gay Science* on the Tube.

In accounts of the erotic, I find Audre Lorde as interesting as I do Bataille. Lorde's femme focus is an antidote to Bataille's crude cocksmanship. Lorde orients the impersonal nature of the encounter towards care and ethics. That said, her blind spot is neglecting the small matter of *filth*. 'Beauty is desired in order that it may be befouled,' as Bataille wrote; 'not for its own sake, but for the joy brought by the certainty of profaning it.' I think here of Proust's kink, which, as his biographer Edmund White tells us, involved soiling and desecrating a photograph of his mother. Excitement can lie in the unforgiveable.

I continued through Gegen's Club Culture exhibition. Three Black drag queens with bodices and silver hoop earrings looked intensely at the viewer, their biceps glistening with sweat. A white man's hands tore his naked torso open to reveal, teeming inside, a bunch of other such hands. Mounted in frames, everything was transgressing its bounds. But all the same, I began to feel guilty. Because against my will, I felt a creeping sense of disappointment.

Being in KitKat's beloved corridors without the musty crowd and smiling faces was like being on a stage set with no audience and no show. Despite the beautifully intense art, finally being back in an unpeopled club only made me miss clubbing all the more.

I bought a beer at the bar and sat on a leather sofa. Along with a dozen or so other socially distanced punters, I was in a room with a red carpet and purple strip lights. A mistress with a leash led in a man on all fours wearing a leather dog mask. On a small stage, they enacted his canine kink. To my left, a screen showed a documentary (*No Democracy Here* by Liad Hussein Kantorowicz). An Israeli man was talking about his BDSM relationship. He described his feelings of humiliation when, before his Israeli friends, a dominatrix demanded that he scream aloud, 'End the Occupation!'

Sex positivity isn't about sensual hedonism. Sex positivity isn't about getting your hole. Sex positivity is about shirking off the shame in sexuality; it means that your sexuality, whether it's vanilla or quote–unquote weird, is something to celebrate. The corollary of this is that, through this occluded aspect of ourselves, we can come to (no pun intended) a better sense of whatever it is we are in the universe. In *Whip Smart*, her dominatrix memoir, Melissa Febos describes how her clients were generally not 'pervs' but ordinary people – executives, workers. Through kink, they found a fresh perspective on being human. But importantly, a sub would never want moral respectability or recuperation. There could be nothing more vulgar than bourgeois social acceptance. Something must always remain abject, forbidden, boundless. Filth matters.

In this spirit, I suppose I should tell you about my queer awakening, my first non-cis-hetero sex. She was super attractive,

I mean intensely pretty. She was wearing a leopard-print bolero, a crop top and denim hot pants. Her hair was pulled back to show off her eyes and cheeks. She was a trans woman, a woman born in a male body (AMAB). She took supplements and had small breasts. When we got back to her flat, she moved to give me oral pleasure but instead I fucked her from behind beside a pile of magazines and a bin spilling over. What, more than anything, I got off on was the filthiness of the sex, which was in disagreement with the straight identity I had previously by rote inhabited.

I had always thought of myself as mostly straight, theoretically bi, internally androgynous. Suddenly that state fell apart. And it felt so liberating. I remember the morning afterwards, as I walked away from her place, along the canal. It was the first time I had had sex with someone other than a cis woman, and I felt afraid my mind might go off-kilter; my mind tends to do that. I was aware of my mental precarity and that anything out of the ordinary could bring on a horrible depersonalization. But instead I experienced the total opposite. As I walked along the canal, I felt so bright, a hum of positivity. I mean, it had been hot and murky and tawdry, but it was also somehow innocent and pure and pleasant.

After this, I realized I could be attracted to different bodies. In particular, I had a thing for genderqueer people. Thinking back on that trans woman's black hair and lips and bony face, I entertained the idea that my desire for her had been motivated by some deep metaphysical narcissism: she was, I realized, in her striking beauty, like an idealized female or non-cis-male version of myself, a body evading any simple gender identity, the realization of something obscurely I longed for. I realized my masculinity at its fullest through becoming woman, and realized myself to my fullest, in erotic play, through quite literally becoming another – whatever that means.

Krüger says of KitKat's ethos, 'It's about the leap into the unknown, into a world that everyone actually wants: into fulfilment.' In this, an element of early 1990s utopianism remains. Consciousness and self-reflection are necessary to build a weekend party into a general ethos. Like Thaur, Krüger is dismissive of those who aren't able to imagine it without drugs. 'If people can only achieve this when they've consumed some substance – that won't work.'

The film's credits rolled. I had reached the end of the Club Culture Day exhibition. Having spent an hour at the COVID-times KitKat, I finished my beer and left. But unbeknownst to myself, the KitKat Club and I were not yet through for that calendar year.

A week before Christmas, I was staying at Indrani's flat and having trouble sleeping. My breathing was shallow. The next morning, at her workplace, Indrani was asked to take a COVID-19 rapid test. I received her text message around noon: her test had come back positive.

Cue panic.

Now, I had to get tested. But where? I wasn't registered in Germany with a local GP. So, where? Where else but the KitKat Club.

The KitKat, I soon remembered, had recently generously reopened as a COVID-19 quick-test centre. You could show up and get tested without booking. Off I went, short of breath, walking a few kilometres to Kreuzberg, to stand on that red carpet; not to dress up, or dress down, or revel, but to have a swab shunted up my nose.

It turned out that I, too, was positive for COVID-19.

I don't remember much about the two weeks that followed. They're a blur, and were mostly spent horizontal. But I do remember having delirious dreams – carnivalesque dreams that were nearly a match for Berlin club-land.

After the Gegen exhibition, my attitude to KitKat changed. The reasons for this were connected to broader occurrences in the club world. Two stories broke that described sexual harassment by one of the founders of Detroit techno, Derrick May. Numerous women alleged that May had preyed on them. The investigative journalist Annabel Ross wrote about it after the behaviour came to light through Michael James, the Detroit musician who co-wrote the classic Detroit techno track 'Strings of Life'. A few months earlier, the famous house DJ Erick Morillo had been charged with sexual battery, after which ten women told similar stories of their encounters with him. This was dance music's long overdue #MeToo moment.

Later, allegations became public that the frontman of the German metal band Rammstein, Till Lindemann, had sexually preyed upon vulnerable women. Meanwhile, he was welcomed with open arms at KitKat. Krüger and Thaur seemed unperturbed about hosting this alleged sexual predator at their sex-positive club. Friends of mine said they'd seen him there often, as well as at other clubs. Eventually, the police dropped their investigation of Lindemann due to insufficient evidence.

By then, I'd heard a couple of other stories concerning KitKat that disturbed me. The first was from my German friend Z–, who spoke about how she'd started going there as a teenager, meeting a much older man, a rich and successful artist, who seduced her, and of how at times, having entered KitKat with him, she would later come to to find herself in another part of Berlin with no recollection of having left the club. The second story was a deeply unsavoury one concerning a prominent KitKat Club figure, pertaining to something that allegedly happened without consent in the 1990s and which came to me from someone credible. After that, I stopped going to KitKat.

Stuck in Berlin that snowy Christmas, lying on the sofa in Indrani's apartment with COVID-19, I read more books than I had in ages. I read Annie Ernaux's *The Years* and reread White's biography of Proust. I also read Jack Fritscher's memoirs of the gay underground in NYC, a scene of which Fritscher was the main literary chronicler. With the light touch and gift for detail of a classical diarist, Fristscher had set down for posterity some of the orgiastic experiences that had happened in gay NYC circles in the 1970s. Fritscher's account, I thought, gave the lie to the psychedelia – the undoing of selfhood – that these men arrived at through sexual experimentation, and to the seriousness with which these men took it, setting up dungeons in their homes:

> Pleasantly stoned, and in stony company, I watched, and, without embarrassment, admit to being a minimalist supporting player in the revels . . .
>
> The men moved from incantatory words to grunts and growls, leaving civilization behind, devolving back to primitive communication of grunt and groan.

One particularly beautiful young man lay on the floor beneath the Grossman sculpture and became an altar around whom the assembled coven gathered to shoot their seed.

No matter how 'sick' people may think this ritual, I can truthfully say I found them to have risen through the chosen medium to an ecstatic state . . .

I don't know what drug cocktail he had swallowed. He was so in a trance state that he seemed not to understand plain English.

My only escape, because for me personally things had gone quite far enough, and professionally the writer in me had seen more than any anthropologist with a government grant would ever see, was to grunt back, offering to hose him off.

He took to the hot shower I sprayed on him and made a game of it.

I'll never forget how the water turned him from primordial ooze as his white skin began to wash through.

I confess I felt like God, an acid god, creating Adam, the human, from the mud of the earth.

The Future Becomes You

I was in the heart of the woods on a grey afternoon, stopped at a fork in the path near a dried-up lake. It was a place where I often paused while walking, taking stock of the altered light quality where the dense tree cover momentarily broke. Around the barren lake, there was an eerie stillness that brought me back to the forest a kilometre across the bog from where I grew up in Donegal, Bonny Glen Wood, where I whiled away so many childhood afternoons.

Before me was a malformed tree. My imagination, enlivened by the music on my headphones, saw in this tree an alien presence. In its amputated appendage, there was a cyclopean eye; in its rising branch, an outstretched arm; in its trunk, a pregnant growth; in its exposed roots, tentacular legs. Standing forth from the surrounding woodland, it looked, I fancied, like a temple's threshold guardian, a statue into whose faceless gaze, in entering, you're obliged to look.

Counter-intuitive though it might seem, on those Sundays in Berlin when I didn't go clubbing I often went rambling in Grunewald, the sprawling forest west of the city. From the anonymity of the woodland, among the forest's pillars, my spirit drank in the same thing as it did from the anonymity of the dark dance floor; in the depths of the woods as on the depths of the dance floor, I became the same anonymous person, mercifully voided of semantics and norms. 'Multitude, solitude: identical terms', as Baudelaire wrote, comparing solitary drifts among urban crowds to anonymous drifts in nature.

Today, in particular, I was walking in Grunewald to douse a fire in my brain. Early in the morning, as I sat pulling up my Nike socks, readying for a stint at Tresor, I noticed on my laptop screen an email from Klaus, the German guy from whom I was renting my twentieth-floor apartment. The news wasn't good, and irritatingly Klaus relayed it cheerfully by attaching a thumbs-up photo of himself on an African street. Along with his new wife and daughter, Klaus had decided to return from Senegal to Berlin, owing to his tighter freelance work circumstances post-pandemic. Would I be so good as to vacate his apartment in four weeks' time?

I felt winded, like someone had punched me. This meant I'd have to try to find somewhere new to live at an impossible time, with Berlin in a housing crisis. Realistically, I wouldn't be able to find anywhere to live, since my bank account was empty, I had no work references and I remained off the books in Germany. It meant, I realized, as I looked out the window, that Berlin was coming to an end. That those orange clouds were coming to an end. That the black windows on the faces of the high-rises across the way were coming to an end. That the distant Ferris Wheel on the horizon was coming to an end. The beautiful red sky and green neon were coming to an end. The soothing hiss of water in the fountain down below was coming to an end. And I, too, was coming to an end.

Now, as I trundled out of the undergrowth, I struck upon a lonely sandy path undulating westwards, deeper into the woods. Kilometres into Grunewald, the forest freed itself of human life, one's reward for penetrating so far. On my headphones, I was listening to the Planetary Assault Systems (PAS) album *Arc Angel* and EP *Plantae*, *Arc Angel* being the first techno release I'd picked up after moving to Berlin, a gift from my former friend Karin. This was techno with which, years later, I was still obsessed. Resonating with the green leaves around me, lucent electronic frequencies swooped, glided, delirious and free. A soft pulse impressed underfoot on the sand where my feet fell.

On the PAS double album *Arc Angel*, in particular, in the persistent lack of any tonal centre, alongside the polyphonic texture of glissandi, and the granulation on tracks like 'Sonar Falls' and 'Message from the Drone Sector', there was sonic sophistication in studied weirdness. It was an uncompromising vision of techno that, as I walked through the woods, enhanced the sensory experience and seemed to set the trees speaking. 'As Planetary Assault Systems, Luke Slater is an innovator of psychedelic mindfuck techno,' went the press release for *Plantae*, a sentence that immediately won me over.

Slater's body of work stretched back to the early 1990s. He was a master of the craft, and when we'd spoken recently over Zoom, I was keen to ask his thoughts on techno's power. For me, techno was not just its formal attributes but what these did to a person. Dressed dapperly in a suit and brimmed hat, and sitting in his studio at the time – all desks and dials and hardware, it looked like a spacecraft cockpit – Slater talked to me first about his most recent L. B. Dub Corp album, *Saturn to Home*. I then asked him whether, as a Berghain resident and long-standing Ostgut Ton artist (the first non-German artist released on the label), playing at the club, with its distinctive spacious main room reverb, affected his music.

'Totally,' he replied. 'These kinds of experiences do affect how I think.' He liked to test out new music at Berghain to see how it sounded. 'Berghain has been really lucky, I think, because the space just is what it is. The way things sound in there to a degree is an accident because the space itself just happens to have this sound.' People had tried to replicate that in different venues, 'but it never really sounds the same. Because it's just the nature of acoustics, right? It has got a sound. And thankfully, it's a really good sound.' That Berghain sound is amply displayed across Slater's later catalogue, from the canonical 'Desert Races' through LSD's 'Process 1' to recent hit 'Say It Loud'.

When I asked Slater about psychedelia – I mentioned to him how I thought *Arc Angel*, beyond genre tags, was one of the great psychedelia albums of recent decades – he was cautious about too neatly associating his music with that culturally loaded term. Historically, Slater noted, psychedelia recalled things like Timothy Leary and LSD overindulgence in the 1960s. 'Which is all valid. But I think that that's possibly its downfall. It seems to get separated out into this [thing of], "well, you're a hippie on LSD and you think everything's like this, or you're a conservative who only drinks."' Slater resisted any over-easy split between different ways of thinking. 'I've felt, especially lately, that this sectioning-off has become more apparent. That's a hard taboo to bust with the idea of psychedelia.'

The video for 'Say It Loud' playfully riffs off a cyborg version of Slater in a hyper-accelerated contemporary city. He once told *Resident Advisor* that PAS at times felt like a separate entity to him with which he communicated. I asked how important futurism was for him as a techno artist. 'I've been asked this a lot,' he replied. 'Back when I started, the idea of other worlds and the future were really strong. Everything I did in the beginning was based around the idea of other worlds rather than anything that seemed to be around me at the time.'

Nowadays, Slater distinguished this other-worlds aspect from heroic sci-fi tropes. 'As much as I like sci-fi, I think the aspect I find important is the imagination of different worlds and different constructs, and of how people are in those constructs; that's always been my kind of thing,' he said. 'As much as I like *Star Trek*, it's good entertainment, but it doesn't quite cut it in the way of something you can apply to where you are now. Whatever it means, I don't know, but I always want to go somewhere else rather than accepting that the here and now is everything.'

Slater's thoughts were illuminating. Liberating strangeness was, for me, techno's appeal. That meant the techno tracks to which I was drawn weren't the modal exoticism of Ben Klock and Marcel Dettmann and, more recently, Ignez. It wasn't techno that had traditional Western musical elements like major/minor keys and so on. No, it was synthetic electronic music with no melody, no harmony, no song structure. It was atonal music like Xenakis and Varèse but affixed to hypnotically repeated pulsations. It was producers like Developer, Kr!z, early Rødhåd, Blawan/Pariah/Karenn, Isabel Soto, Truncate, Adriana Lopez, DVS1, Rrose, ROD, Mike Parker and Temudo, and labels like Clone, Hayes, Modularz, Mote-Evolver, Modwerks, Sandwell District, Klockworks and Ostgut Ton. It was something inhuman or transhuman, related to how Xenakis described modernist music: 'Music is not a language. Any musical piece is akin to a boulder with complex forms, with striations and engraved designs atop and within, which men can decipher in a thousand different ways without ever finding the right answer or the best one.'

On my headphones, in the depths of the woods, Ø [Phase]'s 2012 track 'Binary Opposition (Process 1)' came on. Dating from what I felt was techno's prime psychedelic period, Ø's track grew around a kick drum pulse of Redwood tree magnitude, its sonic textures fading in and out of view. Another track based around this type of explosive kick drum was Len Faki's 'BX3' – on a YouTube upload, it appears mixed with PAS's 'Surface Noise' under the admirable name 'Obliteration of the Berghain' – and the Berghain-inspired colossal kick-drum ethos culminated in the aforementioned 'Process 1' by LSD (a collaboration by Luke Slater, Steve Bicknell and Dave Sumner), the apex, for me, of techno's psychedelic phase, its video recalling Philip K. Dick's cosmic hallucinations.

Alien music like this is a mode of address. As Sun Ra said, it comes 'from the void, the nothing, in response to the burning need for something else'. Good techno addresses that within us which does not find itself reflected anywhere in the everyday world, as with the address made to me earlier by the mutant tree. Stockhausen, like Sun Ra, had also spoken of music in these terms. 'I expect an expansion of consciousness through which one can learn to listen better, discover something, develop oneself,' Stockhausen said, 'especially through alien sound events. The alien is so important for what we are actually looking for.' An other self in you awaits this transmission, a dormant unself.

At Berghain, I usually danced on the podium at the back of the main room dance floor. In part, this was because the sound was better there. But as well as this, it was because it gave a full vista of the club space. Your eyes spanned from the bifurcating red and blue lights to the alien-face Funktion-One speakers hanging at either end of the room. In the right conditions, I often reached ecstasy dancing while staring at the speaker, the music reaching peak abstraction through visual association with the speaker's alien face. And if you're still wondering what I mean by something beyond your everyday self, Maurice Blanchot puts it succinctly: 'the everyday is what we never see for a first time but can only see again, having always already seen it by an illusion that is constitutive of the everyday.'

Ahead loomed the evocatively named Teufelsberg, or 'Devil's Mountain', a hill that's Grunewald's salient feature. Although the Teufelsberg was nowadays all tree cover as thick as a jungle, the hill itself was only a few decades old and comprised rubble and debris from the destruction of Berlin in the Second World War. When I walked its muddy paths, lost in the multilayered techno, smithereens at times appeared underfoot of tiles from decades-old domestic interiors, the ruined everyday of those who underwent the Third Reich's apocalypse. Rising impassive on top of Teufelsberg were three white domes, one large orb above the other two. They had an unreal presence, like the abandoned set of some 1970s sci-fi film; but these three white domes emerging from the forest were, in fact, the ruins of a Cold War-era U.S. listening station.

As I walked along, negotiating the nettles and briars, the derelict station put me in mind of the recent phone conversation I'd had with the techno artist Function, the artist whose music, experienced at Berghain, had originally set me off on this years-long journey through techno. At a time of ever-increasing commercialization of club culture, with some artists advertising luxury brands or pressured to make fools of themselves on Instagram, Function (real name David Sumner) remained for me one of techno's most fascinating artists. Mostly, he let his enigmatic music do the talking and ignored whatever was trendy.

We had spoken a few weeks ago after I had first emailed him the questions I wanted to ask.

'This one about what art and music I'm into right now,' he said over the phone, 'is that one of your initial questions?'

'Yeah, if you'd like it to be.'

'No, I mean, Liam,' he paused; 'I've been going through a really, really powerful spiritual awakening process . . . It's why Function for me is not really at the top of my priority list right now. I've been hit with something that's so powerful that I've needed to listen.' What he went on to tell me about, in confidence, was mind-bending, a transcendental experience. It related, among other things, to clandestine codes inserted in his recent music, quite resonant with the Americans' spy listening station I was now passing.

Existenz, Function's double album of 2019, had world-building scope. After a stressful period in his life, Sumner said, 'I found that the only escape was to feverishly work on music. And then I started making more music than I ever had in my whole life. And then it just started growing into this narrative.' Lost media, as well as autobiographical allusions, were involved, including haunting old crackly late-night television broadcasts on local Manhattan public-access television. When the album was released in September 2019, a few months before the COVID-19 pandemic, weirdness kicked in, blurring fiction and reality.

Occasioning the release was a promotional video featuring a vintage public network television broadcast of two psychics forecasting the future ('Psychic Masters: No Guaranteed Futures', says the on-screen legend). A woman psychic remarks, 'This year is horrible for you,' before she corrects herself. 'It's not this year; it's *next* year. Keep it cool next year; it's not the most nurturing year for you.' Announced just before the COVID-19 plague year struck, it was auspicious. That synchronicity was amplified when the website *Electronic Beats* made the album announcement: 'The Video For Function's New Album On Tresor Is Psychic And May Predict Your Future', said the prescient headline. These disturbing coincidences were only the beginning.

Of the album's compositional period, Function told me that 'the floodgates came down,' and his subsequent EPs seemed more overtly to link secret codes to a weird multiplicity of history he had discovered behind his life. In ways, it reminded me of Philip K. Dick's epiphanic experiences in the 1970s, when he felt an extraterrestrial intelligence communicating to – and through – him. A few of *Existenz*'s cuts sample the strange radio transmissions called numbers stations. As first explored by Akin Fernandez and released on his Conet Project, numbers stations are secret broadcasts made on radio where unknown individuals read series of numbers. Allegedly, they are codes being relayed to intelligence agents in the field, and nobody has ever managed to decipher them. On *Existenz*, tracks like 'Zahlensender' and 'Ertrinken' intone numbers and radio static and Morse code patterns in the musical texture. Their audio quality is crackly and uncanny, as if coming from elsewhere entirely. As Function experienced it, this precipitated a cosmic awakening through synchronicity and tech-gnosis.

Dick said his stories came to him in deep night, when the everyday world had vanished: 'reception is best between 3 a.m. and 4:45 a.m.' – as with techno sets at club nights. Given that techno was auditory sci-fi – or better, experiential sci-fi – I supposed it was natural that there should at times be such crossovers. *Awakening from the Illusory Self* (2021) was the name of Function's most recent EP, and another recent release, on Rrose's Eaux label, had the same tenor. *Subject F (Transcendence)* (2019), it was called, and its blurb was cryptic: 'subject f has transcended. please wait new designation . . . david sumner experiences transcendence – an awakening from the illusory self. hearing. feeling. thinking.'

For some, science fiction as an artistic force was spent in our era, subsumed within commercialized Hollywood scenarios. 'There is no more fiction,' French theorist Jean Baudrillard wrote in *Simulacra and Simulation* (1981). '[Science] fiction will never again be a mirror held toward the future, but a desperate rehallucination of the past.' But a way forward for the genre was suggested by Ursula K. Le Guin, a branching away by which sci-fi endured in an uncannier guise:

> If science fiction is the mythology of modern technology, then its myth is tragic. 'Technology', or 'modern science' (using the words as they are usually used, in an unexamined shorthand standing for the 'hard' sciences and high technology founded upon continuous economic growth), is a heroic undertaking, Herculean, Promethean, conceived as triumph, hence ultimately as tragedy. The fiction embodying this myth will be, and has been, triumphant (Man conquers earth, space, aliens, death,

> the future, etc.) and tragic (apocalypse, holocaust, then or now).
>
> If, however, one avoids the linear, progressive, Time's-(killing)-arrow mode of the Techno-Heroic, and redefines technology and science as primarily cultural carrier bag rather than weapon of domination, one pleasant side effect is that science fiction can be seen as a far less rigid, narrow field, not necessarily Promethean or apocalyptic at all, and in fact less a mythological genre than a realistic one.
>
> It is a strange realism, but it is a strange reality.

Science fiction, or speculative fiction, wouldn't be heroic fantasy but a different way of attending to the everyday: the everyday estranged, reality queered.

A guidebook for me was Paul B. Preciado's *Can the Monster Speak?*, an autobiography of a self whom Preciado presents as having always been a fiction. Preciado describes how he undertook a course of injecting testosterone for three months, 250 milligrams every 21 days, until eventually he opened his mouth 'and a hoarse, gravelly voice came from my throat. I was more startled than anyone, it was as though my vocal tract were possessed by an alien being.' He experienced an accelerated version of the process of gender-formation that all cis people go through, an acceleration that revealed its artifice. The process taught Preciado 'to cease to assume, as you do, what a man is, what a woman is, what a homosexual or a heterosexual is. To free my thinking from these shackles and experience, try to perceive, to feel, to name, beyond sexual difference.' Born into a female body, living in adulthood as a man, equally incredulous of both,

Preciado existed outside the gender binary. He considered the gender binary outmoded, as Newtonian physics was in the age of quantum physics and relativity, and he experienced human life instead as an alien, a Uranian. All of which I found deeply relatable.

I knew that techno addressed another being in me. As Slater had said, many of us in our deepest core yearn for something different, go through our lives yearning for it. At the club, techno played by someone like Azu Tiwaline or Setaoc Mass disorients you; it flows into you; you become one with it. And in the darkness, that's what you want. You invite an alien experience because the alien experience is real, more real than riding the train or staring at your phone or buying groceries in the supermarket or any of the other supposedly real things in the supposedly real world. On the dancefloor, I was androgynous. I was washes of colour. I was red flickering in total darkness. I was a body without a body, vision unloosed from eyes, hearing without ears. I was fields of forces intersplicing, like shoals of fish whose movement generates larger forms. Before it all vanished again.

By now, I was so deep in the forest I felt decentred. I was freed of cardinal points, of forwards and backwards and sideways. I stayed close to the areas with tree cover.

So deep in thought was I, hypnotized by all this as I walked down a dark slope, that I almost didn't notice the first naked body. Human and stocky, male and white, it came out of the undergrowth, strolling nonchalantly. Then came a second, further away, a naked brown woman's body walking towards an expanse of green water. They were forms inseparable from this forest. And when, passing from the tree-cover dark, the sky opened and shimmering water came into view, the scene was as in Cézanne's *The Bathers*. Naked bodies and tree trunks blended in and out of each other.

I sat on the low branch of a tree growing at the sandy lake shore. 'Mugwort' by PAS came on my headphones, intertwined atonal ostinatos. I closed my eyes and became the sounds. Into my head came a line from that androgyne Clarice Lispector: 'Do you ever suddenly find it strange to be yourself?'

At home that evening, I started taking my things and putting them in boxes. Temporarily, I could crash at Indrani's. I removed books from the bookshelf. Should I keep the bulky French–English dictionary I never used or throw it away? Should I sell the Moby autobiography my sister had thoughtfully bought me for Christmas? There were bookshops where you could trade them in for a few quid. I was broke, and now that I didn't know where I was going to be in a few weeks, maybe it was time to start letting things go.

Staving off depression for another day, and feeling calm after my forest techno walk, I reflected again on my conversation with Luke Slater. I had found his outlook inspiring, as an artist who had been through serious mental health issues and who used his music for good. 'There's a long way to go till the myth is busted that big companies have the answers with pills,' he said to me, warning me off pharmaceuticals; 'because ultimately, we're all human and our brains don't all function the same.' For him, as for me these days, music was the drug. 'My early feeling was that I wanted to take my brain to somewhere else and I used music to do that. The sounds change how you think and how you feel. And I've bought into that from day one.' Sobriety these days was my only way of experiencing techno in the club, the purest techno experience by far.

Slater recognized that everyone needs some kind of escape. 'We all need to be able to imagine and to take our brains to other places,' he said. 'And I always like to think if I can affect someone in this kind of surreal way, where they can go on a journey and hopefully it works for them in the same way as me, then that's a tick in my book. And that can be quite subliminal as well. It doesn't really have to be stamped in your face.'

From off the bookshelf I took Le Guin's science fiction novel *The Left Hand of Darkness*. I'd read it a while back and been disappointed by it. While the theme fascinated – in the far-off future of a universe twinning ours, on a remote alien planet, a humanoid race lives that exists outside binary sex and gender, a race whose members are simultaneously male and female – the style, as so often with classic sci-fi, was disappointing, written as it was in corny pseudo-archaic English.

Now, though, as I sat leafing through the pages, I noticed something fascinating, a bizarre coincidence. The name of the prime world from which, many thousands of years ago, all other alien races derived, was Hain. In German, *Hain* is the colloquial name for Berghain. It was one of those synchronicities in which Function had been embroiled. 'We are all men, you know, sir,' the protagonist says to the ruler of Gethen, the alien planet of non-binary people. 'All of us. All the worlds of men were settled, eons ago, from one world, Hain.'

It was a nice idea: Berghain as incubator for future humans, humans who became aliens, aliens freed at last from the gender binary. In the novel, the ambisexual race of Gethen are a deliberate experiment by the denizens of Hain to see the society that would result from eliminating this male/female cis-heteronormative distinction. All I knew was that, while others had identities and classes and orientations, there was no name or category for whatever I was. I barely at times recognized myself in the mirror.

The future becomes you, I thought, putting the book away. Perhaps all this was happening – the tower blocks, the Ferris wheel, the distant lights – because I was a future person set down to write up my impressions of this past time where I was wrongly located, writing them up in a book, an alien ethnographer. People's everyday beliefs to me were as so many cave paintings of bulls and bears and otters. All of it was an extravagant fabulation. And if it was about to end, I knew I had to experience, at least once, the most intense party there was: Snax Club.

Love's Secret Domain

It was six o'clock on a misty Sunday morning. I felt a mix of excitement and unease, as if I were about to ride hungover on a rusty rollercoaster. Disembarking the cab on Rüdersdorfer Straße, I knew I would be entering the building in time to catch most of Boris's climactic Snax Club set. Ahead of me on the dirt path two bald men in blue overalls who were carrying a ladder, whom I'd assumed were in costume for the party, turned out, in fact, to be just two bald workmen in overalls carrying a ladder – an easy mistake to make.

Alongside this men-only party in Lab.oratory and the Berghain main room, the regular Klubnacht was also on in Panorama Bar. Accordingly, as I arrived before the building in the hazy dawn, tired-eyed people dressed in black – rejects – gathered and talked, high or drunk. I walked along with the other men down to the left of the building towards the Lab.oratory entrance. The burly doorman, saucer-eyed, was chastising two men who seemed not to be wearing the appropriate gear, the dress code supposedly being fetish-only. I stepped forward and opened my leather jacket to show my army look and leather wristbands. 'Your costume?' he asked. I said yes. He nodded and I passed in.

Snax Club is held at Berghain twice a year, a men-only so-called pervy party. I was attending for the first time. It was Snax Club's thirtieth anniversary edition, a milestone for the gay techno party out of which – holy buggery leading to immaculate conception – Berghain was born. Boris had once said that during

Snax Club, 'you can actually see the real face of Berghain. You know exactly why that place exists on that night. Then it all makes sense.' That was an endorsement I'd opted this weekend to heed.

In Berlin, I'd already been in the most intense and depraved gay underground spaces. Part of the appeal of attending this enormous *débauche* – aside from helping me to understand Berlin's techno scene better – was in what the extreme environment could do for me, a non-binary man of Preciado's type. While I wasn't gay, I wasn't quite straight either. I was drawn to anything that, through force, could crack open my everyday self and let me see, unfiltered, whatever amorphous thing lay underneath.

Snax Club has elaborate set constructions at each edition, in the ordinarily unopened Halle part of the building. The 2010 programme declared: 'Foucault would be over the moon: Prison – that is the topic of this year's Snax Club. Monitoring, punishing, imprisoning'; while, as the club ethnographer Luis-Manuel Garcia described, the 2014 edition had a military theme: different tents were arrayed around the space 'filled with relevant furnishings and equipment. Throughout the sprawling sex-labyrinth . . . camouflage canvas netting was draped along with other elements that evoked both a battlefield and a training obstacle course.'

In what I'd heard of Snax's elaborate theatricality – scaffolding reaching into the gloom; a boxing ring on the dance floor – it was hard not to marvel at the sense of human life estranged, the everyday world treated as the fabrication it is. It made me think of the extravagant, decadent novel *Against Nature* and its model Robert de Montesquiou's bizarrely decorated *fin de siècle* Paris mansion, with its faux-monastic corners and gold-painted turtle-shell. Aesthetically, it sounded like *l'art pour l'art*, the triumph of artifice, an antidote to the everyday world's dull realism. I was intrigued about what they would come up with this year, as I walked with trepidation down the dark tunnel, entering the pleasuredome, the house that Teufele and Thormann built.

'Michael and Norbert, they appeared out of nowhere,' Stefan Schwanke had told me of Berghain's founders when I'd asked him about it. In a scene as close-knit as Berlin's was in 1994, everyone had basically shared a pill with everyone else. Yet, Schwanke said, he had 'no idea where they were before. All of a sudden, they were asking if they could do their own party at the top floor of Bunker,' though 'none of us had ever seen them.' Another man I spoke to, Ad, a Dutch fetishist active going back to the Mineshaft and Studio 54 days, said the founders obviously had absorbed the international leather scene. 'I'm sure that they also looked around as I did in all in those places.'

The original Snax Club took place, between 1994 and 1996, on the top floor of a fortress-like overground Nazi bunker. A more brutally intense club environment was hard to imagine. The Albert Speer-commissioned building, its walls 2 metres thick, its innards a disorienting labyrinth, was built by forced labour during the Allied bombing, and as the war devolved to its shattering conclusion, thousands of starving women and children were housed there. A warehouse during the GDR, it opened as the club Bunker in 1992, becoming one of Berlin's most notorious (in 2007 the *New York Times* dubbed it the hardest club in the world).

Located on Reinhardtstraße in Mitte near the Death Strip, Bunker tended towards the most musically uncompromising dance music like gabber. For the journalist Ida Krenzlin, who lived nearby, going to Bunker was a psychological ordeal, and she described the experience well. 'You had to get past the bouncer,' she said.

> There were hard gabber techno parties, very excessive. You felt your way from one room to the next, from one floor to the next. It was very dark. You were always going around a corner, up or down another flight of stairs. Sweat dripped from the low ceilings, the strobe lights were blinding, and fog also wafted through the narrow rooms. It was just a matter of luck when you found someone again. The bunker was a labyrinth. Everything was somehow anonymous and broken.

Clubber Uwe Reineke told Denk and von Thülen that the Bunker's scuzzy clientele was 'the subculture within the subculture' – coincidentally, the very phrase used in a contemporary review of the Mineshaft, New York City's notorious gay leather club. 'The Mineshaft changed the character of sex and ritual in the 1970s,' wrote Jack Fritscher, editor of *Drummer* magazine, in the first volume of his memoir *Profiles in Gay Courage*. Snax Club's concept was to merge this type of men-only party with techno.

Andreas Schwartz, who was Bunker's managing director, told me about how things started. 'Werner Vollert – the owner of the Bunker – was approached by them, and then he sent them to me to ask what I thought about it, probably because I'm gay myself and to see if I would approve of it,' Schwartz said. 'So then Norbert and Micha came to see me, and I found it quite amusing because they looked so different at the time. Norbert with his sleek haircut, and then Micha with all his piercings and tattoos – both, of course, highly intelligent.' Bunker had been running a fetish party called the Ex-Kreuz-Club in a small space behind the main building. 'It was very exclusive back then, with people coming from all over Germany,' Schwarz said. 'I assume Norbert and Micha were at those parties and got inspired there. They eventually got their own floor in the Bunker, because we had five floors and so on.' Another old clubber told me of his bemusement, when attending a gabber party at Bunker, at seeing gay men in rubber and leather file past on another staircase: 'None of us had ever seen that before.'

Snax Club's first edition took place in July 1994, followed by a second edition in October. The initial flyers were printed in monochrome. On the second edition's flyer, over the phrase 'no-man's-land', three muscular skinheads are shown in a struggle-cum-embrace. All are topless, with tattoos and leather wristbands, a typical gay skins clone look. No one's face is visible. 'They were playing with the idea of anonymity,' one attendee, Adrian, told me of Snax at Bunker.

Initially, Schwanke said, he appreciated that someone was 'finally' running a worthwhile party in the 'no-doubt impressive' Nazi ruin. When he started attending Snax regularly, it wasn't for sex but for the music. 'What I really liked is they were playing hard techno at a time when funky techno was all the rage. Funky techno and all this boring, pattern-repeating-after-pattern techno. When Snax started, they were the only party playing modern, hard techno that still had variations in its sound, and that was

PERVY PARTY

Sat. 01. 10. 94 Start 11 pm, End ?! am
Bunker Albrechtstr. 24/25 Berlin-Mitte

euphoric techno trance with
djoker daan + dj leo krieger

G rab your favourite outfit. Live your apocalyptic dream. It's served again at SNAX CLUB

Info: DevilTeufelDiable Postbox 30.43.12 10723 Berlin
Men only ! Tickets: DM 18,-

the reason why I went there.' He also brought his straight male friends, and once snuck in a wide-eyed woman friend who crashed the darkroom with a lit lighter ('Norbert laughed about the whole story').

One DJ who played the party was the exceptional selector Benji DF, a resident at the time on the Globus floor of Tresor. 'I just loved it,' Benji told me. 'It was like being zoomed directly into Sodom and Gomorrah. As I remember, the little rooms or dungeons within these floors were all filled with specific "themes".' The male guests, he said, were 'doing unspeakable things to each other but being super friendly and cozy apart from that, even to a straight, kinda normal dude like myself.' Benji said the atmosphere built as he played tracks like Tronikhouse 'Savage and Beyond'; Zero Gravity, 'The Crave'; DBX, 'Super Phreak'; DJ Oz, 'Technozone'; Mover, 'Frontal Sickness 1 and 2'; and Jimmy Crash, 'Crash Course' (tracks I list out so you get a sense of the music there). Eventually, the frenzy came to a head when Benji dropped Nasty Django, 'Fuck Beats' ('the EP's first untitled track'). 'The crowd went completely mental,' Benji said. 'Some guys in front of the DJ booth even took the silly "fick dich dochmal" slogan literally, doing some kind of standing threesome, while "dancing".'

A distinguished academic, a brilliant writer on art and on music, a leatherman and a Sephardic Jew (he had always avoided Berlin before, he said, 'for political reasons'), Adrian was visiting Berlin for the first time in 1994 to speak at a conference on the sociology of the city. While in town, he decided to check out the Snax party, taking a train to Friedrichstraße. After queuing in the late evening, he was admitted, and the party he found there, he said, 'was astonishing'.

In contrast to many other leather parties, great care was directed towards the aesthetics, and in particular, Adrian said, 'the connection of the aesthetic and the erotic'. As the beats pounded and you went from one room to another, the sound from the previous room began spilling in and mixing with the sound in the current room, and the room-by-room spatial sequence had an almost curatorial aspect in its planning. 'There was a succession of rooms, and it was like passing through a succession of fantasies. In one room, there were military cages all around the walls. Guys were at the bottom of the cages, ready for men to come along.' Then you passed into the next room. 'It was *totally* black. It was like a classic darkroom, but bigger. And so, you passed in and explored your way. Eventually, when you reached around at the wall, you searched around and found a door, which you opened and passed through into the next room.' This room was cavernous, full of basins and baths. Finally, Adrian said, you pushed through a door – and you arrived in a lounge bar, the walls decorated in bright pink velvet. At the bar in this pink room people sat on stools and drank cocktails and ate gingerbread, as if in a camp Schöneberg gay bar. 'It felt like a secret party,' he told me.

Robert Mapplethorpe, whose photography documented gay S&M and leather culture and brought it into the mainstream, once remarked that those initials, for him, stood for 'sex and magic, not sadomasochism'. In this way, and in line with 1960s counterculture's injunctions to dissolve the ego, Mapplethorpe in his photography captured the fantastical aspect of the underground gay club environment ('their real faces were transformed into Mapplethorpe masks,' his friend Fritscher remarked of some of the portraits). As well as being sites of pleasure, leather clubs were a zone for exploding the illusion of selfhood. The leather scene always had a dream aspect.

William Eppridge's photograph of leathermen for a 1964 *Life* article fixed the image of this 'secret world', homosexuality as a theatre of exaggeratedly rugged male identity. Arising in the USA after the Second World War, the leather scene idealized the masculinity portrayed by Marlon Brando in *The Wild One* (1953) and the uniformed servicemen that closeted gay men in America spent time around while on military service. Tom of Finland, the most famous erotic illustrator of the hyper-masc stud, said, as a youth, he fantasized about the leather-clad Nazis he had seen serving in Finland during the war, in whose rough-hewn manliness gay men found a refuge from the stereotype of the effete homosexual. At one San Francisco bar, the Black and Blue, a Harley Davidson motorbike was suspended from the ceiling, and at certain ritualized moments, to the strains of Beethoven, the patrons would toast this dramatically lit, quasi-sacred relic. Inasmuch as it was linked to silver-screen fantasy, the leather scene paralleled the drag culture that developed independently over the same period among femme queers in Harlem – queer selfhood as living one's fantasy, authentic truth through fabulation.

In the 1970s, the leather bars in some urban centres developed into gay BDSM clubs. Patrick Moore calls this 'the great experiment' and argues that, in its aestheticization and extremity, underground gay sex clubs like San Francisco's Catacombs and New York's Mineshaft (which one could extend to early Snax Club and its successor, Lab.oratory) hosted a de facto artistic movement, wherein sex became art. The Mineshaft was a theatre of pleasure, deliberately planned for a *mise en scène* of bodies in architectural distributions, where, according to Fritscher, 'homomasculine men came out to try everything to make up for time lost in the closet, and to create erotic interaction, no matter how existentially extreme, to achieve fully human male pleasure.' The erotic dynamic was set 'so far beyond the boundaries of civilization,' he wrote, 'that a man had to have self-discipline not to get swept away in action or voyeurism too extreme for himself, but not for the other guy.' In a 1982 interview, partly with this in mind, Michel Foucault said: 'From the idea that the self is not given to us, I think that there is only one practical consequence: we have to create ourselves as a work of art.'

Artwork was, naturally, a key source of inspiration in this aestheticization of selfhood. A 1978 poster for the New St Marks Baths in New York, the largest gay bathhouse in America, tapped into the archaic fabulation schtick (what writer and academic Ben Miller calls 'primitivist homomythopoetics'). The poster shows a fantasy scene of a heroic, strapping man with a moustache, torn clothes and bulging groin riding a monstrous dinosaur. Man and steed are surrounded by muscular alien men, bald clones of each other, creepy yet seductively ripped, who reach towards him. The heroic lone white male has his counterpart in the wretched bald aliens, and the wretched bald aliens have as their further cousin a huge reptilian monster acting as a steed. Repurposed from a 1950s comic, its artist was called Boris – coincidentally, the name of one of Snax Club's longest-playing DJs.

In his interview with *Resident Advisor*, Boris conflated the Snax Club guests' butch masculinity with the building's architecture: its bruised concrete walls, its height, its darkness, a vast inside cut off absolutely from the outside world. 'It all goes together with this maleness, this bruteness, this testosterone, that fits right into that building,' he said. Attending, for me, meant opening that zone wherein the human became the alien.

Schwanke thought that, in Snax's early days, its founders Teufele and Thormann weren't totally certain of what its pitch was. 'They didn't want it to be a pure sex party,' he said. 'They wanted it to be a party where you can combine both interests. but they didn't know how to promote it.' Schwanke was at the time a journalist for Germany's main dance music magazine *Frontpage* and also editor-in-chief of *1000 Clubzine*, a punky free what's-on guide for Berlin distributed around the city. In the latter, the first press appeared for Berghain's later founders; Schwanke wrote that, despite a decline in club culture having recently set in in Berlin, here was something exciting happening. 'It's in a bit of a strange setting, but if you focus on the music, there's really something to be discovered there,' Schwanke recalled writing. The organizers were grateful. 'Norbert said, "Thanks so much for directing people our way. Because it has started to become a bit expensive, and there was no money coming in, but we just want to keep it going."'

Snax Club quickly became a fixture in the international gay circuit. At one Snax party, Schwanke bumped into Martin Gore, whom he knew from having worked on a Depeche Mode tour. 'I was really surprised, because he used to live in Berlin in, I think, '85 or '86, then he left and said he didn't see any reason going back, because the whole scene turned towards heroin.' Others remembered seeing Jean Paul Gaultier at Bunker – some of his fashion took inspiration from gay BDSM. When asked in 2016 about his times partying in Berlin, Gaultier was coy. 'I've had a lot of crazy nights, especially at Berghain and KitKatClub. Both embody eccentricity, extravagance, and freedom. It's like a dream in there.' A less coy acquaintance wrote me: 'Get hold of J-P G. He was everywhere. One felt stalked by him. I had a Backstreet chum who conserved some cum stains of him on his chaps as "designer cum". You should interview him.'

Gaultier did not answer my interview request.

Police raids in 1995 and '96 put paid to Bunker as a club. Snax Club entered a period of wandering that would last until 1998, sometimes holding parties further north in the district of Prenzlauer Berg, in the Pfefferberg complex and in an old dairy plant on Brunnenstraße, with one edition taking place in Tacheles and another at the old site of Planet by the Spree. At times, the sudden influx of burly bald men on the streets made the neighbours afraid that they were neo-Nazis. By this time, Snax Club's flyer design had changed to gay skins fetish photography and Tom of Finland-style cartoon pornography – bodies bound, torsos tied, liquid splashing, leather wrapping, piercings and pleasurable pain – some of which I now saw projected onto the decayed power plant's walls, as I stood in my army gear, readying to enter the fray. One abject flyer showed a close-up of a multiply pierced cock; another, a group of clones *in flagrante delicto*.

Below the projections, as in a gym changing room on a remote space station, were massed male bodies, changing into or out of their fetishwear. Empty plastic bags lay all around. The cloakroom guy took my bag and with a marker marked my wrist. In terms of constructions, there wasn't much. Nearby was a tarpaulin-covered darkroom tower with a staircase leading down to the ground floor. But other than that, there was seemingly nothing. Walking out of the tower, on my way to the club proper,

I almost got lost in a labyrinthine, dimly lit series of corridors. In the Lab.oratory, tech house was playing. The usual fisting and sex were going on, but that was nothing out of the ordinary. I walked on towards the Berghain main room.

Teufele and Thormann, the founders of Snax and Berghain, are the Thomas Pynchons of the club world (there are no public photos of them). Ad, a long-standing Lab.oratory attendee I spoke to, had had filthy sessions there with Teufele back in the day, and he derided the pollution of the hardcore gay scene with mainstream attention. 'It was an unwritten rule,' he said; 'you have to hide it because it's such a treasure. The secret of the formula, probably found itself [*sic*], but Michael taught me to "never, ever be judgemental."' A smallprint text on Snax's old flyers listed the contact address for a Snax mailing list under the organizer's pseudonym 'DevilTeufelDiable'. One resonance of the surname 'Teufele' ('Devil' in German), organizer of theme nights like 'Fausthaus', was with Aleister Crowley's adoption of the 'Great Beast 666' epithet. Crowley's magickal method of consciousness expansion, too, based around transgressive sex in a space he called 'la chambre de cauchemars', was not unlike what went on at Snax; and Sven Marquardt's autobiography even had a Crowley epigraph: 'Balance every thought with its opposition. Because the marriage of them is the destruction of illusion.'

The DJ Daniel Wang, who knew the two owners, wrote a classic account about the opening night of the Berghain building in 2004. Wang said that the club (initially still called Ostgut) owed its personality to its two founders, who, at the time of writing, were both in their late thirties. Wang's description of them suggests a productive antithesis:

> Michael (multiple tattoos and piercings, New Balance sneakers, always cheerful and an enthusiast for all kinds of new music) and Norbert (a successful former fashion photographer – without any tattoos or piercings – who handles more of the financial and legal aspects, and whose bookish appearance belies a boundless imagination for planning fetish events).

Both founders had a background in the arts, and given their concept for Berghain, influenced by leather spaces, as a 'club as a work of art' (as they'd told Wang), I'd found it useful to consider other arts in which they were involved.

Teufele told the writer Philip Sherburne in 2007 that he attended theatre, opera or ballet a couple of times a month, alongside running his techno club. More attuned to music than visual art, Teufele oversaw the setting up of Ostgut Ton, Berghain's in-house record label and artist agency (which closed down not long after he left the organization). 'Michael speaks softly in heavily accented English,' Sherburne noted, 'and gestures generously with arms swathed in spiraling ink; his enthusiasm is infectious. (He seems like a bit of a character, which makes sense: you'd have to be to run a club like Berghain.)' Of Ostgut Ton's releases, Teufele said that

> the idea about the label is that we start with no stars, just our residents . . . If you buy a record it's a special thing, so if you have the artwork to go with it – I think it's really important in these downloading times, it's another way to give people something valuable.

One techno artist I spoke to recalled Teufele wearing a T-shirt of their musical project and eagerly asking about the mixes of their new album, which he'd listen to in his car.

Berghain would collaborate a couple of times with Berlin's Staatsballett, fusing techno and high art. 'The Staatsballett *publikum*, their audience, is really traditional,' Teufele said, 'and the company is really focused on classical technique and classical repertoire, but the young dancers are really hungry to make new things. So I said OK, I can speak with some producers, with four or five acts, and each one said "Yes, we'll make a track!"' It was clear that Teufele's musical sensibility informed the concept of, first, Snax, and thereafter Ostgut and Berghain, each of which succeeded through becoming synonymous with high-calibre techno. 'There's one thing that Mischa said that I always remember,' DJ Aroma told me, quoting Teufele (Aroma was for a while in the 1990s a booker of sorts for Snax and Ostgut): '"Gay people like to listen to horrible music!" That meant it was very hard for him to be at a gay party, but he was a gay man, so he wanted to have a nice party with nice music. And I understood that, because back then, [gay music] was like Marianne Schöneberg and Schlager.'

Teufele's business partner Thormann was a fashion photographer. Under the artistic *nom de plume* Northor, some of his photos were used as cover art for Ostgut Ton releases. For the compilation album *Shut Up and Dance! Updated* (a soundtrack to the Berghain/Staatsballett collaboration), Thormann shot the ballerina Xenia Wiest in a pose that, to me, recalls the Scottish gay punk ballet dancer Michael Clark, who, marrying *sur les points* classicism with a mohawk and assless chaps, embodied, as Berghain did, a new age. The photo on the cover of Len Faki's

2007 EP *Mekong Delta* is a black-and-white head shot of a crew-cut woman with a flower in her mouth. It seems to be a white lily of some kind, its stamen extending obscenely. In Thormann's image, I found an echo of Yukio Mishima's series *Ordeal by Roses* (shot by photographer Eikoh Hosoe), specifically, the photo of Mishima staring into the camera with a white rose in his mouth. ('Everyone says that life is a stage,' Mishima writes in the gay novel *Confessions of a Mask*. 'But most people do not seem to become obsessed with the idea, at any rate not as early as I did.')

Then, there was the cover of the 2020 album *Scanning Backwards* by industrial techno artist Phase Fatale. Its pink colour, easy on the eye, seems to invite us in. The image shows an X-ray of a human pelvic area. The concept is refined, recalling Helmut Newton's 1979 'X-Ray of Woman's Skull with Van Cleef and Arpels Necklace' and his series for *French Vogue* showing X-rays of a nude woman posing seductively. But as you'd expect, Thormann takes things further than a skeleton in high heels: here, we're looking at an X-ray of a man being fisted. It's a photo apparently taken for an old Snax Club flyer.

Apollo and Dionysus, you might say: the marriage of refinement and chaos. That synthesis was everywhere evident in the artworks with which Teufele and Thormann decorated their love-child, Berghain. Among these artworks, not least was a brawny Dionysus statue erected at the foot of the main staircase. A threshold guardian – you had to pass by it in order to enter the club – it showed an idealized naked, frenzied man, pointing a cornucopia into the infinite black above, swallowing all the energy and excess and filth and insatiably wanting more. Berghain's infinite black above was not unlike what Mishima's *Mask* narrator describes when, recounting a troubling erotic

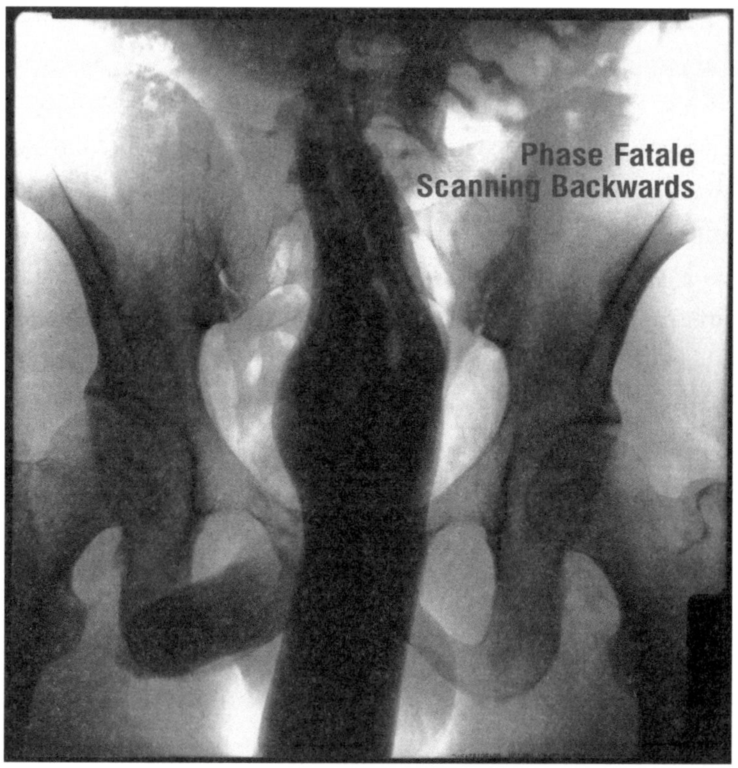

dream, he tells us of a 'perfect cube of empty night, ceaselessly swaying and leaping, to and fro, up and down ... boldly reigning over the cloudless noonday of early summer'. In terms of direct influence, the Dionysus appeared to be an homage to a famous leather-clad version of Michaelangelo's David that used to stand in the entrance of Fe-Be's in San Francisco, Folsom Street's first leather bar, opened in 1966.

Nowadays, though, with Teufele gone, the iconic Dionysus lay buried in Berghain's garden, covered in ivy, replaced at the foot of the staircase with a bland statue of a PA speaker. As for Teufele, having retired from the organization in the late 2010s, these days, I'd been told, he was content to farm orchids in a garden in rural Brandenburg.

Everyone likes Boris, and his Sunday morning Snax Club set was buoyant. It ranged from minimal techno to bouncy jacking stuff. But as I looked around me on the dance floor, the Snax Club guests looked palpably withered and dumbstruck and totally un-avant-garde. They barely danced or even moved. Mostly, they were G-zombies. Above their bare chests and harnesses, their eyes were dead. And most wore identical cookie-cutter harnesses and jockstraps. Experimentation, fetishism and breaking free from the binary were not on the agenda. Whatever I was looking for, I wouldn't find it here.

As I've said, reading Preciado's account of being a trans man had felt liberating. 'I am the multiplicity of the cosmos trapped in a binary political and epistemological system, shouting in front of you,' Preciado wrote. 'I am a Uranian confined inside the limits of techno-scientific capitalism. I am not a man and I am not a woman and I am not heterosexual I am not homosexual I am not bisexual. I am a dissident of the sex-gender system.' His account of walking down the street, newly gender-coded as a man, focused on pretending to be a man, was more or less how I'd felt my whole life. This transgender text put into words my experience of selfhood, which had always felt half incredulous and half dysphoric.

Fritscher, as editor of *Drummer*, was one of the authors of gay leather culture. When we'd corresponded, I'd told him that this was what interested me: sex not just for itself but as a portal for making-strange, finding one's true alien self (an aspect in common, of course, with techno music as post-human art). By way of a reply, he'd sent me a eulogy he'd written for Rex, the recently deceased Mineshaft artist. Fritscher referred there to gay leather culture as 'homosurrealism'.

One artist Thormann and Teufele admired was Bastille (in 1997 they'd organized an exhibition of his work in Friedrichshain). Bastille's gay BDSM paintings show orgiastic visions that, in their conflation of sexual extremity and alienness, resemble a more out-there H. R. Giger. Bald slaves on their knees, bound in chains, resemble alien greys. Muscular male forms, naked and exposed, fuse with metal beams and pipes going into and out of every bodily opening. Gay male sex, in modernity, makes of the human a *tabula rasa*. If, in one Bastille illustration published in *Toy* magazine in 1985 (and seemingly the model for a promotional Snax Club photo in 2001), the text referenced the reversion of humans to beasts, the aesthetic equally exaggerated the human to the point where it becomes alien. The gay man, over his flesh mask, dons a leather mask to escape the everyday heteronormative illusion.

I'd first come across this attitude as a teenager in the more transgressive aspects of William S. Burroughs's fiction. *Naked Lunch*, an explosion into shards of the surface of everyday life, was inconceivable without Burroughs's experience as a gay man on the societal margins. For Burroughs, 'romantic love was disgusting.' He felt equally repelled by homonormativity, as shown in a passage about New Orleans in *Junkie*:

> In the French Quarter there are several queer bars so full every night the fags spill out on to the sidewalk. A room full of fags gives me the horrors. They jerk around like puppets on invisible strings, galvanized into hideous

> activity that is the negation of everything living and spontaneous. The live human being has moved out of these bodies long ago. But something moved in when the original tenant moved out. Fags are ventriloquists' dummies who have moved in and taken over the ventriloquist. The dummy sits in a queer bar nursing his beer, and uncontrollably yapping out of a rigid doll face.

Everyday life is a tissue of illusions. Speaking to people is ridiculous. Having dinner is ridiculous (snacks). The human subject – here, the normative gay male – lives out a fake existence, unconsciously animated, à la *Invasion of the Body Snatchers*, by the malign power of an alien virus. Only his sexuality, harnessed in its full power, can help dispel the illusion of being human.

At the extreme end, this developed into pig-human sexuality. Queer cultural theorist João Florêncio points out how many names in gay male slang relate to the animal: bears, cubs, otters, giraffes, gym rats and so on. But while 'most other categories are predicated on physical attributes – what bodies look like, the qualities of their physique – gay "pigs" are instead defined by their behaviour.' In the gay subculture, 'Being a pig entails committing oneself to sexual excess, to pushing beyond boundaries of propriety and corporeal integrity; being a pig thus positions a man for membership in a sexual avant-garde, and, unsurprisingly, some men advertise their pig status with tattoos, T- shirts, and various forms of braggadocio.' Of Teufele, the charismatic Snax Club co-founder, Ad said: 'I did have quite an intense session [at the Lab.oratory] with the heavily pierced (superpig) owner, that I remember fondly.' 'I really looked up to him. He was a tall, impressive guy with a bald head and all these huge piercings. He was a really interesting guy who helped me along.' Against knee-jerk prudish moralizing, Florêncio insists upon the fundamentally political nature of leather and pig sexuality. This is especially the case in the age of PrEP, the anti-HIV drug. 'Those same drugs', he writes,

> also seem to have afforded gay men the chance of engaging in new creative modes of unproductive expenditure, intimacy, and sexual sociability that appear to veer away from the capturing forces of the apparatuses of production, accumulation, and capitalization of identity that have come to define neoliberalism as a highly coded economic programme predicated on a double-gesture of decoding and recoding of desire.

On the dance floor around me, the muscle men were in a stupor. They were basically like Odysseus' crew on Circe's island. Most had been in Berlin all week by this stage, partying every night, so the air stank of chemical sweat. None had the faintest interest in the music. Snax Club wasn't some glorious avant-garde fetish ritual; it was a boring gay circuit party, full of dead-eyed ventriloquists' dummies.

I went to leave. But I couldn't find my way out. Up and down I walked, to and fro, from inner to outer shadow, on the ground level in the Halle complex. It was a maze of rooms and passageways. I kept feeling sure I'd finally found the way out, only to end up back at the same spot again several minutes later. In long corridors, rotating single-bulb lights were directed onto concentric circle cut-outs, the rotary motion making circle silhouettes move around the walls, casting shadows of people's bodies as they passed by. Wandering in darkness past the alcoves with cages, shrubs, spare tyres and industrial objects became disorienting to the point of psychedelia. Male forms lurked in the recesses.

The experience rang a bell, but I couldn't quite recall why. Later, it snapped into surreal sense. Someone else who had attended told me that this labyrinth was, in fact, a reconstruction of the layout of the original Snax Club party at Bunker in 1994. All those decentred corridors looping back upon themselves were an homage to the layout of the very first party Teufele and Thormann had thrown, the party Adrian had told me about. I marvelled at the low-key aesthetic ambition of this. Silently reconstructed inside the Berghain building, twilit and dream-like, the construction reminded me of the metamorphs from Stanislaw Lem's sci-fi novel *Solaris*: an alien planet sensing and simulating human life as art.

When I got home, I was exhausted. I'd barely slept, even before entering this umbral underworld. By midday, I was lying on Indrani's sofa in camo pants and white vest, legs akimbo, eyes drooping, surrounded by boxes containing my possessions. Wild as it was, Snax Club, as things in Berlin went, had been a more normative experience than I'd expected. 'Massification' was the derisive word Adrian had used for Snax Club these days, meaning an overblown Ridley Scott-type commercial production, in contrast to the more subtle, nuanced, selective, horizontally distributed secret party he'd first attended.

Adrian had written a brilliant text about that party, later collected in his book *Future Imperfect*. Comingling past and present tenses, fiction and memoir, first and third person, drama and theory, the text seemed to meditate on his experience as a Sephardic Jew, in Germany for the first time, engaging in BDSM play with a German man in that Speer-commissioned Nazi bunker.

> 'I want to be your slave.'
>
> The voice was hoarse with desire, just as you might expect in a pornographic story. Neither too heavy nor light toned, its richness cut by the breathless sigh, a slight Berlin accent in his English. David was struck by this, by the man's ability to be so direct in another language, immediate in his response to the question that had just been put to him.
>
> 'What do you want?', he had asked, 'what do you want?'
>
> Had the man replied, 'I want to be free', it would have made no sense at all.
>
> Around them the spaces of the club are wrapped with sounds and filled with lights, the dance-floor techno muted in this distant corner of the concrete bunker, beating off the attracting shield of leather, toungueing latex and lashing round tattoos.

Lucid yet opaque, this text presents and withholds the event for the reader's gaze, as if the text itself were the darkness in which the bodies and words appeared and disappeared. It reminded me of something the queer theorist Guy Hocquenghem had written: 'The exceptional richness of the vocabulary indicating the male homosexual deserves at least to be mentioned: queer, fag, fairy, queen (using the masculine or feminine gender arbitrarily), etc., as if language were exhausting itself in trying to define, to name the unnamable.'

When Snax Club, at the end of 1997, relocated to an old freight train warehouse in a derelict part of the Friedrichshain district, it found a lasting location, a place with a rental lease. Sticking initially to their Snax Club brand, Teufele and Thormann ran various parties there throughout 1998, including a gay rock party called Gang Bang Riders and a mixed-genders kinky club night called sin.o.lax. Then, in January 1999, having gone back to the drawing board, they launched two new clubs at their Friedrichshain site: a gay fetish club called Lab.oratory and a mixed-genders club called Ostgut (the latter named after the Ostgüterbahnhof, the former Eastern goods railway station they'd taken over). Ostgut, during the period it was open (until January 2003), became Berlin's best nightclub and it established the template for Berghain. That template, as I now realized, had as its chief feature the decentring of heteronormativity within a techno space, through synthesizing gay leather and techno club lineages.

Attending Snax Club had shown me that, a good Uranian, I preferred the mixed and gender-fluid clientele of a regular Berghain Klubnacht or that of another queer Berlin party. Nonetheless, time seemed almost up for me. I was homeless and broke and would have to move back to Ireland. As such, reading a couple of Internet guestbook entries written upon the occasion of the closure of Lab.oratory in 2003, I appreciated the poignancy of those men who, the world rapidly changing around them, had felt like they had lost a home:

NAME: ████

EMAIL: ████████████

DATUM: Dienstag, 7 Januar, 2003 um 00:06:09

[. . .]

The end of an era, perhaps the era of East Berlin and its wall, its abandoned factories and its lab. Things are changing, there are Fist shows in straight discos, leather-guy shows are vaguely copied by straight people without understanding all the mechanics and customs, 25-year-olds are sniffing poppers, and what about tomorrow? The Lab was the place where I pushed back the boundaries of my sexuality to discover more and more pleasure. It was MY SECRET GARDEN . . . demolished by men . . . from the building site, the same men who made me jut in the Lab's backrooms. I hope a new place will be found, just as trippy as the old one.

NAME: ████

EMAIL: ████████████

DATUM: Samstag, 4 Januar, 2003 um 09:40:21

My Ostgut. It was a cold winter night when I set off with a friend to go to the SNAX in Berlin. The party was held at a different place each time, so you never knew exactly where you were going. There was a lot of word-of-mouth propaganda going on at the time . . . We knew we had to get to Ostbahnhof, from there it was only a few metres, we were told. We just followed the men who looked like us . . . The uncertainty of being let in, the clearly perceptible booming of the basses already in front of the door made my heart beat faster. Then the first flashes of light when the door opens to be a bit closer to this magical place . . .

It was never boring, we were always well taken care of. We should collect all these anecdotes so that this place is not forgotten.

Fabulations

In a book like this, this is usually where the protagonist, having sunk into dejection, is unexpectedly propelled into clarity through a so-called *peak experience*. The mountain is scaled, transcendence comes, finally he sees things as they really are! So, since it looked like my journey in Berlin was ending, and since I had a publisher now and the publisher was insistent my book finish with a climax, one Sunday morning in late summer I set out to engineer said peak experience. Really and truly, I needed to finish my book. And it was a good omen that one of my favourite DJs was playing, the Chicago-born club queen Honey Dijon, a link via Derrick Carter and Frankie Knuckles back to Larry Levan and the Loft. Coming with me for this final excursion was my Portuguese techno-aficionado friend Tânia.

My journey seemed to have reached a natural endpoint. On a personal level, I'd said goodbye to my twentieth-floor high-rise apartment and was staying with Indrani. By now, too, I'd realized what techno meant to me. No small part of that related to my figuring out, late in the day, that I was autistic.

Although the autism diagnosis was an armchair one, coming from a clued-in family member, once I'd had time to process it, I embraced it. Being autistic was a wonderful gift and a horrid curse. It made sense of so many things. If I'd gone through life feeling like I was nobody and nowhere, it was because the everyday world was the world of neurotypical people, and whatever world I should inhabit was a wholly other one. If I'd gone through life feeling like an alien, it was because in a way I was one, wired not as others were but more like a cyborg.

Being autistic means waking up every day having to deliver a speech to an assembly without having your notes prepared. Being autistic means waking up every day in the cockpit of a Boeing 747 without having any aeronautical training. Autism means life as perma-surrealism, a lifelong acid trip. It means being obliged to pretend to be a person when, deep down, you know you're not a person. I felt my life could be summed up by putting a twist on a classical Latin saying: everything human was alien to me.

So, you move from Ireland to Berlin and end up living in a haunted squat on the edge of the city. Thereafter, you discover something remarkable: a bizarre black box, a house of alien experience. You're drawn to return, regularly, alone, to this place of permanent night. It's perfect for autistics, because you no longer need to pretend to be normal, as therein, there is no normal. Gender is nonsense. 'That my heart beats in my breast is enough,' as Lispector writes. 'The impossible living of the "it" is enough.' You become what you are, entrained nothingness experiencing itself rhapsodizing. Whatever that is.

In *Inventing Ireland*, Declan Kiberd wrote that 'post-colonial artists, born as copies, were determined to die as originals.' He was talking about Irish literary modernism and the sober lunatic world-building of Joyce and Beckett. But I realized much the same could be said of queer dance floor self-invention (Leigh Bowery, Aérea Negrot) and of the afrofabulating of Sun Ra and Jeff Mills. 'I think of myself as a complete mystery to myself,' Sun Ra said – an autistic take *par excellence*. Techno recognized and maintained that innate mystery. My season in Berlin's club scene taught me to re-evaluate pretty much everything I had taken for granted about myself. That was what clubbing could do for you.

The other reason my journey had reached a natural end was because I had found some clarity on the origins of Berghain. Those origins were in Ostgut, the club's predecessor, where Teufele and Thormann had set out its conceptual blueprint. Talking to artists who'd been part of the original project when it had started back in late 1998 had helped me to see that Ostgut basically *was* Berghain, on a more familiar scale and located in a smaller, less flashy building. Two artists I spoke to were the DJs Aroma and Disko. Encountering them made me realize that, first, the same tensions had played out there between commerce and subculture as were repeating now, and that, second, Berghain was forever ending and forever beginning.

Growing up as a gay club kid in West Berlin in the 1980s, Disko had been going out from an early age. But, he told me, around the time the Wall came down and the first acid house clubs opened, 'what surprised me at these places like UFO or Planet, and all the other one-off parties that happened at the time, was that it was what I called "social architecture".' Disko said there was a 'kind of non-spoken agreement that you built this vision of how the world could be'. Beyond hedonism, clubbing had a utopian element. The enthusiasm Disko shared for creating new forms of social arrangement and even identity led him to become one of Berlin's most in-demand DJs, then one of the figures behind E-Werk.

E-Werk, which opened in 1993 and ran until 1997, was a superclub housed in an old GDR power station near the Brandenburg Gate. In scale and architecture, E-Werk was a forerunner of Berghain. Glamourous and labyrinthine and colourful, E-Werk had a prominent queer component, and its concept marked an apex for the first wave of post-reunification club creation. Initially, E-Werk felt to some like a club-as-cathedral, all tiled walls and vaulted ceilings and myriad dark nooks and crannies in which to get lost. Yet eventually, Disko said, he became jaded with what had evolved there into an over-commercialized version of club culture. E-Werk hosting the MTV Awards had made him unsure of whether the original spirit remained. 'I left the circus behind,' as he put it.

Then, at the end of 1998, Ostgut opened in the then-undeveloped East Berlin district of Friedrichshain. In that warehouse, Disko found the spirit of social architecture reprised. Ostgut, he said, 'was the follow-up to E-Werk in a way, but it was distinctly different for sure. I mean, it had a more serious vibe and [was] more industrial; not as colourful, not as diverse, too. It was way more sombre, in a way.' Disko knew Teufele and Thormann from E-Werk, where the two founders had first met and often partied, and he appreciated their professionalism. 'I enjoyed working with both Norbert and Mische very much,' Disko said, 'because they didn't bullshit around. You know, they were not out of their heads all night. They knew what they were planning and they knew what they wanted. And they were always very open about it, which was a huge relief.' Teufele and Thormann were 'serious guys', said Disko, but they were also 'underground, so it didn't feel like selling out or anything. I felt that it was a good time to support an idea like that.'

In the mid-1990s, Aroma – a talented DJ who had moved from Munich to Berlin to study cultural anthropology, and who would later be listed as one of *Tendances* magazine's top 20 DJs

– had been a de facto booker for Snax Club. She subsequently became one of Ostgut's first resident DJs. 'They knew what kind of club they wanted to do,' Aroma said of Teufele and Thormann. 'They always said, "We loved E-Werk, and E-Werk doesn't exist anymore, so we have to make a new one and it has to be gay."' In developing their concept, Teufele had asked Aroma's advice. 'I remember one evening that was really nice,' Aroma told me. 'I met with Mischa on one of the roofs, which now is the Universal building. Because he was asking me, "Oh, would you mind talking about the club that we're planning?" And I said, "No, no problem, let's do it. Let's go get two beers and sit on the fifth floor and watch the sunset."' On a rooftop by the Spree, Aroma and Teufele sat into the evening discussing the new club. 'And this is how it started.'

Ostgut opened on New Year's Eve 1998/9 and its subsequent story has been well documented. During its lifespan it was 'the epicenter of Berlin nightlife', said DJ Daniel Wang. 'Ostgut didn't look left and right at what was fancy or hip at that time,' said Ben Klock of why the club appealed. 'They just did what they liked.' By 2001, even the *Berliner Zeitung* was reporting on Ostgut, calling it 'sophisticated and excessive'. At a time when dance music had reached peak commercialization (as typified by the Love Parade and mainstream big-beat acts like Fatboy Slim), it 'kind of felt like going back to the original idea of what a techno club would be', Disko told me, 'after years of debauchery and it just becoming more commercial in a way'. Surprisingly, though, for the club that would eventually be reincarnated as Berghain, the most successful club in the world, at the beginning it was a flop. 'I was really surprised that they managed to go on for so long when they started Ostgut,' Schwanke said. 'No one was going there. There were weekends where there would be, like, twenty people on a Saturday night.' Sven Marquardt, who was working the door, remarked: 'The rush we knew from Snax Club didn't materialize at Ostgut at first.' Initially, Ostgut was exclusively gay. 'But it never seemed like their choice,' Schwanke said. 'Rather, [the owners] seemed to have only gays as friends so that became their first regulars.'

By summer 1999, the club's future was in doubt. 'Rumours in the club said that the financial situation was really on edge,' Aroma said, 'and I can tell you from my fees, that it was or must have been.' Teufele and Thormann decided to make an all-or-nothing gamble. For electronic dance music, Berlin's main draw was the Love Parade, which attracted punters in the millions, and that July weekend, to draw some of the crowd to Ostgut, they assembled a glitzy three-day line-up featuring the likes of Sven Väth, C. J. Bolland, Richie Hawtin and Luke Slater. 'I remember Norbert calling me and being totally proud of the line-up he managed to get for that weekend,' Aroma said. Of Luke Slater's live set that weekend, Disko recalled it was 'super loud, super hard, undanceable, but kind of true to the original idea of what Underground Resistance used to do. And that was very remarkable because I thought, *well, what the fuck are you doing*? Nobody can dance to that shit. But he was happy.'

As were the owners. That weekend was the turning point for the club's fortunes, and soon after the queues extended – and, with it, the clientele gradually changed. By 2003 (setting the tone for Berghain a couple of years later), the *Berliner Zeitung* was calling Ostgut 'the best club that currently exists. Even the Paradise Garage in New York couldn't have been wilder, more beautiful and more wonderful in the '80s.' Others were less effusive. When Ostgut flourished, Schwanke said, 'it was exactly as at E-Werk (the mix of people), except for that ridiculous corporate outfit I told you about [the gay clone look that became a signature of the Ostgut and Berghain dance floor]. E-Werk always was about individuality, a crass opposite to the clone armies at Ostgut.' Aroma was similarly ambivalent. For her, Ostgut in its early days was a model for the kind of social architecture Disko had mentioned. 'I told you that the nineties were extremely sexist and that we female-read people often had to put up with a lot of implicit and explicit sexism,' she said. 'That was completely different and pleasant at Ostgut.' There, Aroma never felt different or marginalized, even though she was often the only female-presenting person among the gay men. 'It was great for me, because it just felt different without this constant sexism. I could completely express myself with my clothes without being stared at greedily, and it never felt like I had to give some kind of "female performance", whether in the audience or backstage.' At the time, she didn't reflect too much on it, 'but it was a great opportunity to really express myself artistically and personally.'

Everything has to evolve. And while showing no ill will towards the organization to whose stratospheric journey she contributed, Aroma said she grew disillusioned with Ostgut once success began attracting what she considered more stereotypically ego-driven elements. At the outset, 'it was a place of freedom and equality and experimentation,' she said. 'It was about physical experiences, letting go, going on a journey together with lots of other people. Few rules, a lot of respect and a lot of openness.' This changed for her when increasing success and popularity altered the crowd and vibe. 'When at some point everyone just wanted to stay up as long as possible, and the bouncers became "important people", which had previously been mostly self-regulating, the open atmosphere was over.' Some ambitious DJs, she said, insisted on playing self-indulgent twelve-hour sets and there was harder drug use.

Teufele and Thormann had a clear concept from the start, which they maintained until their split in the mid-2010s. 'They had a vision,' Disko said, 'and they followed it through pretty severely, in a way.' And no less apparent was the tension within that between aesthetic idealism and hard-nosed entrepreneurship, a Scylla and Charybdis that was unavoidable from the start. My conversations with Disko and Aroma informed how I felt about my own journey. Everything is always beginning and ending. Everything is cyclical, and cycles mean renewal. But everything is also iterative, and iterations mean degradation.

As was my wont, I had set my alarm for ridiculous o'clock on Sunday morning and taken care to arrive at Berghain at an early-bird hour. But, to my dismay, as I came in view of the grimacing building, I saw an hours-long queue had already formed there. It was some time before Tânia joined me, and we waited impatiently, shoulder-to-shoulder amid the moody black-clad children.

'How's your book going?' she asked beneath her red beret: 'are you finished?' I cherished Tânia as one of the most down-to-earth club heads I knew, a barometer for good music who could also rattle off some Seamus Heaney.

'Almost. I'm trying to finish off my book with a peak experience. But I find it weird sometimes, going out when you know you are writing about it. I mean, I guess you'll probably end up in this chapter, too.'

'With some what?' she asked absently, as she licked closed a cigarette.

'A peak experience. You know, like when you're emerging through the clouds on the top of a mountain and suddenly, *bam*, you see everything.'

Tânia shook her head. 'Not sure I do.' I realized that, when you said these things out loud, they sounded kind of stupid, more like something from a book than real life.

'I feel it will be timely, your book,' she continued.

'Why do you say that?'

'I feel we are now in a different phase with the club. Maybe it's time for this book.'

Recently, I had similarly wondered whether my book might inadvertently be a Berghain obituary, published to coincide with the club's expiration. When Tânia and I had attended one recent Klubnacht to see the Berghain debut of Kaiser, one of the techno scene's hot new names, the experience really was a stinker. Kaiser had played a set of wishy-washy, middle-of-the-road techno to a cheering audience of normative young professionals. No gay guys graced the dance floor. Looking around us at the rest of the crowd in the main room, despite cosplaying in their pricey off-the-rack designer fetishwear, they were clean-cut. The vibe felt eerily like an episode of *Friends* ('the one where they go to Berghain').

Partly, this was because Berlin post-pandemic was morphing into London. Gentrification had accelerated. People at the club talked to you about crypto rather than weird art. Moneyed young professionals were in, subcultural oddballs were out. Squats like XB Liebig had been evicted and new apartments were becoming unaffordable. Changes had come in that suggested Berghain recognized the new Berlin and was embracing it. Although I felt ambivalent about that (like the club was betraying me), I knew at base Berghain was a business, and a good business knew when to evolve with the times.

Warmly as Aroma remembered Ostgut, she pointed out nonetheless that, in contrast to when full-time staff part ways with an organization, DJs, when freelance, aren't afforded financial compensation or a safety net. 'The balance of power in the scene was extremely asymmetrical, and I simply didn't have the strength, the money or the supporting crew around me to create the kind of place I wanted,' she said. Eventually, she checked out of the ever-more-commercialized industry. 'I think I also understood back then that it's mostly not about art,' Aroma said; 'it's always about selling drinks.' These days, she felt that the places where that wasn't the case and where a club really was a social sculpture were few. 'I guess I probably expect too much from the club scene, but that's how techno and house started for me and I still don't want to give it up as I experienced it. It used to be an open artistic playground, but for many reasons it's not anymore in most cases. In today's scene, there are still a few exceptions, and they are great, but it's not the ones you find on Instagram, TikTok, *Resident Advisor* and the like.'

Described in these terms, once the mystique wore off, the club-as-brand struck me as a humdrum capitalist platform. Guests and artists, essentially, were interchangeable content creators within the experience being sold.

Tânia had asked the people behind us for a lighter. We started chatting with them to pass the time in this insufferable queue.

'Do you . . . uh . . . like Berghain?' a rosy-cheeked woman asked me.

'I do. I'm quite fond of it.'

The second woman, lanky with crow-like eyebrows, eyed me suspiciously. 'You are from California?'

'Irish. Are you Irish too?'

She gave me a look of death.

'I didn't think so from that accent,' I said cheerfully.

They told us that they had been drinking champagne late last night and had swung by Multisex before coming here (Multisex was one of the pretentious new quote–unquote *queer parties* where Berlin's young demimondaine went to be seen; I was usually glad when it was on, because it sucked away some of the more obnoxious types from Berghain).

'We are not sure about this queue,' the lanky crow woman continued.

'Oh, this is nothing,' I said. 'Back in November, people were queuing, like, seven hours to get in. One guy I know even queued for twelve hours.' I had in mind Andreas, one of my favourite Berghain friends, a pure soul and music head whom I hadn't seen in months, since the last birthday party Klubnacht, when, sensing I was starving, he'd appeared out of nowhere and given me a banana as Dasha Rush was playing.

'What is your limit?' the rosy-cheeked girl asked me.

I told her I could do four hours max, because I would lose respect for myself after that. 'But some people get obsessed with this place.'

Of course, I was obsessed with the place myself. Even if I couldn't help feeling that, for me, it was ending.

'Oh!' Tânia said an hour later, looking down at her phone.

'What?'

'Julien is working today.' Julien was Tânia's quiet friend who worked in the Berghain ice-cream bar. 'He put someone else's name on the guest list, but he said that person didn't show up.'

'So we can take their place?'

Tânia nodded. Without further ado, we migrated from the gigantic main queue into the short guest-list queue, which ran by the right-hand side of the club entrance by the love sculpture.

'Whose name is on the guest list?'

'Kim's,' Tânia replied. 'But I will pretend that it's my name, and you are my plus-one. You will have to pay. And it is not guaranteed that you get in. But actually they never reject the plus-one.'

I had a vague sense of déjà vu. But I quickly forgot about it when, rudely, two tall fashionista men shoved into the queue before us. Their expensive jewellery jangled as they cut in rather than going behind.

'Alright if we cut in in front of you?' they asked without making eye contact.

'No,' I shot back.

The white club bro with a joint in his mouth affected to be shocked. 'That's not very *Berghain* of you.'

As often, I wondered what Berghain meant.

'Do you mind going behind us?' I asked.

They stayed where they were, and the Black American man in designer D&G sunglasses acted particularly affronted. 'How long is he going to Berghain?' he scoffed to his friend. 'Three weeks?'

My anxiety pulsed. Rather than talking to each other, for the rest of the queueing, they kept muttering derisive insults at me. Tânia was uncomfortable but said nothing, and I felt guilty that, inadvertently, I had attracted hostile attention towards us. Eventually, I calmed down by telling myself the bouncer must have seen the two skipping and would reject them. But of course, they waltzed straight in.

Finally, it was our turn.

'You, fine,' said the stocky ginger-bearded bouncer to Tânia, once she'd given the fake name. Then, he quickly threw his eye over me in my red sleeveless jacket. 'Not him. Sorry.'

My heart hiccupped. Tânia and I glanced at each other. 'Have fun,' I said, ruefully turning away.

Not for the first time, but maybe for the last, I was doing the walk of shame away from the building.

Two other people I'd spoken to had told me recently of how Berghain had opened them up sexually. Even if Berghain was, in fact, ending, that was an enduring legacy, for them and me and many others.

When Heiko, a young IT worker from Magdeburg, relocated to Berlin in 1999 at the age of 22, he had no friends in the city. By chance, he became acquainted with a group of gay men at the Love Parade ('they adopted me'), and one subsequent weekend he received an invitation that ended up being, he told me, 'literally life-changing'. 'Heiko, there's a really cool new club in town, and it's gays only,' his friend told him. 'But they have a night on the Thursday or Friday that is gays plus friends.' Heiko queued up outside what seemed like a 'no-name' club, an illegal warehouse party. The exterior was unmarked. Once he and his friend were inside, he was taken aback by this new club. 'Essentially, I was stuck in a big factory building, all industrial, dusty. And hard techno.' When Heiko walked through the darkness to the central dance floor, he found himself in an unusual environment. 'Just guys,' he said.

The club was Ostgut, and that night, Heiko spent hours dancing among the burly semi-naked men. 'The music was good,' he said, 'industrial techno.' He started dancing and felt respect from the other men. 'There was gentle flirting on the dance floor,' he said, 'and I always took it as a compliment, but they were just glances and stuff. Then, the partying, the dancing with each other was completely different, because it was kind of skin on skin. That was just mind-blowing to me.' The word Heiko used is one I was familiar with when people talked about Berghain. 'Just free, I felt free. Like I could be myself.'

One of Ostgut's innovations, for a mixed club, was darkrooms, carried over from Snax Club and the gay leather scene, where darkrooms facilitate anonymous sex. Interviewed in the documentary *Feiern*, the writer Thilo Schneider said that this aspect of Ostgut was

> totally surreal. It was right next to the dance floor, separated by curtains, so you could see the strobe lights and hear the music. Somehow it rather sharpened my senses. In there I could forget who I am. I did things I'd never have done before, ever. To use and be used like a piece of flesh – but always respectfully.

Another guest, Frank, a young straight man from a tiny Bavarian village, told me of his amazement when he was first brought into the darkrooms and witnessed, lit slightly from above, a man being fisted. The vision he described was like a debauched living Caravaggio or Bernini. 'I respect these things,' Frank said. 'Everyone can do whatever he wants to do, no problem.'

Later, Heiko had his queer awakening in the darkrooms of Berghain, when he was partying with a girlfriend.

> I was sitting there, she was going down on me, occasionally kissing me. Then suddenly, I got kissed, and someone else was blowing me. Then suddenly, there was not just two hands on me. There was three, four, five, six hands on me. And then I was kissing someone. Then I was being blown. Then I was touched. And at that moment I realized, actually, I'm slightly bisexual. When I'm horny, I do not give a fuck about gender. That was another breakthrough moment, in that dark room. So this is why I still think a club that offers this kind of freedom is fucking amazing. Because it allows people to experience this freedom. Then, they realize it might become a need for some people; for me, it's more of a want occasionally. But it means, this is part of me. And I don't have to define myself as gay or bi or whatever.

Ostgut and Berghain exposed its straight guests to gay underground culture in a way that, in a heteronormative society, rarely happens.

Guy Hocquenghem, in *Homosexual Desire*, points out that, in itself, desire knows no subdivision into human-made categories like heterosexual and homosexual. Therefore, he argued, modern heteronormative society experiences something like the return of the repressed: divided artificially from an aspect of their nature, straight people become fascinated with gay culture. 'The margins close in on the norms of sexuality and gnaw at them persistently. Every effort to isolate, explain, reduce the contaminated homosexual simply helps to place him at the centre of waking dreams.' Following on this, the architectural theorist Johann Andersson has argued that Berghain can be considered a de facto anti-gay-conversion-therapy machine. It wasn't the worst theory by a long shot. People's 'erotic horizons expand and multiply through the combination of chemicals and a multi-sensory overload of pleasurable stimuli', he wrote. 'Since this sexuality is specific to the event, we might think of sexual orientation as located inside the building instead of inside individual bodies.'

The other person I'd talked to recently was S Ruston, the DJ and activist, who told me about how clubbing in Berlin had eventually led to their non-binary awakening.

When Ruston first visited Berghain in its early years, they were a straight, AFAB, Bristol-based bass-music DJ with an antipathy to four-to-the-floor. 'I was a Panorama Bar fairy,' they told me of their partying days. 'I didn't understand Berghain. It was the Ben Klock and Marcel Dettmann era of techno, and I didn't like it.' Soon, fascinated by the club, they relocated to Berlin, where during the weeks they lived and worked in a space with other DJs like Dasha Rush and at weekends they partied.

In Panorama Bar, which back then was still heavily queer, Ruston had their first queer experience. 'I met this really hot girl, and that was the moment. I remember coming back to London and coming out as bisexual, and then sort of going back to hetero life for a while and thinking it was just a flash in the pan.'

They were fascinated with the gay BDSM club Lab.oratory. 'I went there one New Year's when it was open,' Ruston said.

'I was wearing big bunny ears, and I knew [the Ostgut Ton label boss] Nick Höppner at the time, and I remember, I was looking up at the swing above and he's like, "You want to go up there?" And I was like, "Yeah!" And he chatted to some gay guys and they all lifted me up on this swing as Fleetwood Mac "Tell Me Lies" came on, and I was swinging, and everyone was like . . . ! It was a moment.'

Ruston began experimenting with their gender presentation. 'I identified as a woman then and not many women knew that we could go there [on occasional special nights]. And so I went once, and yeah, went into the Victorian toilet, pissed on someone, thought it was fucking amazing (also just loved the fact that I didn't need to queue for a pee!).' Another time, they decided they weren't very good at male drag. 'So, I dragged up as a twink in drag. I wore an overly feminine cosplay pink wig, and I covered up my neck so no one could tell if I had an Adam's apple or not.' They went with two of their gay friends. 'One was quite androgynous. And we just got super high, and we all ended up making out on the swing. Then, before I know it, there's all these people stood around us. It was incredibly voyeuristic.'

Ruston began to realize they were not within the gender binary. Initially, they told me, 'I didn't even know what that was. But throughout my life, I've definitely . . . I feel like I went through my twenties wanting to be a boy. Even as a teenager, wanting to be a boy, wanting to behave, wanting to assimilate, then being in Panorama Bar, watching all the gay guys . . . Probably at that point, I would have transitioned, had I known. I think my thirties were about trying to come to terms with my womanhood, and then hitting my forties and being like, "Oh fuck, I'm non-binary."'

These days, Ruston plays clubs all over the world, and the day we spoke in Friedrichshain over a drink, they were getting ready to leave Berlin for good. In their later Berlin years, as a member of the Lecken feminist and non-binary party collective, they worked to bring queer strategies from the dance floor into the everyday world. When performing, they often wore a mask over their face, and in their musically adventurous sets, I found a refreshing example of the underground Berlin experimentation I'd always loved, but which, in the bigger clubs, felt like it was becoming an endangered species.

My indignation from the walk of shame was still faintly sizzling as, an hour later, Indrani and I, in the summer breeze, strode northwards from Ostkreuz station. Ahead of us was a tall bald person, dressed splendidly in purples and pinks, sauntering in the same direction. No prizes for guessing where they're going, I thought. Two parties that had kept alive the queer underground spirit were Buttons and Lecken, and as it happened, a club listings group on Telegram told me that today Buttons and Lecken were holding a joint eighth birthday party at Oxi. Since, after my Berghain rejection, I was already in Friedrichshain, I thought I might as well go. Indrani – who for various reasons avoided Berghain – said she would join. It may not deliver a peak experience, but it was worth a go.

'Why isn't Buttons at ://about blank anymore?' Indrani asked.

'The owners of ://about blank are Antideutsch. Pro-IDF.'

'Oh,' Indrani said. 'That's a shame.'

'Yes.' Those days, during the Gaza genocide, living in Germany often felt like being in a country of brainwashed people. Germany was enabling another genocide, the genocide of the Palestinian people; yet few if any of the white German clubbers I knew said a word about it, preferring business as usual, promoting themselves online, complaining about Trump, partying at the weekend. It was disturbing. For what it was worth, I was wearing red and green and black today.

Indrani and I passed onto the graffitied sidestreet leading to Oxi. Thankfully, there was no queue at the door, where a Brown trans woman asked us if we had been at Buttons or Lecken before. After we covered our phone cameras with yellow stickers, I showed the security man the contents of my *TOLKA* magazine tote bag ('formally promiscuous' the bag said). An Australian cashier with eyes madly dilated was chewing gum as she welcomed us with a stamp. 'Body horror,' Indrani said, perturbed, as there appeared stamped on our wrists a vulva with an eye inside it. I liked how it recalled Georges Bataille's *Story of the Eye*.

In the Oxi garden, it was a relief to find a very queer crowd. On the primary-colours-draped wooden decking, there were naked men and topless women, trans women and men, people whose gender was non-binary, butch lesbians and femme lesbians, gay clones and twinks, black and brown and yellow and white, chubby and skinny – everyone, basically. Indrani pointed out how much freedom there was. 'I love how expressive people are in how they dress,' she said. That aspect was joyous, people owning their narrative (*auto-nomous*, self-naming). Indrani said it reminded her of the bar in *Star Wars*. People did look like aliens from all over the galaxy, assembled for the common joy of intoxication and music and dance.

Though there was no longer a resident DJ at Lecken, Ruston still kept a motto that appealed to me: rave as praxis, non-binary as practice. 'What I liked about those questions at Lecken,' Ruston had told me, 'was always how can we bring queer utopia outside? How can we let these moments bleed out and permeate this neurotypical, hetero culture?' In this regard, they mentioned Lecken had had a reading group ('Paul B. Preciado and Virginie Despentes, all of that stuff'). Rave could be a site of conscious, embodied self-reflection. It was the same attitude that, over the course of my own journey through Berlin club culture, allowed me to realize the other, non-binary self inside me.

I felt wistful at the thought that all this might be ending, that I might be moving back to Dublin. After a while, I sat on the steps above the dance floor. I would later tell Indrani that these three or four hours were therapeutic. I reflected on what it all meant. Going to the club, for minorities, meant being afforded the licence to fabulate yourself – to render yourself fabulous; to tell a narrative of your own true self through artifice; to fashion a self who's realer than the so-called self you're obliged to act out on a daily basis in the outside world, with its tyrannical normality; to harness a self who's a citizen not of this world but of a world to come. It wasn't simply escapism. It was manifestation, calling into being a future that could house you.

Exhibitionistic, a woman who looked like Milla Jovovich in *The Fifth Element* pumped her ass, then bent over, showing everyone her red knickers. 'Eat Me' was on the black T-shirt of her friend, a butch dyke with angular cheekbones in baggy denim jeans and thick black boots. By the end, it started raining, pleasant summer rain. Because I had wasted so much time in the Berghain queue, Indrani and I had missed most of the DJs (Sally C and Objekt among them). The set we caught was Dirty Daddy Don B2B Jacob Meehan, and it gravitated around tech house, foregoing old Hi-NRG and disco and Italo and foregrounding instead a driving repetitive groove and bassline. 'Professional Widow' by Tori Amos capped off our party. But still I had the itch; still I felt unresolved. Still I craved a *peak experience*.

As we collected our things from the cloakroom and Indrani wound down to go home, I wound up for one last try.

In 2014, around the time that he and Michael Teufele were starting to diverge (one bone of contention, I'd been told, was Claire Danes's hyper-cringe Berghain-effusing appearance on *The Ellen Show*), Norbert Thormann appeared as a speaker at a Berlin business and culture conference, where he spoke publicly about Berghain and his views on Berlin club culture.

When Ostgut was forced to close to make way for a commercial development (on the site was built what is now the Uber Arena), the two owners were offered a new club location. It was a nearby abandoned GDR thermal energy plant, designed in Romantic style and built in the 1950s as part of the Soviet Union's flagship Stalinallee project. 'We were immediately excited about the building,' Thormann told that conference. 'True, it was in a ruinous state, but the details of the building and the layout of the rooms matched our conception of what a club should look like.' In ways, its grandly austere architecture was similar to Bunker, making a natural throughline from their first parties. 'The place had also been empty for twelve years and was there for the taking.'

Publicly in 2003, Teufele and Thormann said their project of a mixed club was finished. 'No, the Ostgut will not be re-opened,' they told the *Berliner Kurier*. 'Most of our thirty-plus employees will go straight into unemployment.' Privately, plans may already have been forming. Suggestively, the last track played in the old Panorama Bar, by Boris, was Frankie Goes to Hollywood's version of 'Ferry Cross the Mersey'. Sven Marquardt recalled that, at the last Ostgut staff meeting, a couple of the bartenders left early as they already had new jobs. 'However,' he said, 'they missed the announcement at the end of the meeting that there may be a new location, and that things can continue for those who are still up for it.' Teufele and Thormann announced their ambition: 'With the new one, we will create clubbing history!'

'The power station was built as a heating and power plant and was part of the Stalinallee building complex,' Thormann said, noting that, where heat and electricity had previously been generated in this building, today it was electronic music. 'We integrated many of the artefacts from past usage into the club: old switch cabinets, for instance, were converted into a bar, porcelain insulators serve as decorations, and so on.' Ben de Biel, owner of the nearby club Maria, told me he'd previously been offered the same building. 'They showed me the building and I looked at it with my partner. And honestly, it was too big for us. It was full of pipes and stuff.' De Biel said a man working for the beer company Becks brokered a sizeable bank loan for Teufele and Thormann, unprecedented at a time when banks didn't generally see nightclubs as secure prospects.

The new Ostgut, as it was still initially called, opened on Friday, 15 October 2004, with a party in Panorama Bar (the Berghain space opened two months later, when the club also received its new name). Writing his report of the opening for *Discopia*, Daniel Wang said the ground floor immediately took one's breath away, resembling 'the entryway of a modern museum'. The ground-floor coat-check area was flanked by the huge wall-length monochrome artwork in tiles I've already mentioned, Piotr Nathan's *Rituals of Disappearance*, showing a monochrome vista of natural disasters (it was sold off in 2017). 'The point is obvious,' Wang noted: 'violent, incomprehensible, yet beautiful forces of nature beyond human control. It is a simply brilliant choice, as revelatory as a dream.' The high-art sensibility continued in the Panorama Bar itself, where three large Wolfgang Tillmans works were mounted on the back walls.

Regarding Berghain's success, Thormann later gave due credit to the original founders of Berlin's post-reunification club scene. 'Berghain continues the tradition of the first techno clubs that, after the fall of the Wall, took over empty buildings in order to fill them with music.' At a time when lot of spaces in the eastern part of the city had lost their uses and importance and their future was uncertain, 'the real pioneers were the people from E-Werk, Tresor, and so on. We are, so to speak, the direct descendants of those pioneers. Today, that underground movement plays a central role in shaping the image of Berlin.'

Wang described the crowd at Berghain's opening night as 'predominantly European, but of every size and hue'. There were, he said, a handful of Asians, Latin Americans and Black people, and several people speaking a mixture of Japanese and idiomatic German. There were also 'two crazy dark-skinned Thai queens with dyed blond hair in a corner, longtime Ostgut regulars, wearing a mixture of Dolce & Gabbana and Wild & Lethal Trash'. By Sunday morning, the crowd had settled into the cocoon familiar to anyone who used to enjoy the early Panorama Bar at Berghain. 'What one notices more than anything,' Wang concluded, 'is a complete lack of pretention.' For me and others these days, it felt quite different. The crowd Wang described had mostly migrated to other parties, and the closest I'd found to the old Panorama Bar was Horse Meat Disco Berlin.

Honey Dijon, a genius musician, summed up the tension at Berghain between art and commerce. On the one hand, as a femme trans woman DJ from Chicago associated with the club since the old Ostgut days, she intimately understood Berghain's ethos, artistically and sexually, as she summed up to Ash Lauryn:

> People love the word 'no'. Being turned away from something makes you want it even more. And there's a reason behind people [being] turned away. The reason people were turned away is because Berghain is a gay club, and they didn't want people in that club that were not comfortable with how people chose to express themselves freely. They didn't want people in there as tourists or sexual tourists. They didn't want people in there that didn't contribute to the culture of the club. Berghain is utopia. Berghain is freedom of expression. Berghain is no body shame. Berghain is no sexual shame. Berghain is a serious music emporium. Berghain is dark. Berghain is wet. But most of all, Berghain is fun.

On the other hand, during the COVID-19 lockdown, the superstar Honey Dijon had been one of the celebrities partying at Soho House following a Bottega Veneta fashion show held behind closed doors at Berghain. While most Berliners were miserably, neurotically confined at home, videos circulated online of the fashion label's post-Berghain afterparty, with celebrities and models and shallow glamorous types living it up. The police seemingly looked the other way.

At that 2014 business conference, Thormann had given a cautiously optimistic picture of Berlin as it was rapidly gentrifying. 'At the moment, Berlin offers a number of opportunities for pioneers. That can be seen in a club scene that is always reinventing itself and the large number of new start-ups.' But, like Hegemann, he warned city planners not to carve up the city in the name of easy money.

> Space, however, is becoming more and more limited, and rents are becoming extremely high. As a result, creatives are being forced out of the inner city. That will change Berlin's image a lot. When space is being allocated – especially in the case of specialized properties and exceptional objects – the fast buck should not be the first priority but rather what is advantageous for the city.

Of that changing city, Ellen Allien had told me, 'I was born in Berlin. I'm a part of it and I'm very proud to be a part of it. And we keep on going.'

It was almost night-time as I walked up to the building alone. The sky was crimson, the air cool. There was only a short queue and I stood in it.

By the Berghain entrance, I saw the graffiti art of Freddie Mercury. Freddie appeared in drag, as he looks in the video for 'I Want to Break Free', with a corona. He was pink and fabulous, femme and butch, like a heterodox religious icon looking into you as you passed into this other realm. His gaze reminded me of an embarrassing teenage memory, when, at a party at my cousin's Donegal home, I was so terrified of being around the other people that I shut myself in a bedroom alone for hours, this happening after I'd spent an afternoon with my cousin watching their double-VHS of Queen videos. Such a stereotypical autistic scenario: always looking for that safe space, such as the space, here, where Freddie reappeared at the doorway; the ruined space that may, now, once more have been ruined.

I rounded the railings. 'Bitte,' the bouncer Mischa said. I was waved in the door.

Inside, the club was a noxious mess. It was wall-to-wall bodies, balmy heat, cigarette tips brushing off your arm, people tripping over your feet, mobile phone screens glaring, toilets like the sinking *Titanic*. On the main dance floor, where Honey was due to play in ten minutes, I was dismayed to see that you couldn't even move: it was all straight men with white pearl necklaces and straight women in sunglasses staring at their phones. On the back podiums, the gay men crowded like clowns in a clown car. It was, as they say, a meat market. I had texted Tânia but there was no sign of her or her friends. I knew Honey would deliver, though – she always did – and in anticipation of the Everest scale of this sought-for *peak experience*, I went into the Klobar and sat recharging my batteries in a cushioned seat.

In narratives like this, I'm generally not one for climactic Hollywood endings. In reality, the volcano remains dormant and the alien mothership doesn't come down. Yet, aware that this might be my last time in the club, I sat for a while in the cushioned seat and stared at my surroundings – the area where, that night years ago, Jürgen had sat gabbing about his corporate ayahuasca retreat. How long ago that was! I stared at the tattooed bodies walking by; at the two men having sex at the bar; at the flashing lights through the archway beyond. I had to admit, even if Berghain was becoming a diluted version of itself, it was still pretty insane.

Then came a cheer: Honey had started. A deep, rolling bass groove kicked in, reverberating through the building. And everything *did* click, finally.

I got up and went out and, passing through the main bar, managed to find a space near the front of the dance floor, underneath the totem-pole speaker stack. Half an hour in, the bodies were molten: they congealed, an undulating sea of fire, churning in waves. The music became the DJ, the DJ became the vast dark room, and the vast dark room became the sound system. All was one. 'She's like a machine,' I tried to mouth to a lanky smiling face beside me, but my mouth had melted away. Way off in the middle of the dance floor, as if on a life raft on stormy seas, Till's moustache and skinny shoulders appeared, then were swallowed up again in the furious swell. Above the dance floor, the hanging Funktion-One speaker stack stared down ominously.

I looked at the nearby DJ booth. Honey Dijon, her maple leaf peaked cap pulled down over her face, was rocking as she leant forward and worked the CDJs and mixer. Behind her, Thormann sat smiling. Honey seemed oblivious to the ecstatic dance floor crowd: her attention was focused on her instrument. It reminded me of a great jazz soloist in the midst of crafting a frenzied filigree of sound. 'Natural jazz is a classical form all its own,' Sun Ra said in a 1969 *Downbeat* article; 'it is a rare art that cannot be duplicated. It is a communication point to somewhere else.' The communication here, I thought, was directed at the future. Immersed in a fluvial, amniotic dance floor, we were the beautiful freaks gestating that Honey gave birth to. The nowhere was the womb, the –

A hand roughly groped my ass.

I flashed around. No one looked back. Just smiling faces, sweating bodies, facing the DJ, a molten mess. I felt upset.

My mind clouded over. The music pounded on. Trying to forget it, I locked into my dance groove again. A minute later, exasperatingly, my ass was groped again. This time, the illusion was gone for good. I left the dance floor and went upstairs to the Panorama Bar toilets.

Thirty minutes later, breathing deeply, trying to calm myself, I was locked alone in a toilet cubicle. I sat there feeling my muscles ache and hearing metallic doors slam. Dawn's fingers reached under the door.

My Berghain night was over.

This used to be a place where I came to flee from normativity; now, it was becoming normative through and through.

This used to be a place that reflected me back to myself; now, it did not reflect me back to myself at all.

This used to be a place where the hours turned into days; now, it was a place I'd exhausted in thirty minutes.

This used to be a place for delirious psychedelia; now, it was as rote as going to the supermarket.

This place, that used to be unique, had started morphing into Turnmills or Pacha. Or maybe I was just having a bad night and being a drama queen.

Then, staring at the floor, I had a strange sense of déjà vu. That puddle, that dirt, those patterns. This summer dawn. This toilet cubicle.

Yes, I'd been here before.

I was sheltering, by wild coincidence, in exactly the same toilet cubicle as the night all those years earlier. I was sitting in the same place as the night when I'd first fallen into Berghain during Function's set, the night of my thoughts of techno as the art of nowhere. I had the uncanny impression that I had been deposited here again after a fever dream from which, Dorothy-style, I'd just awoken.

I could have laughed at the corniness, following my peak experience deflation, of this trope. My journey had ended right back at its beginning – in the squalor of a toilet cubicle, no less. But it was real. This was no metaphor. I had been written right through, inscribed by the club's ink, mine the hand guiding the pen. And I was perhaps no longer the same me.

I was a fabulation.

An alien.

A character in a story.

A wicked dose of circular reasoning.

Note on the Text

While almost everything in this book happened, it didn't exactly happen in the order in which I've laid it out. I used the raw material of my experience the same way as would the producers of a trashy reality TV programme. Those of you who used to watch *Keeping Up with the Kardashians*, and who also kept up with celebrity gossip, would have noticed how two incidents that, in real life, happened several months apart might be presented beside each other on the show as if they happened the same week, for reasons of dramatic expediency. I've done the same thing here.

This story is only my own; I don't speak for anyone else. People's names and identities have also at times been altered.

For playlists related to *Berghain Nights*, scan the QR code.

Bibliography

TechNoWhere

Harraway, Donna, 'A Cyborg Manifesto: Science, Technology, and Socialist-Feminism in the Late 20th Century', in *Simians, Cyborgs and Women: The Reinvention of Nature* (New York, 1991), pp. 149–81

Keeling, Ryan, 'The Art of DJing: Sunil Sharpe', *Resident Advisor*, https://ra.co, 12 May 2020

Osborne, John, 'The Beats', in *A Companion to Twentieth-Century Poetry*, ed. Neil Roberts (Oxford, 2001), pp. 183–96

Rubin, Mike, 'Infinite Journey to Inner Space: The Legacy of Drexciya', *Red Bull Music Academy*, https://daily.redbullmusicacademy.com, accessed 1 December 2021

Savage, Jon, 'Techno City: An Evaluation of the History of Cybotron', liner notes essay in *Cybotron – Interface: The Roots of Techno* (Southbound, CDSEWD 069), 1994

Shklovsky, Viktor, 'Art as Device' [1917/1919], in *Viktor Shklovsky: A Reader*, ed. and trans. Alexandra Berlina (London, 2016), pp. 73–96

Walmsley, Derek, interview with Jeff Mills, *The Wire 300*, February 2009

Wang, Daniel, 'Ostgut, Berlin: Daniel Wang's Scene Report from the German Capital', *Discopia*, IV (2004), available at https://archive.ph, accessed 1 November 2024

Your Roots Are Fabulous

Agi, Yuzuru, review of Kraftwerk's *The Man-Machine* LP, *Rock Magazine*, 1978

Banks, Mike, interview on Detroit Public Radio about Kraftwerk, audio excerpt available at www.facebook.com/DarkEntriesRecords, 13 May 2020

Bradshaw, Peter, et al., '"You Can Smell the Sweat and Hair Gel": The Best Nightclub Scenes from Culture', *The Guardian*, www.theguardian.com, 18 February 2021

Brewster, Bill, and Frank Broughton, *Last Night a DJ Saved My Life: The History of the Disc Jockey* (New York, 2000)

Burns, Todd L., interview with Robert Hood, *Red Bull Music Academy*, 2019, www.redbullmusicacademy.com/lectures, accessed 1 November 2024

Channel 4, UK, *Pump Up the Volume: A History of House Music*, documentary (2001)

Coney, John, dir., *Space Is the Place* (1974)

Cosgrove, Stuart, liner notes to *Techno! The New Dance Sound of Detroit*, 10 Record Compilation (Virgin Records, DIXG 75), 1988

Denk, Felix, and Sven von Thülen, *Der Klang der Familie: Berlin, Techno and the Fall of the Wall* (Berlin, 2014)

Dighton, Mark, 'High Priests of Hi-Tech Living Bring Mission Control to Detroit', *Michigan Daily*, 28 July 1981

Drew, Eris, 'Integrations No. 1: Panorama Bar, Sunday, Nov. 19, 2023', *Journal of the Motherbeat*, https://journalofthemotherbeat.substack.com, accessed 1 December 2024

Düchting, Hajo, *Paul Klee: Painting Music* (London, 2016)

Eshun, Kodwo, *More Brilliant than the Sun: Adventures in Sonic Fiction* (London, 1998)

'Florian Schneider Interview Silverstar Club 1988', uploaded to YouTube by Kraftwerk Archives, www.youtube.com, 18 March 2023

Grossman, Lloyd, 'Pink Floyd: The Dark Side of the Moon', *Rolling Stone*, 24 May 1973

Henke, James, 'Yellow Magic Orchestra: The Japanese Technopop of Yellow Magic Orchestra Is Poised to Invade America', *Rolling Stone*, www.rollingstone.com, 12 June 1980

Kent, Nick, 'John Foxx: The Quiet Man in the Market Place', *New Musical Express*, 1 March 1980

Klee, Paul, *The Diaries of Paul Klee, 1898–1918*, trans. Pierre B. Schneider, R. Y. Zachary and Max Knight (Berkeley, CA, 1992)

McLuhan, Marshall, *Understanding Media: The Extensions of Man* [1964] (Abingdon, 2001)

'Madonna Interview 1984', www.youtube.com, 7 September 2009

Marsh, David, 'MC5 Back on Shakin' Street', *Creem*, October 1971

Morley, Paul, 'The Heart and Soul of Cabaret Voltaire', *New Musical Express*, 29 November 1980

—, 'Waiting for the End with That Old Yellow Magic', *New Musical Express*, 26 July 1980

O'Brien, Glenn, 'Eno at the Edge of Rock', *Interview Magazine*, VIII/6 (June 1978), transcript available in 'New Again: Brian Eno', www.interviewmagazine.com, 22 November 2016

Petridis, Alexis, '"Grace Jones Was in a State": Legendary Producer Trevor Horn Relives His Mega-Hits', *The Guardian*, www.theguardian.com, 24 October 2022

Press release for Kraftwerk, *The Man-Machine* LP (Capitol Records, E-ST 11728), 1978

Renkichi, Hirato, 'Manifesto of the Japanese Futurist Movement [1921]', trans. Miryam Sas, *Cabinet Magazine*, 13 (Spring 2004)

Savage, Jon, 'Techno City: An Evaluation of the History of Cybotron', liner notes essay in *Cybotron – Interface: The Roots of Techno* (Southbound, CDSEWD 069), 1994

Schober, Ingeborg, 'Kraftwerk: Techno-Boogie aus der Neonröhre', *Sounds* (March 1977), available at https://sounds-archiv.at, accessed 1 January 2025

Sherman, 'Sweet Sole Music', interview with Kevin Saunderson, *New Musical Express*, 1991, reproduced on the Facebook page of Drexciya Research Lab, www.facebook.com, 29 October 2024

Rave New World

Adorno, Theodor W., 'The Aging of the New Music', trans. Susan H. Gillespie, in *Essays on Music*, ed. Richard Leppert (Berkeley, CA, 2002), pp. 181–202

Berger, John, *Portraits: John Berger on Artists* (London, 2015)

Chesterton, G. K., 'A Defence of Nonsense', in *A Defence of Nonsense, and Other Essays* (Madrid, 2013)

Drew, Eris, 'Integrations No. 1: Panorama Bar, Sunday, Nov. 19, 2023', *Journal of the Motherbeat*, https://journalofthemotherbeat.substack.com, accessed 1 December 2024

Kabin, Benjamin, 'What Elon Musk Really Thinks of "Silicon Valley"', NBC *News*, www.nbcnews.com, 4 April 2014

Sen, Paul, dir., 'Equinox', *Rave New World*, aired 6 November 1994

Various authors, Blackout series, *Mixmag*, https://mixmag.net/features/blackout, accessed 1 December 2021

Vreeland, Lisa Immordino, Bent-Jorgen Perlmutt and Frédéric Tcheng, dirs, *Diana Vreeland: The Eye Has to Travel* (New York, 2011), DVD

The Art of the Dance Floor

Brembs, Tilman, *Zeitmaschine/Analog Rave II* (Berlin, 2024)

Coultate, Aaron, 'Wall Mural from Berghain to Be Sold Off', *Resident Advisor*, https://ra.co, 17 March 2017

Denk, Felix, and Sven von Thülen, *Der Klang der Familie: Berlin, Techno and the Fall of the Wall* (Berlin, 2014)

Etiman, Yusuf, and Kathrin Hain, eds, *Berghain: Kunst im Klub* (Berlin, 2015)

Hoffmann, Felix, and Heiko Hoffmann, eds, *No Photos on the Dance Floor! Berlin 1989–Today* (Munich, 2019)

Isherwood, Christopher, *Farewell to Berlin* (London, 2022)

Mishima, Yukio, *Confessions of a Mask*, trans. Meredith Weatherby (London, 2017)

Pine, B. Joseph II, and James H. Gilmore, 'Welcome to the Experience Economy', *Harvard Business Review* (July–August 1998), available at https://hbr.org, accessed 1 January 2025

Steyerl, Hito, 'In Defense of the Poor Image', *e-flux Journal*, 10 (November 2009)

Tanizaki, Jun'ichirō, *In Praise of Shadows*, trans. Thomas J. Harper and Edward Seidensticker (London, 2001)

Biomorphism

Cagney, Liam, *Gérard Grisey and Spectral Music: Composition in the Information Age* (Cambridge, 2024)

Novalis, *The Novices of Sais*, trans. Ralph Manheim (Brooklyn, NY, 2005)

Velour, Sasha, *The Big Reveal: An Illustrated Manifesto of Drag* (London, 2023)

Winfrey, Oprah, interview with RuPaul Charles, *Super Soul Sunday*, 21 January 2018, full interview available at www.facebook.com; the full audio (as a podcast) is available at www.oprah.com, as well as on other podcasting platforms

Party Like It's 1999 BCE

Adam, Hans Christian, *Berlin: Portrait of a City* (Berlin and London, 2022)

Andrawis, Michael, dir., *Tresor Berlin: The Vault and the Electronic Frontier*, digital documentary film (2005)

Baudrillard, Jean, *The Mirror of Production*, trans. Mark Poster (St Louis, MI, 1975)

Birgit, Richard, Robert Klanten and Stefan Heidenreich, eds, *Icons: Localizer 1.3* (Berlin, 1998)

Collin, Matthew, 'Techno Is the Sound of Europe', *i-D Magazine*, 99 (December 1991)

Cosmic Cowboy, interview with Joey Beltram, *Melody Maker*, 19 October 1991

Debray, Cécile, Rémi Labrusse and Maria Stavrinaki, eds, *Préhistoire, Une énigme moderne* (Paris, 2019)

Denk, Felix, and Sven von Thülen, *Der Klang der Familie: Berlin, Techno and the Fall of the Wall* (Berlin, 2014)

Dillard, Annie, *The Writing Life* (London, 1990)

Hölderlin, Friedrich, *Hyperion and Selected Poems*, trans. Willard. R. Trask (London, 1990)

Madson, Ryan, 'Zones: Post-Industrial Aesthetics and Environments after *Stalker*', *Offscreen*, XXVII/3–5 (May 2023)

Metzger, Rainer, ed., *1920s Berlin* (London, Los Angeles, CA, New York and Paris, 2017)

Red Bull Music Academy, 'Jeff Mills on His DJ Style, Minimal Techno and Early Productions', www.youtube.com, 16 April 2018

Toffler, Alvin, *Future Shock* (New York, 1970)

Club Oblivion

Baudelaire, Charles, *Selected Writings on Art and Literature*, trans. P. E. Charvet (London, 1992)

Benjamin, Walter, *The Arcades Project*, trans. Rolf Tiedemann (Cambridge, MA, 1999)

Carroll, Lewis, *Alice's Adventures in Wonderland and Through the Looking Glass: And What Alice Found There* [1865 and 1871] (London, 2010)

Cotz, Liz, 'The Body You Want: An Interview with Judith Butler', *Artforum*, XXXI/3 (1992), pp. 82–9

Holleran, Andrew, 'Tragic Drag', in *Chronicle of a Plague, Revisited: AIDS and Its Aftermath* (Boston, MA, 2008), ebook

Lawrence, Tim, *Life and Death on the New York Dance Floor, 1980–1983* (Durham, NC, 2016)

—, *Love Saves the Day: A History of American Dance Music Culture, 1970–1979* (Durham, NC, 2004)

Lispector, Clarice, *Água Viva*, trans. Stefan Tobler (London, 2014)

McLuhan, Marshall, *Understanding Media: The Extensions of Man* [1964] (Abingdon, 2001)

Nietzsche, Friedrich, *The Will to Power*, trans. Walter Kaufmann (London, 1973)

Proust, Marcel, *In Search of Lost Time*, vol. III: *The Guermantes Way*, trans. Mark Treharne (London, 2003)

Valéry, Paul, *Selected Writings of Paul Valéry*, trans. Denis Devlin et al. (New York, 1963)

Wang, Daniel, interview with Discodromo, *Groove*, https://groove.de, 6 November 2015

Wilde, Oscar, *The Picture of Dorian Gray* [1890] (London, 2010)

In Praise of Filth

Anonymous, 'Interviews – Fabio Boxikus from Gegen', *Attack Magazine*, www.attackmagazine.com, 21 December 2020

Bataille, Georges, *Erotism: Death and Sensuality*, trans. Mary Dalwood (San Francisco, CA, 1986)

Bernhard, Thomas, *Gathering Evidence and My Prizes*, trans. David McLintock (New York, 2011)

Burroughs, William S., *Naked Lunch* [1959] (New York, 2009)

Edkins, Jenny, *Face Politics* (Abingdon, 2015)

Febos, Melissa, *Whip Smart: The True Story of a Secret Life* (New York, 2010)

Fritscher, Jack, *Mapplethorpe: Assault with a Deadly Camera: A Pop Culture Memoir, an Outlaw Reminiscence* (New York, 1994), available at https://jackfritscher.com, accessed 1 December 2024

Hussein Kantorowicz, Liad, dir., *No Democracy Here* (2018)

Karmakar, Romuald, 'The Dissidents: THE KITKAT CLUB, Germany', www.youtube.com, 10 April 2018

Kohler, Sebastian, and Julian Würzer, 'KitKat-Gast spricht über Lindemanns Besuch im Fetisch-Club', *Berliner Morgenpost*, www.morgenpost.de, 18 July 2023

König, Ben-Robin, 'KitKatClub nach Till-Lindemann-Besuch: Die völlige Abwesenheit von Anstand und Grenzen', *Groove*, https://groove.de, 26 July 2023

Lewis-Williams, David, *The Mind in the Cave: Consciousness and the Origins of Art* (London, 2002)

Lorde, Audre, *Sister Outsider: Essays and Speeches* (Berkeley, CA, 1984)

Nietzsche, Friedrich, *The Will to Power*, trans. Walter Kaufmann (London, 1973)

Oberländer, Jan, 'Nächte im Kitkatclub: "Wenn man die Leute in normalen Klamotten reinlässt, wird nur das Normale passieren"', *Tagesspeigel*, www.tagesspiegel.de, 23 May 2020

Pound, Ezra, *The Cantos* (New York, 1996)

Ross, Annabel, 'Women Provide Accounts of Sexual Harassment and Assault by Derrick May', *Resident Advisor*, https://ra.co, 13 November 2020

Schiller, Friedrich, *Letters on the Aesthetic Education of Man* [1794], trans. Keith Tribe (London, 2016)

Thaur, Simon, 'About Me', www.innovative-productions.info, accessed 1 January 2025

—, 'Philosophy + Portrait', *Innovative Productions. Simon Thaur*, www.innovative-productions.info, accessed 1 November 2021

White, Edmund, *Marcel Proust: A Life* (London, 2009)

The Future Becomes You

Baudelaire, Charles, *Paris Spleen*, trans. Louise Varèse (New York, 1970)

Baudrillard, Jean, *Simulacra and Simulation* [1981], trans. Sheila Faria Glaser (Ann Arbor, MI, 1994)

Blanchot, Maurice, 'Everyday Speech', trans. Susan Hanson, *Yale French Studies*, LXXIII (1987), pp. 12–20

Dick, Philip K., *We Can Remember It for You Wholesale: The Collected Short Stories of Philip K. Dick*, vol. V (London, 1987)

Electronic Beats, 'The Video for Function's New Album on Tresor Is Psychic and May Predict Your Future', www.electronicbeats.net, 2 September 2019

Le Guin, Ursula K., *The Carrier Bag Theory of Fiction* (London, 2019)

—, *The Left Hand of Darkness* (New York, 2019)

Lispector, Clarice, *Água Viva*, trans. Stefan Tobler (London, 2014)

Preciado, Paul B., *Can the Monster Speak?*, trans. Frank Wynne (London, 2021)

Press release blurb for *Plantae* by Planetary Assault Systems (O-Ton 123), www.berghain.berlin/en, accessed 1 November 2024

Press release blurb for Subject F (Transcendence) by Function (Eaux 1491), https://rrose.bandcamp.com, accessed 1 November 2021

RA Exchange, 'EX.324 Luke Slater', podcast interview, *Resident Advisor*, https://ra.co/exchange/324, 20 October 2016

Stockhausen, Karlheinz, 'We in Music Are Like Physicists', available at *Scribd*, www.scribd.com, accessed 1 December 2024

Sun Ra Arkestra, the official X account, https://x.com/SunRaUniverse

Xenakis, Iannis, *Music and Architecture: Architectural Projects, Texts, and Realizations*, trans. and ed. Sharon Kanach (New York, 2008)

Youngquist, Paul, *A Pure Solar World: Sun Ra and the Birth of Afrofuturism* (Austin, TX, 2016)

Love's Secret Domain

Burroughs, William S., *Junkie* [1953] (London, 2008)

—, *Naked Lunch* [1959] (New York, 2009)

'Clubsterben in Berlin: Maria, Kiki Blofeld, Non Tox, Kato, Bunker', *Berliner Zeitung*, www.berliner-zeitung.de, 8 January 2019

Denk, Felix, and Sven von Thülen, *Der Klang der Familie: Berlin, Techno and the Fall of the Wall* (Berlin, 2014)

Florêncio, João, *Bareback Porn, Porous Masculinities, Queer Futures: The Ethics of Becoming-Pig* (Abingdon, 2020)

Foucault, Michel, *Ethics: Subjectivity and Truth*, trans. Robert Hurley et al. (New York, 1997)

Fritscher, Jack, *Inventing the Gay Gaze: A Memoir of Essays and Interviews* (Profiles in Gay Courage), vol. III (2025), available at https://jackfritscher.com, accessed 1 December 2024

—, *Leatherfolk, Arts, and Ideas: A Memoir of Essays and Interviews Published* (Profiles in Gay Courage), vol. I

(2022), available at https://jackfritscher.com, accessed 1 December 2024

—, *Mapplethorpe: Assault with a Deadly Camera: A Pop Culture Memoir, an Outlaw Reminiscence* (New York, 1994), available at https://jackfritscher.com, accessed 1 December 2024

Garcia, Luis-Manuel, '"With Every Inconceivable Finesse, Excess, and Good Music": Sex, Affect, and Techno at Snax Club in Berlin', in *Dreams of Germany: Musical Imaginaries from the Concert Hall to the Dance Floor*, ed. N. Gregor and T. Irvine (New York, 2018), pp. 73–96

Hocquenghem, Guy, *Homosexual Desire*, trans. Daniella Dangoor (Durham, NC, 1993)

Huysmans, Joris-Karl, *Against Nature*, trans. Patrick McGuinness (London, 2003)

Löhle, Edith, 'Jean Paul Gaultier on Fashion, Beauty, and Love (at any Age)', *Refinery 29*, www.refinery29.com, 5 October 2016

Lowder, Bryan, 'Gays in the Woods: History and Identity with Ben Miller', *Outward*, Slate's LGBTQ podcast, https://slate.com/podcasts, 6 November 2024

Marquardt, Sven, *Die Nacht ist Leben: Autobiographie* (Berlin, 2014)

Mishima, Yukio, *Confessions of a Mask*, trans. Meredith Weatherby (London, 2017)

Moore, Patrick, *Beyond Shame: Reclaiming the Abandoned History of Radical Gay Sexuality* (Boston, MA, 2004)

Morrisroe, Patricia, *Mapplethorpe: A Biography* (New York, 1995)

Preciado, Paul B., *An Apartment on Uranus*, trans. Frank Wynne (London, 2020)

RA Exchange, 'EX.234 Boris', podcast interview, *Resident Advisor*, https://ra.co/exchange/234, 22 January 2015

Rifkin, Adrian, *Future Imperfect* (London, 2021)

Sherburne, Philip, 'Techno', *Pitchfork*, https://pitchfork.com, 8 May 2007

Tzortzis, Andreas, 'In a Berlin War Bunker, Christian Boros Creates a Showcase for Art', *New York Times*, www.nytimes.com, 12 June 2007

Wang, Daniel, 'Ostgut, Berlin: Daniel Wang's Scene Report from the German Capital', *Discopia*, IV (2004), available at https://archive.ph, accessed 1 November 2024

Welch, Paul, 'Homosexuality in America', *Life*, 26 June 1964

Fabulations

Andersson, Johann, 'Berghain: Space, Affect, and Sexual Disorientation', *EPD: Society and Space*, XL/3 (2022), pp. 451–68

Classen, Maja, dir., *Feiern* (2006)

Fiofiri, Tam, 'Sun Ra's Space Odyssey', *Downbeat*, 14 May 1969

Hocquenghem, Guy, *Homosexual Desire*, trans. Daniella Dangoor (Durham, NC, 1993)

'. . . im Ostgut. Schön war's . . .', *Berliner Kurier*, www.berliner-kurier.de, 4 January 2003

Industriekultur Berlin, *Berliner Forum für Industriekultur und Gesellschaft 2012, 2013 ,2014*, https://industriekultur.berlin/termin/forum, accessed 1 September 2024

Kiberd, Declan, *Inventing Ireland: The Literature of a Modern Nation* (Cambridge, MA, 1995)

Lauryn, Ash, 'Berlin – Techno: A Social History', BBC podcast, www.bbc.co.uk, broadcast 26 July 2022

Lispector, Clarice, *Água Viva*, trans. Stefan Tobler (London, 2014)

Marquardt, Sven, *Die Nacht ist Leben: Autobiographie* (Berlin, 2014)

Peters, Harald, 'Der Mond scheint auf unseren Traum', *Berliner Zeitung*, www.berliner-zeitung.de, 4 January 2001

Preuss, Sebastian, 'Neues Ostgut öffnet am Sonnabend', *Berliner Zeitung*, www.berliner-zeitung.de, 17 December 2004

RA Exchange, 'EX.123 Ben Klock', podcast interview, *Resident Advisor*, https://ra.co/exchange/123, 22 November 2012

Rycenga, Jennifer, 'Interview with Sun Ra, November 2, 1988. Conducted by Jennifer Rycenga, in San Francisco. Transcribed and edited by Dan Plonsey', http://danplonsey.com, accessed 1 November 2024

Wang, Daniel, 'Ostgut, Berlin: Daniel Wang's Scene Report from the German Capital', *Discopia*, IV (2004), available at https://archive.ph, accessed 1 November 2024

'Wohin Leute', *Berliner Zeitung*, www.berliner-zeitung.de, 14 September 2001

List of Illustrations

Every effort has been made to contact copyright holders; should there be any we have been unable to reach or to whom inaccurate acknowledgements have been made please contact the publishers, and full adjustments will be made to any subsequent printings.

Acknowledgements

Thank you first and foremost to Pascal Porcheron at Reaktion for his faith and expertise, and to Olivia Davies and Kate Walsh at United Agents for their trust and guidance. Thanks, too, to Simon McFadden, David Hayden, Emma Devlin, Nicola Napoli, Liam Harrison, Seán Hayes, Catherine Hearn, Niamh Dunphy, Nathan O'Donnell, Adrian Duncan, Brendan Mac Evilly, Peter McNamara, Luke Clancy, Antonia Schmidt, Daisy Alioto, Eoin Murray, Luke Turner, Elsa Kiourtsoglou, David Horan, Ben Miller and the Berlin Writers' Workshop, Romain Pinteaux and the Archives of the Schwules Museum Berlin, Vincent and Ann Cagney, Éamonn, Mairead and Evelyn, and Indrani.